Augsburg College
George Sverdrup Library
Minneapolis, MN 55454

The Germans after World War II
an English-language bibliography

The Germans after World War II

an English-language bibliography

BARBARA DOTTS PAUL

G. K. HALL & CO.
70 LINCOLN STREET, BOSTON, MASS.

All rights reserved.
Copyright 1990 by Barbara Dotts Paul.

First published 1990
by G.K. Hall & Co.
70 Lincoln Street
Boston, Massachusetts 02111

10 9 8 7 6 5 4 3 2 1

Library of Congress Cataloging-in-Publication Data

Paul, Barbara Dotts.
    The Germans after World War II : an English-language bibliography / Barbara Dotts Paul.
    p. cm.
    Includes bibliographical references.
    ISBN 0-8161-8994-3
    1. Germany–History–Allied occupation, 1945–Bibliography. I. Title.
Z2240.3.P38   1990
[DD257]
016.94053'144'0943 – dc20   89-26939
                                                                    CIP

The paper used in this publication meets the minimum requirements of American National Standard for Information Sciences–Permanence of Paper for Printed Library Materials, ANSI Z39.48-1984. ∞™

MANUFACTURED IN THE UNITED STATES OF AMERICA

Contents

The Author vi

Acknowledgments vii

Introduction ix

1. German Experiences 1
2. Foreign Observers 19
3. Civilian Relief Efforts 53
4. Journal Articles 61
5. Fiction by Germans 103
6. Non-German Fiction 115
7. Films about Germany 127
8. Historical Studies 141
9. Bibliographies Consulted 159

Index 167

v

The Author

Barbara Dotts Paul has been a librarian for over twenty years at the University of Wisconsin--Stevens Point. She is coeditor, with her husband, Justus F. Paul, of *The Badger State: A Documentary History of Wisconsin.* She has a master of arts degree in history from the University of Nebraska and a master of science degree in library science from the University of Wisconsin--Madison.

Acknowledgments

This bibliography had its beginning in 1978 when my husband and I took our three children and his parents to West Germany for a visit. My interest was aroused by Germany's re-creation of historic buildings after the destruction of World War II. I wondered what life had been like after the war and why my mother-in-law's German friends were still grateful for the food parcels she had sent them once private aid was allowed. When we returned home I began to read about the postwar period and to keep notes. Eventually my family was asking what I planned to do with all those note cards. Thanks to G.K. Hall, this bibliography is the result.

In the process of looking for books in English that reflect daily life in Germany in the immediate postwar period, I have visited more than a dozen libraries. For me no trip is complete without at least one library visit. Nevertheless, since it is impossible to travel everywhere, I have depended upon the InterLibrary Loan Department of the University of Wisconsin--Stevens Point University Library, staffed by Kathy Halsey and Christine Neidlein, to find books that I needed to examine because of their ambiguous titles and subjects. Arne Arneson, Director of the University of Wisconsin--Stevens Point University Library, has assisted me with the complexities of compiling and printing a manuscript using a computer. I have appreciated his tutoring.

My husband and grown children, Jay, Becky, and Ellen, have been supportive and encouraging, and I have appreciated their willingness to listen to my enthusiasms and frustrations. Finally, I would like to salute the generations of anonymous shelvers who have carefully reshelved books from the 1940s in the Cutter bins in the University of Wisconsin--Madison Memorial Library basement. Their exactness has meant that the books were waiting for me to find many years later.

Introduction

The bibliography presents sources in English for studying the lives of ordinary Germans in the immediate post-World War II period. With the renewed interest in social history, there is a need for access to English-language materials that allow the social scientist to investigate and analyze relationships between historical events and the everyday activities of ordinary people who helped to shape those events. Social scientists have traditionally divided the history of Germany in the 1940s into two distinct periods. The first covers the Nazis and World War II. The second concentrates on the beginnings of the cold war and the economic recovery of West Germany after the currency reform in 1948. Most of the sources for the study of the period from 1945 to 1948 are buried within more traditional bibliographies.

This period of defeat, disgrace, and deprivation forms a bridge between the ideas and goals of the Third Reich and those of modern, democratic West Germany. How did the Germans pick up the pieces of their lives and begin to rebuild both physical shelter and emotional health? Their zero hour, "die Stunde Null," when the country hit bottom, seemed to go on for three years, with no hope for the future. How, when the Allies implemented the currency reform, were Germans able to take advantage of the opportunities presented and rebuild their economy? Such questions can be answered only by examining primary sources from the early postwar period.

Although that time of hunger and misery is an engrossing topic for Germans, there has been little interest in translating their published works into English. This increases the importance of having access to the books that have been translated. The immensely consequential issue of the legal, social, economic, and political implications of the absorption of the fifteen million ethnic Germans expelled from their ancestral homes is one that has been almost ignored outside of Germany.[1] The few sources in English that are available are difficult to track down in traditional bibliographies or with usual subject headings. They are cited here. In addition, most bibliographies list memoirs and journals of famous people but ignore those of ordinary people. Here the famous people are omitted unless their writings describe daily living in the early postwar period.

---

[1] Alfred M. de Zayas, *Nemesis at Potsdam* (London: Routledge & Kegan Paul, 1979), xix.

Introduction

It should be noted that there is some overlap between this bibliography and those relating to the World War II Jewish Holocaust, particularly on the subjects of civilian relief work and the writings of foreign observers. People who came to Germany to help the refugees and displaced persons often also aided Jews who had been released from concentration camps and were waiting for an opportunity to leave Germany forever. So, in that respect, some entries duplicate those found in Holocaust bibliographies. Although many Germans had tragic experiences after the war, and the pain and death of any innocent person is deplorable, it is not possible to compare the postwar suffering of Germans with that of European Jews who were swept into the intentionally genocidal nazi bureaucracy of the Third Reich.

Unconditional Surrender

For most Germans the end of the war and the beginning of the peace was not clearly defined. The last few weeks of war merged with the first weeks of peace, accompanied by the terror of bombs and the brutality of conquering troops, the uncertainty of shelter and food, and the agony of not knowing if loved ones still lived. For some in the west the war ended early when their town or village was captured. For example Aachen fell to American troops on 21 October 1944.[2] For others, in desperate flight westward away from the Soviet army, the war ended when they were overrun by Russian soldiers headed toward Berlin and the center of the Reich. In Berlin itself, seat of nazi power, the siege in the last days of the war ultimately involved two and a half million men. Weakened after years of Allied bombing raids, the city was pulverized by the Soviet bombardment and survivors were reduced to a state of barbarism.[3]

General Alfred Jodl, who arrived in Reims, France, to negotiate the end of the war, delayed signing the unconditional surrender because he knew over a million German soldiers and civilians were trying to reach western lines to surrender to the British and Americans rather than to the Soviets.[4] The years of anti-Russian propaganda, the knowledge of the actions of the German army when it invaded Russia, and the atrocities already committed by Soviet troops in East Prussia had thoroughly frightened the Germans. In most instances their fear of revenge was substantiated. Earlier in the winter of 1944-45 Admiral Dönitz had been given credit for rescuing over two

---

[2] Douglas Botting, *From the Ruins of the Reich* (New York: Crown, 1985), 9.
[3] Ibid., 52.
[4] Ibid., 87.

Introduction

million soldiers, sailors, and civilians from the northern coasts of East Prussia, Pomerania, and Mecklenburg when they were cut off from western Germany by Soviet front lines.[5] The Germans who were thus saved from Soviet labor camps formed part of the foundation on which modern, democratic West Germany was built.

When the war was finally over, the greatest war machine in the history of Europe had disintegrated and the German people were worn out. They were tired of the years of nationalistic propaganda, rationing, mandatory winter relief drives, bombing raids, Gestapo threats, and war deaths for the glory of the fatherland. They hoped for peace, the chance to reunite their families, and opportunities to find or rediscover peacetime occupations. They understood that losing the war meant being occupied by the victors, and some were looking forward to being in the areas controlled by the British and Americans. The realities of daily life in occupied Germany were, however, worse than could have been imagined, and gradually, as the news about the death camps spread, the Germans realized that they were pariahs and were despised by the world for their leaders' villainy.

The summer of 1945 found millions of people on the roads, despite the Allies' attempts to prohibit travel and control the traffic. When the war ended many families were separated, with men in army and home-guard units and children in rural camps escaping the bombing raids on cities. Many German civilians were refugees from the bombed cities, and hundreds of thousands of families had fled the Soviet invasion of the eastern provinces. Foreign slave laborers in factories and on farms declared themselves liberated when the Allies moved into their areas. Often their first thoughts were to take revenge on the local people. After supplying themselves with food and clothes, the liberated Russians, Poles, French, Belgians, Dutch, and Yugoslavs headed on foot toward their homes. The roads were thick with people moving east and west. German civilians were seen as legitimate prey for former slave laborers, former concentration camp inmates, and occupation troops. Whether the conquerors were French, British, American, or Soviet, each army had its ruthless soldiers who regarded the Germans as fair game. Property was especially vulnerable to being "liberated." Some people collected souvenirs, some needed basics for survival, and others destroyed things in mindless rampages.

Most German cities were silent ruins with no recognizable landmarks or street signs. Everywhere was the stench of bodies beneath the bombed buildings. People followed paths through the piles of rubble as though

---

[5] Ibid., 109.

Introduction

among trees in a forest. The few people still there lived in cellars, caves burrowed into the ruins, and in rooms hanging on half-demolished buildings and reachable only by ladders. In all, more than a quarter of the living units in Germany had been destroyed or damaged.

Train tracks had been bombed and less than half the engines and coaches were usable. Rolling stock from all over Europe had been brought into the Reich and now had to be returned, but German train stock in other countries was kept by those countries. In the ports, the wharves were destroyed and the channels were blocked with mines and sunken ships. Most bridges over rivers had been blown up, including all twenty-two rail bridges across the Rhine.[6] In the towns and cities electricity, water, sewer, and telephone lines were disrupted. The Allied military governments repaired these vital services as quickly as possible, in part to prevent epidemics.

The occupied country was divided into four parts, to be controlled by the British, Americans, French, and Soviets. Berlin, also, was divided into four sectors, with a jointly run Control Commission to listen to disputes and solve common problems. Civilians were officially locked into the zone where they were. They could travel no more than six kilometers from their homes and could not communicate with anyone in another zone. All their elementary civil rights were suspended, their bank assets were frozen, and they could be detained, searched, arrested, and shot at will. They were subject to compulsory labor and were initially forbidden to converse casually with their conquerors.[7]

When planning for the postwar occupation, the Allies had agreed that Germany should be managed in such a way that it could not recover to rearm and again declare war on its European neighbors. This included dismantling military industries and curbing others. The postwar planners did not realize the interdependence of agricultural and manufacturing production in Germany, nor how the economy of Europe was tied to that of the defeated country. Consequently, industrial stagnation and embargoes on importing raw materials affected coal and agricultural production, as well as manufacturing.

The Reichsmark continued to be the official currency, with many prices fixed by the occupation governments at prewar levels. With labor conscription in effect, people had to hold authorized jobs in order to qualify for ration stamps. Unable to earn enough money to keep their families from

---

[6] Ibid., 125.
[7] Ibid., 123.

Introduction

starving, workers had to take time off from their jobs to hunt for food. Factory owners paid their employees partially in goods in order to keep workers. The goods could be bartered for food and other necessities.[8] This circle of hopelessness went round and round with people seeing no end to it. Meanwhile, chronic undernourishment adversely affected the energy people had for work, politics, and intellectual pursuits. They fixed their attention on feeding their families and surviving another day.

The military governments realized the value of education. Efforts were begun in all four zones to find teachers and texts that were untainted by fascism. For young people, school was a desirable place to be, an opportunity to learn about the world and to prepare for a future occupation. But bombed buildings, absent teachers, and few texts made school unattainable for many. Many schools served a warm meal to the children at lunch. Even though this often was their only meal of the day, in cold weather they had to stay home because they had no shoes.[9]

The traditional morality of middle-class Germany was forgotten in the three years after the war. Stealing became an accepted method of supplementing one's subsistence and bartering was absolutely necessary for survival, even though trading on the black market was illegal. With each zone occupied by Allied soldiers with time on their hands and money to spend, it was not surprising that many German women felt forced to trade sex for a warm place to sleep or food for their families. In general, Germans were obedient and servile when dealing with the military governments because their instincts for self-preservation forced them to suppress their natural resentment.

Expellees From Eastern Europe

Although the war ended in May of 1945 for the Allied armies, for many ethnic Germans life became a nightmare of unimaginable suffering that did not end for many years. This was a direct result of agreements reached by the Allies at the Potsdam Conference, which was held in July and August of 1945 in a suburb of Berlin. The victors agreed to the principle that ethnic minorities could be transferred from one country to another if the minority

---

[8] Gustav Stolper, *German Realities* (New York: Reynal & Hitchcock, 1948), 97.
[9] *What We Saw in Germany* (London: S.P.C.K., Sword of the Spirit, 1948), 13-14.

Introduction

threatened the sovereignty of the host country. At the same conference the Allies agreed that eastern provinces of the German Reich would be temporarily administered by the Soviet Union and Poland until a formal peace treaty was signed. The repercussions of these clauses were more far-reaching than any politician could have imagined.

In every country of central and eastern Europe where the German Reich had sent its armies and oppressed the population, the opportunity for revenge was seized. Women, children, and old people of German ancestry were targets of irrational violence. They were killed outright or tortured, they were forced into prison camps where they starved to death, or they were turned out of their towns and villages and loaded into freight cars headed west. It made no difference that they were citizens of the country and their ancestors had lived there for centuries. The Potsdam agreements presented an opportunity for Czechoslovakia, Yugoslavia, Romania, Poland, and the Soviet Union to get rid of their ethnic Germans and seize their property. In the part of Germany east of the Oder and Neisse rivers Polish militia patrolled the roads and lent support to the gradual infiltration into the area of Polish refugees who had lost their homes through war or who had been expelled from the eastern provinces of Poland by the Soviets.

Starting in the winter of 1945 with those voluntarily fleeing the oncoming Russian troops, the occupied zones of postwar Germany became the destination of millions of people who arrived with scarcely any possessions, with fragmented families, and broken health. The experiences of the expellees depended on circumstances rather than on any planning they might have done. Even when the expulsions were conducted dispassionately, the people were at the mercy of the weather, poor transportation, and roving bands of robbers and thugs. Thousands of refugees poured into Berlin daily, though the ruined city and its relief agencies could not cope with them. In despair they piled up in railroad stations and transit camps.[10]

When Great Britain and the United States realized the enormous consequences of the Potsdam agreements, they tried to modify the effects and temporarily halt the population transfers through the winter months. Their efforts were ignored. Adding to the catastrophe, the expellees were ineligible for aid from the world organization that most logically should have been able to help, the United Nations Relief and Rehabilitation Administration.[11] This put the responsibility on the private charitable

---

[10] De Zayas, *Nemesis at Potsdam*, chap. 6, 103-30.
[11] United Nations Relief and Rehabilitation Administration, *U.N.R.R.A.: The History* (New York: Columbia University Press, 1950), 2:508-10.

Introduction

organizations within the western zones of Germany and in the United States and Great Britain. German churches had kept the respect of disillusioned civilians, so after the war their relief agencies became the principal tools for aiding the expellees. The Evangelical Hilfswerk and the Catholic Caritas built solid organizations that operated across zonal lines, collecting and distributing many thousands of tons of food and clothing.[12] In addition, after several months of interdiction, the American military government finally allowed concerned Americans to send relief parcels into the U.S. zone.

Contemporary British and American magazines published only a few articles on the fate of the fifteen million expellees because people were not interested. Most viewed German suffering with indifference. They were tired of hearing about the war and its consequences. Nevertheless, religious journals such as *Christian Century* continued to remind their readers that as Christians they had an obligation to help the people of Germany.

German Attitudes

After the war, the expectations that victors and vanquished had of each other soon proved to be wrong. Germans who welcomed the end of the war and the arrival of the western Allies had anticipated new beginnings of political and economic life, aided by the generous and just Americans. The people who had silently opposed the stranglehold of nazism felt as if they were being liberated. It was a shock to them to discover that the outside world considered them to be sadistic Nazis. The Americans, on the other hand, expected opposition, both undercover and overt, and the docility of the Germans surprised the army commanders. The discovery of the concentration camps, however, juxtaposed with healthy, well-clothed civilians, heightened the U.S. army's resolve to be stern and formal occupiers.

On the part of the Americans, the likeable children, the clean and cooperative civilians, and the peaceful atmosphere softened the hearts of the U.S. soldiers. It became impossible to maintain the fraternization ban. This was recognized by the soldiers long before the official orders were modified, so from the beginning American military personnel were forced to watch the circumvention of unenforceable regulations. This incongruity was not lost on the Germans. Military government in the U.S. zone also had the task of determining who was reliable among the civilian population so that Germans

---

[12] Stewart W. Herman, *Rebirth of the German Church* (New York: Harper, 1946), 263.

Introduction

could be employed in the many jobs that needed to be filled. This process, called denazification, was intended to be a fair, uniform method of separating the active Nazis from those who had refused to support the regime. It had an elaborate structure of questionnaires and judicial hearings, but because of the numbers of people involved, it was impossible to treat everyone equally. After years of effort, denazification left both Germans and Americans dissatisfied with the results.

Another goal of American occupation personnel was to change the ideas implanted in the people during the years of nazi rule. The democratic system of government, liberally spiced with American culture, seemed the perfect antidote for years of nazi propaganda. The notion that newer, richer, and bigger automatically meant better was a common one among U.S. soldiers and civilians. Americans had little appreciation for the rich Germanic culture that had existed long before the Nazis and that, in the eyes of Germans, stood apart from the crude fascist state.

In the opinions of the defeated Germans, the occupation was a period of misery caused as much by the occupiers as by the loss of the war itself. As the months went by without improvement in their physical and economic conditions, the people who lived in the American zone became discouraged. Their high hopes for American assistance evaporated and they became resentful and angry. It seemed to the Germans that the American occupation had very little continuity of purpose and was riddled with mismanagement and corruption. The harsh orders of 1945 were modified again and again, although industrial dismantling continued at the same time that private food parcels were being sent from the United States. Democracy was preached throughout the zone but the occupation government was autocratic. The flip-flop of U.S. policies was especially noticeable in relations with the Soviet Union. The friendship and alliance of 1945 dissolved into defensive reactions to Soviet intransigence within two years.[13]

Germans soothed their guilty consciences by saying that the American occupiers behaved as badly as the Nazis had. The Allied bombing raids had killed innocent civilians for simple revenge rather than to achieve a purpose. The civilian deaths and the destruction of German cities had been as horrible as the nazi extermination of the Jews, in the opinion of some Germans.[14]

---

[13] Norbert Muhlen, "America and American Occupation in German Eyes," *Annals of the American Academy of Political and Social Science* 295 (September 1954): 54-55.

[14] Kurt H. Wolff, *German Attempts at Picturing Germany, Texts* (Columbus: Ohio State University, 1955), 33-34.

Introduction

The atrocities of the expulsions triggered by the Potsdam Conference were judged to be more than enough retribution for German war crimes. By 1947 many Germans were sure that the food shortages in the British and American zones were intentional. The conquerors planned to have millions of Germans starve to death to reduce the population and to lessen the future threat of a revived Germany.[15] Each brutal or senseless act of cruelty by occupation soldiers confirmed these attitudes. Germans also condemned occupation personnel who trafficked in the black market and used their affluence to buy sex. In the same vein, it was convenient to blame the lower moral standards of the postwar years on the occupiers' policies of too little food and too few consumer goods. Some Germans even condemned imported American movies for encouraging young people to act like Chicago gangsters and western outlaws.[16]

No German had good words for the denazification process. Despite the best intentions, the realities of administration were capricious and unjust. Everyone knew people who were falsely accused and punished, and others who were guilty but went free. Some persons who were useful to the military governments were employed despite their backgrounds. When people were condemned for supporting the Third Reich it seemed that they were being punished for what would be praised as loyalty and patriotism in the victors' countries. In addition, each zone administered and regulated its own denazification policies, so the consequences of having supported the nazi regime differed from zone to zone. The Soviets were especially pragmatic about former associations. They accepted repentance and active support of the new zonal government as proof of being denazified, while the other zones were more strict.[17]

American occupation planning experts had agreed that one facet of the reeducation process would include the sharing of American culture as well as the encouragement of democratic values using examples of American political accomplishments. This one-way street of cultural infusion was deeply resented by many Germans. Not only did they not understand some U.S. cultural offerings, they were convinced that the rich traditions of Germany were far superior. While Americans promoted famous statesmen such as Washington and Lincoln, Germans honored great musicians, artists,

---

[15] Ibid., 19.
[16] Muhlen, "America and American Occupation in German Eyes," 55.
[17] Wolff, *German Attempts at Picturing Germany, Texts*, 31-32.

Introduction

authors, and philosophers. Such comparisons encouraged Germans to view Americans as unintellectual and shallow.[18]

The stereotypes of Americans as naive, ignorant, uncultured, materialistic, and flaunters of wealth allowed Germans to cling to their feelings of cultural and moral superiority, despite all their tribulations. They applauded their own abilities to withstand and triumph over the suffering and hardships of the postwar period. They believed that only Germans had the courage and determination to live in the rubble. Their understanding of Americans and the United States was poor, and few extended themselves to learn more because daily life was so difficult that they had little energy to look past their immediate circumstances. German newspapers and journals frequently published articles extolling the greatness of three aspects of their civilization: der Geist (spirit), die Seele (soul), and die Kultur (culture). These concepts became the focus of German pride and honor during the period of defeat and disgrace.[19] In a sense they were the rallying points that bound Germans together and allowed them to feel intellectually superior to their conquerors. This helped them to survive. As social scientists pursue the lives of ordinary people looking for clues that will help interpret and define aspects of mid-twentieth century history, they will need easier access to the sources that reveal those lives. This bibliography is intended to increase such access.

---

[18] Ibid., 24-26; Verena Botzenhart-Viehe, "The German Reaction to the American Occupation, 1944-1947," Ph.D. diss., University of California, Santa Barbara, 1980, 140.
[19] Botzenhart-Viehe, "German Reaction to the American Occupation," 136.

Chapter 1

German Experiences

The war ended at different times for Germans, depending on where they were. Those on the western edge of the Reich saw Allied troops capture their cities in late fall of 1944. Others fled the Soviet advance in the winter of 1944-45, and still others were in the siege of Berlin in April and May of 1945. For most there was not a sharp demarcation between war and peace. One hesitantly became the other, and both were full of danger and death.

Although most Germans spent the early postwar years in one of the four occupation zones, many former soldiers were prisoners of war in British, U.S., Soviet, or French prison camps. Each man's experience was unique, and each survivor brought that experience back to Germany as he tried to reintegrate himself into family, work, and community.

This chapter includes war and prison memoirs, as well as those relating personal struggles to survive the early postwar years. In addition to memoirs it includes the philosophical and historical works written by Germans explaining the popularity of nazism and Hitler and interpreting the events of the occupation years.

German Experiences

1 ADENAUER, KONRAD. *Memoirs, 1945-1953*. Translated from German. Chicago: H. Regnery, 1966. 478 p.
    Includes a chapter on his experiences at the end of the war. He describes the destruction of Cologne, the general chaos, food shortages, and his part in the postwar government of the city.

2 ANDREAS-FRIEDRICH, RUTH. *Berlin Underground, 1938-1945*. Translated from German. New York: Holt, 1947. 312 p.
    An employee of the Ullstein publishing house, the author was also a member of an anti-nazi group that hid people who were being hunted by the Gestapo. In Berlin at the end of the war, her knowledge of Russian kept her alive.

3 BARTH, KARL. *The Only Way: How Can the Germans Be Cured?* Translated from German. New York: Philosophical Library, 1947. 122 p.
    Originally writing in the spring of 1945, the Swiss theologian offers suggestions for rescuing Germany from its past mistakes.

4 BECKER, HANS, pseud. *Devil on My Shoulder*. Translated from German. London: Jarrolds, 1955. 216 p.
    Sent to Siberia as a prisoner of war, Becker was released with other German nationals and reached Germany in the spring of 1950.

5 BERNHARD, THOMAS. *Gathering Evidence: A Memoir*. Translated from German. New York: Knopf, 1985. 340 p.
    Memories from the immediate postwar years in Austria. His family life was difficult, with rationed food, crowded living conditions, long work hours, and too little money.

6 BLÜCHER von WAHLSTATT, KURT. *Know Your Germans*. Translated from German. London: Chapman & Hall, 1951. 188 p.
    A German view of the history and national characteristics of the German people, which explain the Third Reich and World War II.

7 BROWN, LIANE I. *Refuge*. Greenville, S.C.: Unusual Publications, 1987. 199 p.
    Liane and her family fled East Prussia ahead of the Soviet troops but were overtaken in a small town east of Berlin. Over the next year, Poles moved into the area and the Germans were forced to leave for Berlin and the Soviet zone.

8   BUTTERWORTH, EMMA M. *As the Waltz Was Ending.* New York: Four Winds Press, 1982. 187 p.

   A ballet dancer describes her war years in Vienna. Her description of the difficulties encountered by the people of Vienna while the Soviets occupied the city is informative. The book ends with the arrival of American troops in July of 1945.

9   CHESNEY, INGA L. *A Time of Rape.* New York: Prentice-Hall, 1972. 255 p.

   An autobiographical account of a young girl's experiences in Berlin at the end of the war. She supplies many details of residents' efforts to stay out of the way of the Russians. Bartering possessions with farmers for food was a common experience. When the Americans assumed control of the sector where she lived, Chesney went to work for them because she spoke both English and French in addition to German.

10   CHRISTEN, PETER. *From Military Government to State Department: How a German Employee Sees the Work of the United States Military Government and the State Department in a Small Bavarian Town, Its Success and Its Handicaps.* Erding, FRG: Wagner, 1950. 129 p.

   After being released from a prison camp in the United States, Christen returned home and went to work for the U.S. military government. He gives his impressions of the Americans, the Bavarians, and the war years.

11   COMMITTEE AGAINST MASS EXPULSIONS. *The Land of the Dead.* New York: Committee Against Mass Expulsions, 1947. 32 p.

   This pamphlet was written and published in the United States to inform the American public about the expulsions. The Committee also published other pamphlets on the same subject: *Men without the Rights of Men* (1948) and *Tragedy of a People* (1948).

12   DAY, INGEBORG. *Ghost Waltz: A Memoir.* New York: Viking Press, 1980. 244 p.

   Day is especially effective in explaining her confused state-of-mind after the war. Subconsciously, she was unable to stop hating Jews after the years of believing nazi propaganda.

13 DIETRICH, HERMANN R. *Creating a New State: German Problems, 1945 to 1953*. Translated from German. Cologne: Comel, 1953. 67 p.

    A political history of the postwar period, describing the occupation and the beginnings of the Federal Republic.

14 DOERNBERG, STEFAN. *The First Steps into a New Germany*. Dresden: Verlag Zeit im Bild, 1965. 63 p.

    Photographs of the destroyed cities and their rebuilding.

15 EICH, HERMANN. *The Unloved Germans*. Translated from German. New York: Stein & Day, 1965. 255 p.

    Philosophical explanations of the rise of Hitler and the war, from the German point of view.

16 EINSIEDEL, HEINRICH, GRAF von. *I Joined the Russians: A Captured German Flier's Diary of the Communist Temptation*. Translated from German. New Haven, Conn.: Yale University Press, 1953. 306 p. British title: *The Shadow of Stalingrad*.

    Einsiedel was captured by the Soviets during the war and became a member of the Free Germany Committee. Released from a prison camp in 1947, he broke with the Communists in 1949.

17 EMMRICH, KURT. *The Invisible Flag*. Translated from German. New York: John Day, 1956. 250 p.

    A personal account of experiences in a medical unit on the eastern front during the final phases of the war.

18 FEHLING, HELMUT M. *One Great Prison: The Story Behind Russia's Unreleased P.O.W.s*. Translated from German. Boston: Beacon Press, 1951. 175 p.

    Includes a personal account of the author's six years in a Soviet prison camp as well as many documents and official announcements about German prisoners in the Soviet Union.

19 FERNAU, JOACHIM. *Captain Pax*. Translated from German. London: Constable, 1960. 134 p.

    A German officer on the eastern front was captured by the Soviet troops. He conveys the emotions of his fellow soldiers regarding the war.

20 FITTKAU, GERHARD A. *My Thirty-Third Year (a Priest's Experience in a Russian Work Camp)*. Translated from German. New York: Farrar, Straus, Cudahy, 1958. 263 p.

Autobiography of an East Prussian Catholic priest who was captured by the Soviets at the end of the war and sent to a Siberian work camp.

21 FORELL, CLEMENS, pseud. [JOSEF M. BAUER]. *As Far As My Feet Will Carry Me*. Translated from German. New York: Random House, 1957. 347 p.

One of many autobiographies written by German soldiers who were prisoners of war in the Soviet Union. Bauer eventually escaped through Iran and reached home in December 1952.

22 FRAENKEL, HEINRICH. *Farewell to Germany*. London: B. Hanison, 1959. 142 p.

After spending the war years in exile in Britain, Fraenkel returned to Germany several times in the immediate postwar period. When he decided to become a British citizen he wrote the book to explain why.

23 _____. *A Nation Divided*. London: Yates, 1949. 87 p.

A moderate and balanced view of German war guilt and punishment, German economic recovery, and Soviet domination of the eastern zone.

24 FRANCKE, GUNHILD. *Last Train West*. London: Hodden & Stoughton, 1977. 102 p.

Describes being evacuated from Silesia with the retreating German army. In western Germany her family struggled to overcome the cold, hunger, and primitive living conditions they were experiencing.

25 FRISCH, MAX. *Sketchbook 1945-1949*. Translated from German. New York: Harcourt Brace Jovanovich, 1977. 301 p.

A diary of sorts, recording observations of life in the immediate postwar period in Germany.

26 FURMANSKI, H. R. R. *Life Can Be Cruel*. New York: Vantage Press, 1960. 61 p.

An East Prussian's survival after being captured on the eastern front in 1942. He was released from a Soviet prison camp in 1949 and traveled to Germany to find that only a niece had survived in his family.

27 GARTHAUS, ILS M. *The Way We Lived in Germany during World War II: A Personal Account*. Perth, Aust.: Arale, 1977. 172 p.
Autobiography of a dancer. Not reviewed.

28 GERMAN FEDERAL REPUBLIC. BUNDESMINISTERIUM FÜR ANGELEGENHEITEN DER VERTRIEBENEN. *The German Expellee Problem: Lectures Delivered at the International Conference Called by the League of Red Cross Societies at Hannover, 9.4-14.4.1951*. Bonn: Federal Ministry of Expellee Affairs, 1951. 44 p.

An example of the informative English-language pamphlets published by the Federal Republic since 1949. Other titles include: *Some Facts about Expellees in Germany* (1949) and *Care and Help for Expellees, Refugees, Victims of Material War Damage* (1956).

29 GLASER, HERMANN. *The Rubble Years: The Cultural Roots of Postwar Germany, 1945-1948*. Translated from German. New York: Paragon House, 1986. 372 p.

A cultural and social history of the postwar period. Glaser uses quotations to illustrate the reactions of the public and responses of the arts to conditions at the end of the war.

30 GOLLWITZER, HELMUT. *Unwilling Journey: A Diary from Russia*. Translated from German. Philadelphia: Muhlenberg Press, 1953. 316 p.

Describes his years in Soviet prison camps after being captured at the end of the war. He served in many kinds of labor camps, including one at an asbestos mine. A Lutheran pastor, Gollwitzer ministered to his fellow prisoners.

31 GÖTTINGER ARBEITSKREIS. *Emigration: A Means of Solving the German Problem?* Göttingen: Göttinger Arbeitskreis, 1950. 16 p.

An informative pamphlet by the Göttingen Research Committee, an organization formed to do research on the expulsion. It has published other works in both German and English.

32 GRAU, KARL F., ed. *Silesian Inferno: War Crimes of the Red Army on Its March into Silesia in 1945, a Collection of Documents*. Translated from German. Cologne: Informations- und Dokumentationszentrum West, 1970. 210 p.

A collection of documents that describe the crimes of the Soviet armies as they invaded the Silesian province of Germany.

33 GRIMM, HANS. *Answer of a German: An Open Letter to the Archbishop of Canterbury*. Translated from German. Dublin: Euphorion Books, 1952. 237 p.

  Originally written as a response to a message sent to Germans in 1945 by the archbishop. Grimm defends recent German history.

34 GRÜN, MAX von der. *Howl Like the Wolves: Growing Up in Nazi Germany*. Translated from German. New York: Morrow, 1980. 285 p.

  Intersperses memories of his childhood and youth with the reality of Hitler's Germany, illustrated with documents and photographs.

35 HAHN, LILI. *White Flags of Surrender*. Translated from German. Washington D.C.: Robert B. Luce, 1974. 354 p.

  Having a Jewish mother made Lili vulnerable. She served a prison sentence for passing rumors, saw her mother imprisoned, and traded sex to keep her mother's name off the deportation lists. Good descriptions of daily life in Frankfurt during the war.

36 HÄRING, BERNHARD. *Embattled Witness: Memories of a Time of War*. New York: Seabury Press, 1976. 116 p.

  Catholic priest traveled with the German armies as a medic while saying mass and counseling the soldiers without permission. At the war's end on the eastern front, the author posed as a Polish priest to avoid being sent to Siberia as a prisoner of war.

37 HASENACK, WILHELM. *Dismantling the Ruhr Valley: A Menace to European Recovery (ERP)*. Translated from German. Condensed and revised. Cologne: Westdeutscher Verlag, 1949. 100 p.

  Examines the economic consequences of postwar reparations in the Ruhr Valley from a German point of view.

38 HAUSER, HEINRICH. *The German Talks Back*. New York: Holt, 1945. 215 p.

  Writing in the summer of 1945, the author explains why after six years in the United States he has decided to take his family back to live in a defeated and impoverished Germany.

39 HECK, ALFONS. *A Child of Hitler: Germany in the Days When God Wore a Swastika*. Frederick, Conn.: Renaissance House, 1985. 207 p.

    A sensitive account of the author's rapid rise through the ranks of Hitler Youth until, near the end of the war, he was in charge of hundreds of boys on the western front. The last chapter covers the postwar period.

40 HORNSTEIN, ERIKA von. *Russians in My Home*. Translated from German. London: Angus & Robertson, 1960. 222 p.

    Describes her family's experiences at the end of the war in an east German village. The U.S. troops occupied it first, then turned it over to the Soviets.

41 HORSTMANN, LALI von SCHWABACH. *We Chose to Stay*. Boston: Houghton Mifflin, 1954. 206 p. British title: *Nothing but Tears*.

    Anti-nazi landowners chose to stay on their estate east of Berlin when the war ended. The author's husband was imprisoned and killed by the Soviets because he was a landowner.

42 INSTITUT ZUR FÖRDERUNG ÖFFENTLICHER ANGELEGENHEITEN. *Europe and the German Refugees*. Translated from German. Frankfurt am Main: Institut Zur FÖrderung Öffentlicher Angelegenheiten, 1952. 94 p.

    Essays discussing economic, social, and psychological consequences of the expulsions. Describes how the refugees try to help themselves. Includes an English-language bibliography.

43 JAENICKE, WOLFGANG, ed. *From Scratch ... a Report in Pictures on the Industries Built Up by the Expellees in Bavaria*. Munich: Staatssekretär für Flüchtlingsangelegenheiten, 1951. [79] p.

    Photographs of the various ways expellees have supported themselves in Bavaria.

44 KALOW, GERT. *The Shadow of Hitler: A Critique of Political Consciousness*. Translated from German. Chicago: Quadrangle Books, 1970. 144 p.

    Describes the philosophical basis for German national thought and how some beliefs need to be eradicated as no longer valid.

45   KANTER, TRUDI. *Some Girls, Some Hats, and Hitler: A Love Story*. Suffolk: N. Spearman, 1984. 254 p.
     The autobiography of an Austrian. Not reviewed.

46   KAPS, JOHANNES, ed. *Martyrdom and Heroism of the Women of East Germany: An Excerpt from the Silesian Passion, 1945-46*. Translated from German. Munich: Christ Unterwegs, 1955. 155 p.
     Not reviewed.

47   _____, ed. *Martyrdom of Silesian Priests, 1945-1946: Scenes from the Passion of Silesia*. Translated from German. Munich: Christ Unterwegs, 1950. 120 p.
     Not reviewed.

48   _____, ed. *The Tragedy of Silesia, 1945-46: A Documentary Account with a Special Survey of the Archdiocese of Breslau*. Translated from German. Munich: Christ Unterwegs, 1953. 576 p.
     Testimony collected by the Catholic church documenting the invasion of the Soviet troops, Polish excesses, and the expulsions of the ethnic Germans.

49   KARDORFF, URSULA von. *Diary of a Nightmare: Berlin 1942-1945*. Translated from German. New York: Day, 1966. 256 p.
     After spending most of the war working in Berlin, Kardorff fled the city in February 1945. In the fall, she illegally entered the Soviet zone of Berlin to help her mother cross to the west.

50   KERN, ERICH. *Dance of Death*. Translated from German. New York: Scribner, 1951. 255 p.
     A personal narrative of soldiering on the eastern front. Kern is critical of nazi totalitarianism.

51   KNEF, HILDEGARD. *The Gift Horse*. Translated from German. New York: McGraw-Hill, 1971. 384 p.
     The actress describes growing up in nazi Germany. After the war, she acted in some of the first German motion pictures that were licensed by the Allies.

52   KOEHN, ILSE. *Mischling, Second Degree: My Childhood in Nazi Germany*. New York: Greenwillow Books, 1977. 240 p.
     An autobiographical account of how her Social Democratic parents survived the war by splitting up and protecting Ilse from the

knowledge that her father's mother was Jewish. When she was old enough, she reluctantly participated in Hitler Youth activities.

53   KÖHLER, ALBERT, ed. *We Thank You. Wir Danken Euch*. Mindelheim, FRG: Selbsthilfe-Verlag, 1949. 95 p.
Not reviewed.

54   KONSTANTIN, PRINZ von BAYERN. *After the Flood*. Translated from German. Philadelphia: J.B. Lippincott, 1955. 224 p.
The royal prince of Bavaria records unusual war and postwar experiences of people he knows.

55   KRÜGER, HORST. *A Crack in the Wall: Growing Up under Hitler*. Translated from German. New York: Gromm International Publications, 1982. 242 p.
Describes growing up in Berlin and serving in the army. He reveals his feelings as he gradually becomes disillusioned with nazism.

56   KURTH, K. O., ed. *Documents of Humanity during the Mass Expulsions*. [Collected by the Göttinger Arbeitskreis.] Translated from German. New York: Harper, 1954. 184 p.
A radio appeal was made by the Göttingen Research Committee for reports of good deeds done for expellees by Allied prisoners and forced laborers or by individual Poles, Czechs, and Russians. These helpful acts are gathered into this collection.

57   LEHNDORFF, HANS von. *Token of a Covenant: Diary of an East Prussian Surgeon, 1945-47*. Translated from German. Chicago: H. Regnery, 1964. 328 p. British title: *East Prussian Journal, 1945-47*.
Details his precarious survival as the Soviets invaded East Prussia, ravaged the countryside in revenge, and gradually established their control. He escaped being killed or hauled off to a Siberian labor camp on several occasions.

58   LEONHARD, WOLFGANG. *Child of the Revolution*. Translated from German. Chicago: H. Regnery, 1958. 562 p.
Writes of his long training in the Soviet Union and his return to Germany after the war with other fellow Communists to help lead the eastern zone into a "new age." Disillusioned, he defected in 1949.

German Experiences

59   *Letters from Germany.* Introduction by Oswald G. Villard. Human Events Pamphlets, no. 5. Washington D.C.: Human Events, 1946. 28 p.

   Letters collected in Germany and sent to the United States by military personnel stationed in the American zone. The Germans offer little criticism of the Allies, exhibit willingness to admit war guilt, and declare their readiness to build a new Germany.

60   LÖWENSTEIN, PRINZ HUBERTUS. *Towards the Future Shore.* London: Gollancz, 1968. 448 p.

   An autobiography of a German nobleman who took his family into exile in the United States in 1933. They returned to Germany in 1946 to cast their lot with their native country. The prince wrote stories and dispatches for American newspapers and journals and avoided censorship by sending them through the mail reserved for GIs.

61   LÖWENTHAL, FRITZ. *News from Soviet Germany.* Translated from German. London: Gollancz, 1950. 343 p.

   A defector describes daily life in the Soviet zone in the early postwar years. He was a high-ranking official who was quickly disappointed with communist reality.

62   LUKASCHEK, HANS. *The Expellees in the German Federal Republic and Their Importance to Europe.* Translated from German. Bonn: Bundesministerium für Vertriebene, Flüchtlinge, und Kriegsgeschädigte, 1950. 15 p.

   One of many statistical pamphlets issued by a department of the Federal Republic after 1949.

63   _____. *The German Expellees: A German Focal Problem.* Translated from German. Bonn: Bundesministerium für Vertriebene, Flüchtlinge, und Kriegsgeschädigte, 1951. 35 p.

   Another example of the informative pamphlets issued by the Federal Republic after 1949.

64   McKEE, ILSE. *Tomorrow the World.* London: Dent, 1960. 199 p.

   Autobiography of a typical young German girl growing up in nazi Germany. She conformed when necessary. Her fiancé was killed on the eastern front, and she fled west to escape the invading Soviet troops.

65 MACKINNON, MARIANNE. *The Naked Years: Growing Up in Nazi Germany*. London: Chatto & Windus, 1987. 304 p.

Describes life in Germany during the war years and for two years afterward. Mackinnon was hired by the American military government and then by the British because she could speak English. When the town where she was living was turned over to Soviet troops, she was evacuated with the British.

66 MASCHMANN, MILITA. *Account Rendered: A Dossier on My Former Self.* Translated from German. New York: Abelard-Schuman, 1965. 223 p.

Attempts to accept the truth about nazi Germany and its leaders by trying to clarify her involvement in the Hitler Youth before and during the war.

67 MEINECKE, FRIEDRICH. *The German Catastrophe: Reflections and Recollections*. Translated from German. Cambridge, Mass.: Harvard University Press, 1950. 121 p.

The essay, written in 1946 by a well-known German historian, examines Germany's recent history and suggests that the solution is to return to the ideals of the pre-Bismarck years.

68 MERKL, PETER H. *Germany: Yesterday and Tomorrow*. New York: Oxford University Press, 1965. 366 p.

Merkl explains Germany to Americans while teaching at a U.S. university. He left postwar Germany as a refugee and returned three years later. He describes the attitudes and feelings of the people about the war, the occupation, and economic recovery.

69 MOLDEN, FRITZ. *Exploding Star: A Young Austrian against Hitler*. Translated from German. New York: Morrow, 1979. 280 p.

The author joined illegal Austrian youth organizations in protest over the war. Later he was recruited to spy for the Allies, and after the Americans invaded Austria, he was in the OSS. After a time, he resigned, found his parents in Vienna, and helped his father restart his liberal newspaper.

70 MÜLLER, TRAUDIE W. *The Whip My Homecoming.* Red Hill, A.C.T.: Golden Leaf Publishers, 1986. 319 p.

As ethnic Germans Müller and her children were imprisoned when they tried to return to their home in Yugoslavia after the war. After two horrifying years, they were able to sneak across the Austrian border to freedom.

German Experiences

71 NATIONALE FRONT DES DEMOKRATISCHEN DEUTSCHLAND. *White Book on the American and British Policy of Intervention in West Germany and the Revival of German Imperialism.* Berlin?: Presented by the National Council of the National Front of Democratic Germany, 1951. 199 p.

Describes how the United States is rearming West Germany in anticipation of war. The imperialism of the west threatens the peace-loving people of the German Democratic Republic.

72 NOELLE-NEUMANN, ELISABETH. *The Germans: Public Opinion Polls, 1947-1966.* Bonn: Verlag für Demoskopie, 1967. 630 p.

Survey results of opinion polls taken regularly in western Germany from 1947 to 1966. The polls were conducted by the German Institute for Public Opinion Research and sought opinions about the occupation, the occupation personnel, the German economy, etc.

73 NORK, KARL. *Hell in Siberia.* Translated from German. London: Hale, 1957. 222 p.

Details his life after the war. He was captured by the British in Italy and turned over to the Soviets to provide manpower for the rebuilding of their country. He was in Siberian labor camps for eight years before being released.

74 OBERLÄNDER, THEODOR, ed. *The Expellees Are Working: Picture Report of Reconstruction Work Done by the Expellees in Bavaria.* Gräfelfing near Munich: Verlag für Planung und Aufbau, 1951. 103 p.

Pictorial. Not reviewed.

75 PABEL, REINHOLD. *Enemies Are Human.* Philadelphia: Winston, 1955. 248 p.

A German prisoner in an American camp, Pabel escaped and made his way to Chicago where he became the owner of a bookstore. Eventually the FBI caught him and deported him. Publicity helped him to return to the United States after only five months in Germany.

76 *Refugees Courageous: Help Bavaria Help Her Refugees.* Munich: Staatssekretariat für Flüchtlingswesen, 1950. 31 p.

An informative pamphlet issued by a department of the Bavarian state government. Not reviewed.

77 RODENHAUSER, REINER, and RALPH R. NAPP. *Breaking Down the Barrier: A Human Document on War*. Durham, N.C.: Seeman Printery, 1961. 148 p.

 A former German prisoner describes his philosophy of war and peace, and how peace can be achieved. He weaves in some of his personal experiences as a soldier and prisoner.

78 RÖPKE, WILHELM. *The Solution of the German Problem*. Translated from German. New York: Putnam, 1947. 282 p.

 German social scientist philosophizes about a plan for rescuing Germany from its pariah status among European nations.

79 SALOMON, ERNST von. *The Answers of Ernst von Salomon to the 131 Questions in the Allied Military Government "Fragebogen."* Translated from German. Garden City, N.Y.: Doubleday, 1955. German title: *Fragebogen* (1951).

 The author, a famous writer, sharply criticizes the American military government for its denazification procedures and its general treatment of Germans in the period immediately after the war. Due to an error, he was detained for eighteen months in a prison camp where the treatment was brutal and dehumanizing.

80 SCHACHT, HJALMAR H. G. *Confessions of the "Old Wizard": Autobiography*. Translated from German. Boston: Houghton Mifflin, 1956. 484 p. Reprint. Westport, Conn.: Greenwood Press, 1974.

 Imprisoned by the Nazis after the assassination attempt on Hitler, Schacht was again imprisoned for three years by the Americans while awaiting denazification.

81 SCHAEFFER, KARL-HEINZ. *The Boy Between*. London: Wingate, 1955. 221 p.

 Typical tale of a young Berliner who fought in the German army, worked for the Soviets for a while after the war, and then eventually crossed into the west. He was never very successful in his endeavors.

82 SCHIEDER, THEODOR, ed. *Documents on the Expulsion of the Germans from Eastern-Central-Europe.* Selection and translation from *Dokumentation der Vertriebung der Deutschen aus Ost-Mitteleuropa.* 4 vols. Bonn: Bundesministerium für Vertriebene, Flüchtlinge und Kriegsgeschädigte, 1958-60.

A condensation of a multivolume collection of documents, eyewitness reports, and commentary on the expulsion of the ethnic Germans from eastern and central Europe. Volume 5 and three supplementary volumes of the original German set were not translated into English at the time the rest were published.

83 SCHMELING, MARIANNE. *Flee the Wolf: The Story of a Family's Miraculous Journey to Freedom.* Norfolk, Va.: Donning, 1978. 290 p.
Not reviewed.

84 SCHULENBURG, TISSA HESS. *The Last Days and the First.* London: Harvill Press, 1948. 32 p.

Brief sketches of life as an anti-nazi landowner in eastern Germany at the end of the war. Schulenburg has to hide her sympathy for the French forced laborers on her estate because the local nazi leader watches her all the time. When the Soviet troops approach she persuades a passing army unit to give up its guns rather than to try to defend the village.

85 SCHWARZER, H. RUDY. *My Road to Freedom.* South Yarmouth, Mass.: J. Curley & Associates, 1985. 280 p.

Fifteen at the end of the war, Schwarzer is living in Silesia when the Soviet troops invade. He survives in the eastern zone for a while, then immigrates to Berlin and eventually to America.

86 SHELTON, REGINA M. *To Lose a War: Memories of a German Girl.* Carbondale: Southern Illinois University Press, 1982. 228 p.

Growing up in Silesia near the Czech border, Gina tells about the end of the war and the arrival of the Soviet troops. The womenfolk of her family survived by selling their belongings. When Poles from eastern Poland are settled in Silesia, the German residents are forcibly expelled into the Soviet zone of Germany.

87 SLATER, LISA. *Rape of Berlin.* Brooklyn, N.Y.: Pageant-Poseidon, 1972. 91 p.

Slater experiences the end of the war in Berlin. After living with the Soviets for a while, she seems glad to exchange "being a good German" for "being against Communism."

88 STADEN, WENDELGARD von. *Darkness over the Valley*. Translated from German. New York: Penguin Books, 1982. 163 p.

Describes growing up in a rural area near Stuttgart and having the Nazis appropriate a small valley on her parents' property for a prison camp. She and her mother quietly tried to aid the prisoners as much as possible without being caught. Her family and townspeople took shelter in a cave when the American troops moved into the area.

89 STERNBERG, FRITZ. *Living with Crisis: The Battle against Depression and War*. Translated from German. New York: John Day, 1949. 184 p.

Sees the answers to the economic revival of Germany and Europe to be in socialism and political unity. The Marshall Plan is not effective by itself.

90 STOLL, IRMA. *The Sparrow's Song*. Wheaton, Ill.: Tyndale House, 1984. 132 p.

The experiences of a fifteen-year old East Prussian girl who was captured by the Soviets and sent to a prison camp in Siberia. She attributes her survival to her belief in God.

91 TEMPEL, GUDRUN. *The Germans: An Indictment of My People: A Personal History and a Challenge*. Translated from German. New York: Random House, 1963. 172 p.

A sensitive autobiography as well as an intellectual inquiry into the causes and events of the war and the attitudes of the German people in the postwar period.

92 THOMSON, STEWART, with ROBERT BIALEK. *The Bialek Affair*. London: Wingate, 1955. 203 p.

Bialek tells of being a Communist in the Soviet zone and then losing confidence in its principles. Not reviewed.

93 THORWALD, JÜRGEN. *Flight in the Winter*. Translated from German. New York: Pantheon, 1951. 318 p. Paperback title: *Defeat in the East* (Ballantine Books, 1959).

A narrative account of the last five months on the collapsing eastern front. A condensation of *Es Begann an der Weichsel* and *Das Ende an der Elbe*.

94 TURNWALD, WILHELM K., ed. *Documents on the Expulsion of the Sudeten Germans*. Translated from German. Munich:

Arbeitsgemeinschaft zur Wahrung Sudetendeutscher Interessen, 1953. 308 p.

A collection of sworn statements from Sudeten Germans regarding their treatment by the Czechs from 1945 to 1947.

95 ———, ed. *Sudeten German Picture Book*. Munich: Christ Unterwegs, 1949. 104 p.

Pictorial. Not reviewed.

96 *Two Women and a War: Diary and Pillar of Fire*. [By Grete Paquin and Renate Hagen.] Philadelphia: Muhlenberg Press, 1953. 233 p.

Two personal accounts of life in Germany during the war. The stories are told as a series of events without much introspection.

97 VOGT, HANNAH. *The Burden of Guilt: A Short History of Germany, 1914-1945*. Translated from German. New York: Oxford University Press, 1964. 318 p.

Philosophical background for the recent history of Germany. The author explains her interpretation of why the Third Reich occurred.

98 WATSON, ANN. *They Came in Peace*. Palos Verdes Estates, Calif: T.W. Publishers, 1972. 382 p.

The personal story of an Austrian. Not reviewed.

99 WEISS, WINFRIED. *A Nazi Childhood*. Santa Barbara, Calif.: Capra Press, 1983. 196 p.

Although quite young when the war began, Weiss recalls his life toward the end of the war and through the summer of 1945. With his father away he seeks male companionship first with a Russian worker and then with the American soldiers that occupy his town.

100 WELLS, INGEBORG. *Enough, No More*. London: H. Joseph, 1948. 294 p.

Autobiography of a dancer, actress, and cabaret performer. She writes of her life in Berlin at the end of the war and the beginning of peace. Daily bombings, scarcity of food, the siege by the Russians, and the gradual restoration of calm, law, and order characterize 1945.

101 WENDEL, ELSE. *Hausfrau at War: A German Woman's Account of Life in Hitler's Reich*. London: Odhams Press, 1957. 255 p.

Vividly portrays daily life in Berlin during the war. Deserted by her husband in 1939, she advertised for a new husband so she would not have to board her sons with friends while she worked. After a second marriage in 1942, the family moved to the western suburbs and managed to survive the war. Good descriptions of bombings, rationing, the Russian advance into Berlin, and life after the war.

102   WOLFF-MÖNCKEBERG, MATHILDE. *On the Other Side: To My Children from Germany, 1940-45*. Translated from German. New York: Mayflower Books, 1979. 172 p.

Because her children were in England, the author could not write to them for six years. Instead she wrote letters in a journal that could be saved until the war was over. She and her husband survived the bombing of Hamburg and were eventually reunited with their children.

103   *A Woman in Berlin*. With an introduction by C. W. Ceram. Translated from German. New York: Harcourt, Brace, 1954. 319 p.

An anonymous account of the two months before and after the fall of Berlin. The author, an educated, middle-class person, worked for a publisher. Her frank descriptions include being bombed out, going hungry, being raped by Soviet troops, clearing rubble, etc.

CHAPTER 2

Foreign Observers

Foreigners who observed the ignoble end of the Reich from within its boundaries were there for many reasons. Some had been forced into the country during the war to work as slave laborers in factories and on farms, and others were British and Americans who had married Germans before the war and found themselves trapped in an enemy country when the war started. Thousands of Allied airmen and French infantrymen were prisoners of war within the Reich. Many of these were caught up in the panicked flight westward as German soldiers and civilians tried to escape invading Soviet troops. Of the many prisoner-of-war accounts, only those that tell of marches through German territory or other contacts with civilians are cited in this chapter.

In addition to the foreigners who were there by accident, there were millions of Allied military personnel and war correspondents who entered the Reich on purpose, intending to end the war as soon as possible. For some the war ended late in 1944 when they were assigned to captured towns and cities. For others the hostilities continued beyond the official unconditional surrender of Germany on 7 May 1945.

As the war gave way to occupation, fresh military personnel and civilians of all kinds poured into the Allied zones and Berlin. While some journalists and politicians visited on two-week jaunts to learn the truth about the occupation, others spent many months in Germany observing the people and absorbing the grim atmosphere of the early postwar years. A small group of observers wrote about Germany from the perspective of prewar familiarity and was quite willing to offer advice to the Allies about how to treat the Germans once the war had ended. Some of this group had been born in Germany and had fled the country in the 1930s when the Nazis were in power. All these groups of foreigners are represented in the following citations.

104   AGEE, JOEL. *Twelve Years: An American Boyhood in East Germany*. New York: Farrar, Straus, Giroux, 1981. 324 p.

Agee moved with his mother and stepfather to East Germany when he was eight years old. His stepfather was a Communist who had been in exile in Mexico during the war. For twelve years, Joel tried to fit in with his school and work mates, striving to be a good Communist and GDR citizen. In 1960 his mother's marriage failed, and she and her boys returned to the United States.

105   ANDERSEN, HARTVIG. *The Dark City: A True Account of the Adventures of a Secret Agent in Berlin as Told to Andersen*. New York: Rinehart, 1954. 314 p.

The end of the war in Berlin as observed by an Allied agent behind enemy lines.

106   ANDREWS, STANLEY. *The Journal of a Retread*. 4 vols. N.p., 1971.

The memoirs of a U.S. soldier during the occupation. Not reviewed.

107   AUBERT, LOUIS. *Control of Germany*. New York: Columbia University Press, 1949. 144 p.

Papers prepared for a conference held in the Netherlands in 1947 on economic aspects of occupied Germany.

108   BACH, JULIAN S. *America's Germany, an Account of the Occupation*. New York: Random House, 1946. 310 p.

A roving correspondent for the army magazine *Army Talks*, Bach makes personal observations about the administration of the American zone. He points out the successes and failures. His oddest charge is to put the blame for the GIs' fraternizing on U.S. girls who had conditioned them!

109 BAILEY, THOMAS A. *The Marshall Plan Summer: An Eyewitness Report on Europe and the Russians in 1947.* Stanford, Calif.: Hoover Institution Press, 1977. 246 p.

Using his diary and notes, Bailey reconstructs his personal observations of Germany and its people during the summer of 1947. He also traveled in other countries in Europe.

110 BANNISTER, SYBIL. *I Lived under Hitler: An English Woman's Story.* London: Rockliff, 1957. 264 p.

Married to a German doctor, Bannister was trapped in Germany when the war started. She escaped the Soviet advance into East Prussia and eventually returned to Britain with her son after the war.

111 BELFRAGE, CEDRIC. *Seeds of Destruction: The Truth about the U.S. Occupation of Germany.* New York: Cameron & Kahn, 1954. 232 p.

As part of the U.S. Army's Psychological Warfare Division, Belfrage's responsibility was to find non-nazi Germans to run the licensed newspapers in the American zone. At first there were coalitions of Socialists, Communists, and Catholics. Gradually the leftists were edged out and old Nazis took over, to Befrage's discouragement.

112 BELGION, MONTGOMERY. *Victor's Justice: A Letter Intended to Have Been Sent to a Friend Recently in Germany.* Hinsdale, Ill.: Regnery, 1949. 187 p.

Criticizes the Nuremberg trials and questions their validity. In a war both sides commit criminal acts, with the difference being that the victors punish the conquered. This was a rewriting of a book published in Great Britain in 1947: *Epitaph on Nuremberg.*

113 BERNADOTTE of WISBORG, FOLKE. *The Curtain Falls: The Last Days of the Third Reich.* Translated from Swedish. New York: Knopf, 1945. 154 p.

Count Bernadotte of Sweden spent the spring of 1945 in Germany on behalf of the Swedish Red Cross. This is his account of the disintegration of the Third Reich.

114 _____. *Instead of Arms.* New York: Bonnier, 1948. 227 p.

Directly after the war, Count Bernadotte traveled in Europe on various political and humanitarian missions. These are the notes he had recorded shortly before being killed in Palestine.

Foreign Observers

115   BEVERIDGE, WILLIAM H. *An Urgent Message from Germany.* London: Pilot Press, 1946. 22 p.

Reports from his tour of the British zone of Germany in August 1946. He describes the low food rations, lack of housing, the displaced persons and expellees, and unemployment. The shipyards in Hamburg were being dismantled while he was there.

116   BIELENBERG, CHRISTABEL. *Ride Out the Dark.* Boston: G.K. Hall, 1984. 285 p. British title: *The Past Is Myself.*

Married to a Hamburg lawyer, Bielenberg was swept into the 20 July plot to assassinate Hitler. Her ability to bluff her way through a Gestapo interrogation saved her husband.

117   BOHLEN, CHARLES E. *Witness to History, 1919-1969.* New York: Norton, 1973. 562 p.

As an American diplomat, Bohlen had opportunities to attend both the Yalta and Potsdam conferences. He gives vivid descriptions of people and events.

118   BOUMAN, PIETER J. *The Refugee Problem in Western Germany.* Translated from German. The Hague: M. Nijhoff, 1950. 49 p.

Contemporary account of the problems encountered by the millions of expellees in the western zones. Gives descriptions of self-help that have been undertaken.

119   BOURKE-WHITE, MARGARET. *"Dear Fatherland, Rest Quietly": A Report on the Collapse of Hitler's Thousand Years.* New York: Simon & Schuster, 1946. 175 p.

Bourke-White, a *Life* correspondent, followed the American troops into Germany in early 1945. She records in words and photographs the bombed cities, discarded weapons, and defeated people.

120   BRANDT, KARL. *Germany: Key to Peace in Europe.* Claremont, Calif.: Claremont College, 1949. 109 p.

Three lectures delivered at Claremont College upon returning from a year in Germany. Brandt discusses American foreign policy toward Germany, its reconstruction, and its integration into the European postwar community and economy.

121 _____. *Is There Still a Chance for Germany? America's Responsibility*. Human Affairs Pamphlet. Hinsdale, Ill.: Regnery, 1948. 46 p.

Not reviewed.

122 BRETT-SMITH, RICHARD. *Berlin '45, the Grey City*. New York: St. Martin's Press, 1967. 176 p.

Immediately after the war, Brett-Smith was sent to Berlin with the British occupation forces. He served there from July 1945 to March 1946. He describes the destroyed city, its citizens, the thousands of expellees being driven through, and the uneasy four-part administration by the Allies.

123 *British Zone Review: A Monthly Review of Activities in the British Zone of Germany*. 3 vols. Hamburg: Information Services Division, Control Commission for Germany (British Element), 29 September 1945-20 September 1949.

As an official publication in the British zone, the *Review* contains lots of details of daily life, including the problems the British had in implementing their policies. There are articles on housing, food, fuel, floods, and activities of the British troops. Letters to the editor reflect the thinking of the soldiers stationed there.

124 BROCKWAY, FENNER. *German Diary*. London: Gollancz, 1946. 148 p.

After a two-week visit to the British zone in the spring of 1946, the socialist journalist is convinced that democratic socialism should be encouraged in Germany. He also notes the starving and unemployed people in northern Germany.

125 BRODRICK, ALAN H. *Danger Spot of Europe*. New York: Hutchinson, 1951. 192 p.

An unsympathetic analysis of the postwar period in Germany, including the Allied occupation and the rebirth of German political interest.

126 BROWN, LEWIS H. *A Report on Germany*. New York: Farrar, Straus, 1947. 247 p.

Brown, chairman of Johns-Manville Corporation, was invited to Germany by General Lucius Clay to review the situation and make recommendations concerning the revival of the German economy. He suggests that getting Germany on its feet is essential to the economy of

Europe and that this needs to be done with or without Soviet participation.

127 BUCKHAM, ROBERT. *Forced March to Freedom: An Illustrated Diary of Two Forced Marches and the Interval Between, January to May, 1945*. Stittsville, Ont.: Canada's Wings, 1984. 98 p.

One of ten thousand Allied prisoners forced to march westward in January 1945 to escape being overrun by Soviet troops. Most men lived by supporting one another and getting food from German civilians.

128 BURCHETT, WILFRED G. *Cold War in Germany*. South Yarra, Aust.: Capricorn Printing Co., 1950. 258 p.

Not reviewed.

129 BYFORD-JONES, WILFRED. *Berlin Twilight*. New York: Hutchinson, 1947. 192 p.

Describes daily life in Berlin in 1945 and 1946 after interviewing many people. He also spends several chapters discussing the Allies' investigation into Hitler's last days and death.

130 CASSIDY, VELMA H. *Germany, 1947-1949: The Story in Documents*. Washington, D.C.: U.S. Department of State, Office of Public Affairs, 1950. 631 p.

Arranged topically, the documents present an event-by-event chronology of political developments during the two-year period.

131 CLARK, DELBERT. *Again the Goose Step: The Lost Fruits of Victory*. New York: Bobbs-Merrill, 1949. 297 p.

Clark was the *New York Times* Berlin correspondent from 1946 to 1948. His pessimistic view of Germany includes the failures of the Allied occupation, the efforts to denazify people, and the attempts to reeducate and democratize the Germans. He finds little to admire and much to criticize.

132 CLAY, LUCIUS D. *Decision in Germany*. Garden City, N.Y.: Doubleday, 1950. Reprint. Westport, Conn.: Greenwood Press, 1970. 522 p.

General Clay was deputy military governor and then military governor in Germany from 1945 to 1949. In this book he emphasizes the political and economic aspects of the U.S. occupation and Germany's reentry into the European community.

133 COLE, JOHN A. *Germany, My Host.* New York: Abelard-Schuman, 1957. 284 p.

British title: *My Host Michel.* Describes his stay in Germany in the postwar period. He has useful accounts of East and West Berlin, and goes into detail about the behavior patterns of Germans whom he observed.

134 COLLINS, SARAH M. *The Alien Years: Being the Autobiography of an Englishwoman in Germany and Austria, 1938-1946.* London: Hodder & Stoughton, 1949. 222 p.

Collins spent the war in Berlin and Vienna. Her husband was in charge of a factory which manufactured essential goods. Near the end of the war she and her son sought refuge with relatives in a small Bavarian town. Her husband escaped the Soviets in Vienna and joined her.

135 ———. *Bitter Harvest.* London: Hodder & Stoughton, 1951. 255 p.

Postwar period in Bavaria. Not reviewed.

136 COLLIS, ROBERT, and HANS HOGERZIEL. *Straight On.* London: Methuen, 1947. 178 p.

Reveals the experiences of the British troops who first stumbled onto Bergen-Belsen concentration camp near Hamburg.

137 CONFERENCE ON HEALTH AND HUMAN RELATIONS IN GERMANY. *Health and Human Relations in Germany.* 3 vols. New York: Josiah Macy Foundation, 1950-51.

The conference papers from the first (1950) and third (1951) meetings focus on human relations and mental health. The second-conference (1950) publication contains recommendations but no reports.

138 CONLON, WILLIAM H. *Berlin, Beset and Bedeviled: Tinderbox of the World.* New York: Fountainhead, 1963. 268 p.

Soldier stationed in Berlin. Not reviewed.

139 CONNELL, BRIAN. *A Watcher on the Rhine: An Appraisal of Germany Today.* New York: Morrow, 1957. 320 p.

British journalist who had been in Germany since 1946 is impressed with the miraculous recovery of the German economy. He is concerned, however, that the Germans are becoming arrogant again as they gain economic respectability.

Foreign Observers

140 CONNOR, SYDNEY, and CARL J. FRIEDRICH, ed. "Military Government: Germany." *Annals of the American Academy of Political and Social Science* 267 (January 1950).

    Seven essays by scholars and government officials on different aspects of the U.S. occupation of Germany.

141 DANIEL, EUGENE L. *In the Presence of Mine Enemies: An American Chaplain in World War II German Prison Camps.* Attleboro, Mass., 1985. 112 p.

    Memoirs of an American in Stalag Luft III, in eastern Germany. He marched westward with ten thousand other Allied prisoners to escape Soviet troops.

142 DAVIDSON, BASIL. *Germany, What Now: Potsdam Partition, 1945-49.* London: F. Muller, 1950. 268 p.

    Thinks the four-power occupation of Germany was jeopardized by Anglo-American distrust of the Soviets, and downplays the disruptive actions of the rulers of the east zone.

143 DAVIS, FRANKLIN M. *Come as a Conqueror: The U.S. Army's Occupation of Germany, 1945-1949.* New York: Macmillan, 1967. 271 p.

    Having served in the military government in Berlin, Davis presents the history of the occupation in Germany, combining research with reminiscences.

144 DENEKE, HELENA, and BETTY NORRIS. *The Women of Germany.* London: Published by the National Council of Social Service for the Women's Group on Public Welfare, 1947. 31 p.

    A report made to the Control Commission for Germany (British Element) by two representatives of the Women's Group on Public Welfare.

145 DICKENS, ARTHUR G. *Lübeck Diary.* London: Gollancz, 1947. 349 p.

    Reveals experiences in Lübeck as a member of the British occupation government in the first months of peace.

146 DOBRAN, EDWARD A. *P.O.W., the Story of an American Prisoner of War during World War II*. New York: Exposition Press, 1953. 123 p.

Dobran's prison camp, Stalag Luft IV, near Danzig, was evacuated the first of February 1945. Marching westward, the men came into contact with Russian prisoners, slave laborers, and civilians.

147 DONNER, JÖRN. *Report from Berlin*. Translated from Swedish. Bloomington: Indiana University Press, 1961. 284 p.

The material for this book was collected in the middle 1950s by Donner, who is a Finnish journalist. Although outside the immediate postwar period, the book is useful because Donner emphasizes the personal lives of both East and West Berliners.

148 DOS PASSOS, JOHN. *Tour of Duty*. Boston: Houghton Mifflin, 1946. 336 p.

The author's journalistic "tour of duty" brought him to Germany soon after the end of the war. He traveled from city to city visiting military governors and gathering information about the U.S. occupation through interviews and observations.

149 DUSHNYCK, WALTER, and W. J. GIBBONS. *Refugees Are People: The Plight of Europe's Displaced Persons*. New York: America Press, 1947. 96 p.

Not reviewed.

150 EBSWORTH, RAYMOND. *Restoring Democracy in Germany: The British Contribution*. New York: Praeger, 1961. 222 p.

A former member of the British military government in Germany presents a history of its activities: demilitarization, denazification, food rationing, reeducation, etc.

151 *Economic Policies, Programs and Requirements in Occupied Germany: Answers to Questions Submitted by Members of the Select Committee on Foreign Aid, House of Representatives*. N.p.: Office of Military Government, U.S. Zone, 1947. 177 p.

Not reviewed.

152 *Enactments and Approved Papers of the Control Council and Coordinating Committee*. 9 vols. Berlin, 1945-1948.

Official actions of the Allied Control Council in Berlin.

153   *Europe 1945/46*. 3 vols. London: Wiener Library, 1946.
Volumes 1 and 2 report the German press reaction to the Allied occupation from April to December 1945. Volume 3 is a report of a recent visit to Germany by Louis W. Bondy.

154   *Facts about Occupied Germany*. 11 nos. New York: American Association for a Democratic Germany, 1945-1948.
Issued irregularly. Not reviewed.

155   FAVIELL, FRANCES, pseud. [OLIVIA PARKER]. *The Dancing Bear*. New York: Norton, 1954. 246 p.
In the fall of 1946, Faviell and her son accompanied her husband, an officer in the British army, to Berlin to live. She describes the city and its citizens from the perspective of a comfortably situated foreign dependent.

156   FERGUSON, CLARENCE. *Kriegsgefangener 3074, Prisoner-of-War*. Grosbeck, Tex.: C. Ferguson, 1983. 295 p.
Tells of his officers' stalag being evacuated westward ahead of the advancing Soviet troops. His group was marched to Luckenwalde, southwest of Berlin.

157   FETTER, JOSEPH. *Sudetens, a Moral Question*. New York: William-Frederick Press, 1946. 59 p.
Fetter, an American of Sudeten German ethnicity, explains the expulsion of the Sudeten Germans from Czechoslovakia after the war.

158   *A Four Year Report, July 1, 1945-September 1, 1949*. Berlin: Office of Military Government for Berlin Sector, U.S., 1949. 127 p.
One of many periodic reports by the U.S. occupation forces in Berlin recording the efforts to carry out policies and surmount difficulties, including the Soviet lack of cooperation, the millions of expellees streaming into the city, and the isolation of the city from the western occupation zones.

159   FREEMAN, DEXTER L. *Hesse, a New German State: Arranged for OMGH*. Frankfurt am Main: Druck- und Verlagshaus Frankfurt, 1948. 194 p.
Not reviewed.

160 FRIEDMANN, WOLFGANG. *The Allied Military Government of Germany*. London: Stevens & Sons for the London Institute of World Affairs, 1947. 362 p.

    A German-speaking British military officer spent 1945-47 with the military government in Germany. He describes the government of the four Allies through the Control Council, and the reactions of the Germans to being occupied.

161 FRIEDRICH, CARL J., ed. *American Experiences in Military Government in World War II*. New York: Rinehart, 1948. 436 p.

    A collection of essays from former military government officers in Germany or Japan. They gave their expert opinions on the successes and failures of the occupations.

162 FRITSCH, LUDWIG A. *The Crime of Our Age: A Call to the Clergy and to All Christians in the United States of America*. 2d ed. Chicago: the Author, 1949. 90 p.

    In Fritsch's opinion, Germany continues to be the central defender of Christian civilization. Urges Americans to help save the German people and not condemn them to a country-wide concentration camp.

163 GANT, ROLAND. *How Like a Wilderness*. London: Gollancz, 1946. 160 p.

    Memoirs of a forced march from an Allied prison camp in eastern Germany.

164 *German Book Publishing and Allied Subjects, a Report*. Edward M. Crane, chair, Visiting Committee of American Book Publishers. New York, 1948. 171 p.

    Not reviewed.

165 *Germany, a Series of Photos of the U.S. Zone, Its Towns and Villages*. Photos taken by p. Wolff and Tritschler; introductory text and captions by E. Beckmann. Produced by order of the U.S. Army Exchange Service. Frankfurt [1947?]. [215] p.

    Not reviewed.

166 GOLLANCZ, VICTOR. *Germany Revisited*. London: Gollancz, 1947. 39 p.

    Gollancz, a British socialist publisher, was filled with compassion for ordinary Germans who were on the edge of starvation and lacked decent housing and clothing. This book was written after a two-week visit to Frankfurt in August of 1947. He relates people's stories and describes their living conditions.

167 _____. *In Darkest Germany.* Hinsdale, Ill.: Regnery, 1947. 252 p.
Describes his visit to the British zone of Germany in the fall of 1946. With photographs and words, Gollancz calls the Allies' attention to the defeated people of Germany who are hungry, unclothed, and lack decent places to live.

168 _____. *Leaving Them to Their Fate: The Ethics of Starvation.* London: Gollancz, 1946. 48 p.
In this expanded chapter from his book *Our Threatened Values*, Gollancz raises an ethical question about the levels of food rationing in the British zone.

169 _____. *Our Threatened Values.* Hinsdale, Ill.: Regnery, 1947. 217 p.
Sees the decline of moral and spiritual standards in contemporary life in Britain and in the way she governs her zone in Germany.

170 _____. *What Buchenwald Really Means.* London: Gollancz, 1945. 15 p.
Not reviewed.

171 GORDON WALKER, PATRICK C. *The Lid Lifts.* London: Gollancz, 1945. 96 p.
Gordon Walker was part of the British Army of the Rhine, which invaded northwestern Germany in the spring of 1945. He describes what it was like, including the discovery of Bergen-Belsen concentration camp.

172 HABE, HANS, pseud. [JEAN BEKESSY]. *Our Love Affair With Germany.* New York: Putnam, 1953. 247 p.
Controversial views of the changes of U.S. policy toward Germany in the late 1940s. Habe is critical of the steps toward rearmament being sanctioned in Germany.

173 HAVIGHURST, ROBERT J. *Report on Germany for the Rockefeller Foundation.* N.p., 1947. 136 p.
The report is a result of a two-month visit to the American zone in the fall of 1947. Havighurst visited universities in several cities in the zone, interviewing many Germans. He is sympathetic to their

destitution and recommends that they be helped to become democratic and self-sufficient as soon as possible.

174　HERMAN, STEWART W. *Rebirth of the German Church*. New York: Harper, 1946. 297 p.

　　Sees the revival of religious interests by the Germans to be encouraging. Herman describes the work of the church in trying to help the millions of expellees being forced into the western zones.

175　HEYMONT, IRVING. *Among the Survivors of the Holocaust-- 1945: The Landsberg DP Camp Letters of Major Irving Heymont, United States Army*. Cincinnati, Ohio: American Jewish Archives, 1982. 111 p.

　　Although Heymont worked primarily with Jewish displaced persons, he also had contacts with Germans in the American zone. His genuine sympathy and concern for people often overcomes the remoteness of military government.

176　HILL, RUSSELL. *Struggle for Germany*. New York: Harper, 1947. 260 p.

　　As Berlin correspondent for the *New York Herald Tribune*, Hill comments on the American military government in Germany and the behavior of the American troops. Describing the deplorable conditions, he encourages policy changes that would speed up the rate of German economic recovery.

177　HIRSCHMANN, IRA A. *The Embers Still Burn: An Eye-witness View of the Postwar Ferment in Europe and the Middle East and Our Disastrous Get-Soft-with-Germany Policy*. New York: Simon & Schuster, 1949. 272 p.

　　On an information-gathering mission for UNRRA, Hirschmann visited several European countries. He reports on his observations of displaced persons camps in western Germany.

178　HOEMBERG, ELISABETH S. *Thy People, My People*. New York: Crowell, 1950. 314 p.

　　Diary and letters of a Canadian woman who married a German and spent the war in Germany. Her husband was in the air force. She includes descriptions of the end of the war, her husband's imprisonment, and the hard winter of 1945-46.

Foreign Observers

179   HOLBORN, HAJO. *American Military Government*. Washington, D.C.: Infantry Journal Press, 1947. 243 p.

With a knowledge of German and first-hand experiences in military government, Holborn provides a thorough description of U.S. administration and policy. Many documents are appended.

180   HOOVER, HERBERT C. *Addresses upon the American Road, 1945-1948*. New York: Van Nostrand, 1949. 319 p.

This collection of speeches and reports includes reports on both German and Austrian agriculture and food requirements that President Hoover delivered to President Truman in February and March 1947.

181   HOWELL, FORREST W. *Whispers of Death: Yankee Kriegies*. Moore Haven, Fla.: Rainbow Books, 1985.

Captured by the Germans in 1944, Howell was a prisoner until being liberated just after the war ended. He had little contact with German civilians.

182   HOWLEY, FRANK L. *Berlin Command*. New York: Putnam, 1950. 276 p.

Brigadier General Howley led U.S. troops into Berlin in their first encounters with the Soviets. His personal account of the beginnings of four-power government in Berlin is colorful and candid.

183   HUGHES, WILLIAM R., ed. *Those Human Russians: A Collection of Incidents Related by Germans*. London: Gollancz, 1950. 128 p.

Anecdotal stories gathered on trips to visit Quaker friends who were working in Germany after the war. Hughes was interested in experiences that revealed the common goodness of people.

184   HUTTON, ORAM C., and ANDY ROONEY. *Conqueror's Peace: A Report to the American Stockholders*. New York: Doubleday, 1947. 92 p.

Having been war correspondents in Germany, the reporters retraced their steps through the American zone two years later. They describe the countryside and the German people. They also report on expellees and the behavior of occupation troops.

185 *Information Bulletin: Magazine of the Office of U.S. High Commissioner for Germany.* 9 vols. Frankfurt, 28 July 1945-March 1953.

   A weekly, then monthly publication of the military government of the U.S. zone, giving highlights of policies, German reactions, general information, and comments from American newspapers.

186 *The Integration of Refugees into German Life: A Report Submitted to the Chancellor of the Federal Republic.* By the Technical Assistance Commission on the Integration of the Refugees in the German Republic. 2 vols. Washington, D.C.: National Planning Association, 1951-52.

   An up-to-date statistical report on the employment, housing, resettlement, and social welfare of the expellees.

187 JASPERS, KARL. *The Question of German Guilt.* Translated from German. New York: Dial Press, 1947. 123 p. Reprint. Westport, Conn.: Greenwood Press, 1978.

   Jaspers, a Swiss philosopher, analyzes German responsibilities for the war and offers some advice on dealing with guilt. The book is a condensation of lectures delivered at Heidelberg University shortly after the end of the war.

188 JEROME, V. J. *The Treatment of Defeated Germany.* New York: New Century Publishers, 1945. 106 p.

   The author, editor of *Political Affairs* and a Marxist scholar, gives his point of view on how the Allies should treat Germany when the war ends. He urges a "just peace" that will purge Germany of militarists, Nazis, and industrialists. The labor class should be encouraged to help rebuild their country.

189 JOESTEN, JOACHIM. *Germany, What Now?* Chicago: Ziff-Davis, 1948. 331 p.

   Describes the occupation governments of Germany, the desperate economic situation, and the Allied efforts to rebuild. Cites favorable opinions about early Soviet actions but later finds them guilty of uncooperativeness.

190 KAHN, ARTHUR D. *Betrayal: Our Occupation of Germany.* 2d ed. New York: Kahn, 1950. 224 p.

   Kahn, a former intelligence officer, is quite critical of American actions in Germany. Roosevelt's original plans were softened and old Fascists and nazi sympathizers were allowed to take control of the local German governments and industries. He believes that hysterical fears of the Soviets are the excuse for American policy changes.

191 KEE, ROBERT. *A Crowd Is Not Company*. London: J. Cape, 1982. 240 p.

Tells of life in German prison camps in eastern Germany. Kee's camp was one of many evacuated ahead of the invading Soviet forces. First published in 1947.

192 KEEFE, WILLIAM F. *Two Years Before the Masthead*. Frankfurt am Main: Rudl, 1952. 277 p.

A newspaper editor in occupied Germany. Not reviewed.

193 KEELING, RALPH F. *Gruesome Harvest: The Costly Attempt to Exterminate the People of Germany*. Chicago: Institute of American Economics, 1947. 140 p.

Has collected first-hand, personal accounts of the conditions in Germany in the immediate postwar years. The descriptions of the ruined cities, the dismantling of industry, and the starvation of the people are very striking.

194 KLIMOV, GREGORY. *The Terror Machine*. Translated from German. New York: Praeger, 1953. 400 p.

Klimov is a former Soviet officer in charge of the industrial branch of the Soviet Economic Administration in Germany. He writes of his experiences in the Soviet occupation government and of his reasons for defecting.

195 KNAPPEN, MARSHALL M. *And Call It Peace*. Chicago: University of Chicago Press, 1947. 213 p.

The deputy chief of the education section of the U.S. Office of Military Government offers his criticisms of occupation policies and the efforts to reeducate the Germans toward democracy.

196 KNAUTH, PERCY. *Germany in Defeat*. New York: Knopf, 1946. 233 p.

Knauth, a *Time-Life* correspondent, returned to Berlin in 1945 just behind the U.S. troops. In the immediate postwar period he concentrated on interviewing Germans concerning the 20 July 1944 plot and the deaths of Hitler and Braun. In the early days it was difficult to find repentant Germans.

197 KNOP, WERNER G. *Prowling Russia's Forbidden Zone: A Secret Journey into Soviet Germany.* New York: Knopf, 1949. 200 p.

　　The author, a German exile in Britain during the war, traveled illegally into the eastern zone to get a first-hand view of life in eastern Germany. Parts of the book appeared serially in the *Saturday Evening Post.*

198 KOPELEV, LEV. *To Be Preserved Forever.* Translated from Russian. Philadelphia: J.P. Lippincott, 1977. British title: *No Jail for Thought.*

　　An unusual picture of the war on the eastern front from a Soviet officer in command of an army propaganda unit. His duty was to spread fear of the Red Army among German civilians. He, however, deplored the looting, raping, and torture of Germans by the Soviet troops and was arrested shortly afterward for criticizing these actions.

199 KOSPOTH, B. J. *Red Wins.* London: Macdonald, 1946. 220 p.

　　The author was a British airman in a German prison camp as the war drew to a close. He recounts his adventures trying to reach British lines throughout the spring of 1945, when the Soviets occupied the eastern Reich and were pushing toward Berlin.

200 KRANTZ, PAUL. *Bridges over the Rhine.* New York: Holt, 1947. 317 p.

　　Offers his opinions of how to treat the Germans from his position as a German exile since 1933. He thinks internationalization of the Ruhr area will prevent the Germans from rearming. He also wants to see the encouragement of democratic ideals in postwar Germany.

201 KRAUS, CHARLES H. *In the Wake of Battle.* Washington, D.C.: Georgetown University, 1950. 102 p.

　　Kraus collected histories from several American military government officials who had served in Germany. Examples of problems and solutions are cited.

202 KRAUSE, WALTER C. *So I Was a Sergeant: Memoirs of an Occupation Soldier.* Hicksville, N.Y.: Exposition Press, 1978. 206 p.
　　Not reviewed.

Foreign Observers

203 KRUK, ZOFIA. *The Taste of Fear: A Polish Childhood in Germany, 1939-1946.* London: Hutchinson, 1973. 205 p.

Forced into the Reich with her father at the beginning of the war, Kruk did farm work until released by the Allies in 1945. She spent time in UNRRA displaced persons camps and eventually immigrated to Britain.

204 LEWIS, RICHARD H. *Hell Above and Hell Below: The Real Life Story of an American Airman.* Wilmington, Del.: Delpeake Publishing Co., 1985. 163 p.

Tells of being evacuated from a prison camp near Vienna in April 1945. Marching westward, the German guards deserted their posts and the freed airmen raided farms for food and clothes.

205 LITCHFIELD, EDWARD H. *Governing Postwar Germany.* Ithaca, N.Y.: Cornell University Press, 1953. 661 p.

A group of essays from experts covering most aspects of the American occupation and the recovery of German politics, economics, education, justice, public finance, health and welfare, and legal issues.

206 LUDWIG, EMIL. *The Moral Conquest of Germany.* Garden City, N.Y.: Doubleday Doran, 1945. 183 p.

Recommendations from a Swiss on how to treat the Germans after the war. After sketching a picture of an average German, he urges tight occupational controls, letting them know who is the master. He thinks that it would be appropriate to allow some freedom about 1960, after the rest of Europe is rebuilt.

207 LUNAU, HEINZ. *The Germans on Trial.* New York: Storm, 1948. 180 p.

As a German exile in America, Lunau pleads the case for Germany. The people have been punished enough with their cities in ruins, the economy destroyed, and nonexistent consumer goods. Nazism was not peculiar to Germany but could have developed anywhere.

208 McDOUGALL, IAN. *German Notebook.* New York: Elek, 1953. 168 p.

The author, a British journalist, gives a sympathetic description of German life after traveling there in the early 1950s. Many stories relate to the postwar period.

209 McMILLAN, LEWIS K. *A Report from Inside Germany in Late Summer and Early Autumn, 1949.* Orangeburg, S.C., 1950.
Not reviewed.

210 MacNALTY, ARTHUR S., and W. FRANKLIN MELLOR. *Health Recovery in Europe.* London: Muller, 1946. 180 p.
Describes generally the actions being taken or planned by public health authorities and international organizations to raise the level of health standards in Europe.

211 MAGINNIS, JOHN J. *Military Government Journal: Normandy to Berlin.* Amherst: University of Massachusetts Press, 1971. 351 p.
General Maginnis shares his daily journal of military operations on the drive through Europe to Berlin. He was assigned to occupation duty in Berlin until March 1946.

212 MANN, ANTHONY. *Comeback: Germany, 1945-1952.* London: Macmillan, 1980. 242 p.
Blends personal observations from his years in Germany as correspondent for the *Daily Telegraph* with an analytical study of the events of postwar Germany to tell what happened in the seven years after the war.

213 MANNIN, ETHEL. *German Journey.* London: Jarrolds, 1948. 168 p.
Sympathetic British journalist traveled through the destruction in 1946, seeking old friends and taking notes on the postwar survival efforts of ordinary Germans.

214 MARTIN, JAMES S. *All Honorable Men.* Boston: Little, Brown, 1950. 326 p.
Martin was Director of the Division for Investigation of Cartels and External Assets in the American military government. He is critical of the behavior of American business interests in Germany both during and after the war.

215 MAYER, MILTON S. *They Thought They Were Free: The Germans 1933-1945.* Chicago: University of Chicago Press, 1955. 345 p.
After the war Mayer spent several months in a town in Germany interviewing ten former Nazis about their lives, their beliefs, their jobs in the war, and their attitudes afterward.

216   MELROSE, GEORGIANA. *A Strange Occupation*. Bognor Regis, Eng.: New Horizon, 1983. 190 p.

Without a job when the war ended, Melrose chose to move to the British zone of Germany to work for the occupation government. She started writing and broadcasting radio plays in Hamburg and stayed sixteen years.

217   MENDE, TIBOR. *Europe's Suicide in Germany*. London: St. Botolph Publishing Co., 1946. 100 p.

After traveling in Germany in 1946, Mende describes the political and economic conditions in the western zones. He admits that he has less information about the Soviet zone because communication is poor. Nevertheless, he thinks the Germans have an unfounded fear of the Soviets and that it would be disastrous for Europe to have Germany permanently divided into zones.

218   MERRITT, ANNA J., and RICHARD L. MERRITT. *Public Opinion in Occupied Germany: The OMGUS Surveys, 1945-1949*. Urbana: University of Illinois Press, 1970. 328 p.

Summaries of answers to questions asked by the U.S. Office of Military Government survey teams. No individuals are quoted but the answers reflect the opinions of Germans over a four year period.

219   METCALF, CLAYTON G. *Kriegsgefangenen*. N.p., n.d. 102 p.

Describes being marched west from a prison camp in Poland. His group was evacuated in October 1944. They ended the war in a camp southwest of Berlin.

220   METTERNICH, TATIANA, FÜRSTIN von METTERNICH-WINNEBURG. *Purgatory of Fools*. New York: Quadrangle/New York Times Book Co., 1976. 283 p.

Tatiana and her family were White Russian aristocrats who had fled the Russian Revolution in 1919. She and her siblings were reared within the circle of European aristocracy. Toward the end of the war, she was on her husband's estate in eastern Germany. She fled westward to another estate on the Rhine. Her sister's memoirs are also cited: Marie Vassiltchikov, *Berlin Diaries, 1940-1945*.

221   MIDDLETON, DREW. *The Struggle for Germany*. Indianapolis, Ind.: Bobbs-Merrill, 1949. 304 p.

A factual account of Germany's postwar history by an American journalist assigned to Berlin. He is optimistic that western Germany will be reintegrated into the European community.

222 *Military Government Gazette, Germany, United States Zone of Control*. 16 nos. N.p.: Office of Military Government for Germany (U.S.), 1946-1949.

Both the Americans and British issued official publications with titles similar to this. The exact titles, frequency, and issuing bodies tended to change with the changes in occupation officials.

223 MILLIN, SARAH G. *Seven Thunders*. London: Faber, 1948. 335 p.

This is the sixth volume of Millin's diary of World War II and after, which she maintained through the period of the Nuremberg trials. Not reviewed.

224 *Monthly Report of the Military Governor, Military Government of Germany, U.S. Zone*. 50 nos. N.p., July 1945-August/September 1949.

In addition to the monthly report of the military governor, special reports were frequently appended on topics such as education, property control, the German press, forest resources, tuberculosis, and political activity.

225 MORGENTHAU, HANS J., ed. *Germany and the Future of Europe*. Chicago: University of Chicago Press, 1951. 179 p.

A collection of lectures given by experts on various aspects of postwar Germany at the University of Chicago in 1950.

226 MOSLEY, LEONARD O. *Report from Germany*. London: Gollancz, 1945. 125 p.

Following the British army, Mosley returned to Germany in 1945. He reports his findings as the war ends and the Germans begin to assess their situation.

227 MUHLEN, NORBERT. *The Return of Germany*. Chicago: Regnery, 1953. 310 p.

Conversations with Germans reveal how they felt, how they thought, and what they were doing in the early 1950s. They were generally critical of the occupation and its effects.

228 MURPHY, ROBERT D. *Diplomat among Warriors*. Garden City, N.Y.: Doubleday, 1964. 470 p.

A political autobiography by a diplomat who attended the Yalta and Potsdam conferences and who became the chief U.S. State Department officer in Germany after the war. He worked closely with General Clay in Berlin.

229 NABOKOV, NICOLAS. *Old Friends and New Music*. Boston: Little, Brown, 1951. 294 p. Reprint. Westport, Conn.: Greenwood Press, 1974.

Nabokov was sent to Berlin by the U.S. State Department in 1945 with the task of finding the Soviet officer in charge of cultural affairs. He was supposed to persuade the Soviets to join in an Allied Directorate of Information Control. Although he spoke Russian, his mission failed.

230 NIZER, LOUIS. *What to Do with Germany*. Chicago: Ziff-Davis, 1944. 213 p.

Proposes how to treat Germany after the war. Nizer takes a moderate position on German war guilt, punishment, and postwar occupation policies.

231 NORMAN, ALBERT. *Our German Policy: Propaganda and Culture*. New York: Vantage Press, 1951. 85 p.

After personal experience in Germany with the American occupation, Norman offers a factual history of the military and civilian policies concerning newspapers, magazines, radio stations, motion pictures, and theaters.

232 NOTH, ERNST E. *Bridges over the Rhine*. Translated from German. New York: Holt, 1947. 317 p.

As a German living in France, Noth offers his suggestions for dealing with Germany. He does not excuse its actions but urges the Allies to seek a just and fair peace. Democracy should be encouraged to block the spread of communism.

233 *Occupation of Germany: Policy and Progress, 1945-1946*. Department of State Publication, no. 2783. Washington, D.C.: U.S. Department of State, 1947. 241 p.

Early source of documents, statistics, public speeches, and descriptive summaries for American policies in Germany.

234 O'DONNELL, JOSEPH P. *The Shoe Leather Express: The Evacuation of Kriegsgefangenen Lager Stalag Luft 4, Deutschland Germany*. Robbinsville, N.J.: J.P. O'Donnell, 1982. 106 p.

The Allied prisoners in Luft IV in Pomerania were marched westward in January 1945. Describes the experiences of many prisoners during the march.

Foreign Observers

235 *Official Gazette of the Control Council.* 19 nos. Berlin: Control Council, 19 October 1945-31 August 1948.

This official publication, issued in four languages, contains the rules and regulations that were agreed upon by the Control Council. The frequency varied.

236 PADOVER, SAUL K. *Experiment in Germany: The Story of an American Intelligence Officer.* New York: Duell, Sloan, Pearce, 1946. 400 p.

Padover followed the U.S. troops into central Germany as a member of the Psychological Warfare Division of the U.S. Army. He was to seek out and analyze the views of German civilians.

237 PAKENHAM, LORD. *Born to Believe.* London: J. Cape, 1953. 254 p.

He served in the British occupation in Berlin and then chaired the Anglo-German Association. His concern for the German people was influenced in part by Victor Gollancz's books.

238 PETERS, WILLIAM. *In Germany Now: A Diary of Impressions in Germany, August-December 1945.* London: Progress, 1946. 115 p.

Peters, a German speaker, toured the British zone in the autumn of 1945. He did not think the Germans looked as if they were starving. He was friendly to the Soviets and critical of those who complained about them.

239 PICTON, HAROLD W. *The Ordinary German: A Gathering of Memories.* London: St. Botolph Publishing Co., 1948. 104 p.

A positive view of Germany and its people, reviewing its past history and quoting from letters written in the postwar period that describe daily life there.

240 PIE, ARTHUR B. *Journey into Desolation: The Journal of a 2,000 Mile Tour through the Wreckage of the Third Reich, Shortly After the Nazi Surrender.* Brisbane, Aust.: the Author, 1946. 90 p.

Not reviewed.

241 POLLOCK, JAMES K. *Germany under Occupation: Illustrative Materials and Documents.* Rev. ed. Ann Arbor, Mich.: G. Wahr, 1949. 305 p.

Primarily contains official documents that have influenced the postwar period in some way. Pollock served with the U.S. Office of Military Government.

Foreign Observers

242 *Population of the U.S. Zone of Germany, November 1947.* 2 vols. N.p.: Office of Military Government, U.S., Civil Administration Division, 1947.
   Not reviewed.

243 PRICE, HOYT, and CARL E. SCHORSKE. *The Problem of Germany.* New York: Council on Foreign Relations, 1947. 161 p.
   Essays based on a questionnaire sent to many experts around the world. They cover the economic, political, and cultural problems of rebuilding Germany.

244 PRITTIE, TERENCE C. *Germany Divided: The Legacy of the Nazi Era.* Boston: Little, Brown, 1960. 381 p.
   Discusses the events that led up to the establishment of separate Germanies, including their internal problems and their attempts to rejoin the European community. Prittie was head of the German bureau of the *Manchester Guardian* for a number of years.

245 PROUDFOOT, MALCOLM J. *European Refugees, 1939-52: A Study in Forced Population Movement.* Evanston, Ill.: Northwestern University Press, 1956. 542 p.
   A comprehensive history of the millions of refugees who were forced from their homes during and after the war. The author served with the displaced persons unit of the Allied military effort in Europe.

246 RATCHFORD, BENJAMIN, and WILLIAM D. ROSS. *Berlin Reparations Assignment.* Chapel Hill: University of North Carolina Press, 1947. 259 p.
   These men tried to carry out the dismantling of German industry in accord with the agreements made at the Potsdam conference. The decisions were based on inadequate statistics, but the officers in charge were helpless to change the policy.

247 *Report of the Control Commission for Germany (British Element).* 5 vols. Berlin: British Control Commission, July 1946-September 1950.
   An official publication of the British military government in Germany. Issued monthly.

248 *Report of the United States Education Mission to Germany.* Department of State Publication, no. 2664. Washington, D.C.: U.S. Department of State, 1946. 50 p.

The education mission representatives visited the American zone in July 1946. This report provides excellent contemporary descriptions of German education, the physical condition of the zone, the state of the children, etc. It also makes recommendations to Congress.

249 RICHARDS, PAUL. *Spotlight on Germany.* New York: New Century Publishers, 1948. 46 p.

Reflects the Soviet point of view on the confrontation between east and west in Berlin. The issues were created and intensified by "Wall Street's plan for world domination."

250 RICHTER, WERNER. *Re-educating Germany.* Translated from German. Chicago: University of Chicago Press, 1945. 227 p.

After describing prewar education in Germany, a former German educator proposes necessary changes to be made in the postwar educational system to redeem the defeated country.

251 RIESS, CURT. *The Berlin Story.* New York: Dial Press, 1952. 368 p.

Writing about Berlin from the perspective of a former inhabitant and a present journalist, Riess covers the history of the city from 1945 through the blockade. He incorporates many details from people's lives into the narrative.

252 RODNICK, DAVID. *Postwar Germans, an Anthropologist's Account.* New Haven: Yale University Press, 1948. 233 p.

Findings of five months of fieldwork conducted in two towns in Hesse during 1945 and 1946. The anthropologists were hired by the U.S. Office of Military Government.

253 ROOSENBERG, HENRIETTE. *The Walls Came Tumbling Down.* New York: Viking, 1957. 248 p.

Four Dutch forced laborers were liberated in May 1945 by Allied troops. Their first and only instinct was to head for home, rather than wait to be repatriated. It took them five weeks to travel four hundred miles across Germany to the Netherlands.

Foreign Observers

254   RUST, WILLIAM. *Where Is Germany Going: Impressions of Tour of British Zone in Germany Made During the First Half of February, 1946.* London?: Daily Worker League, 1946. 15 p.
      Not reviewed.

255   SANDULESCU, JACQUES. *Hunger's Rogues: On the Black Market in Europe, 1948.* New York: Harcourt Brace Jovanovich, 1974. 280 p.
      Autobiographical account of a Romanian refugee who was stranded in postwar Germany waiting to immigrate to Canada. He survived by dealing on the black market where greed, shrewdness, and selfishness were the characteristics needed to survive.

256   SCHAFFER, GORDON. *Russian Zone: A Record of the Conditions Found in the Soviet Occupation Zone of Germany.* New York: Published for the Cooperative Press by SRT Publications, 1947. 192 p.
      Notes with enthusiasm the progress being made in the Soviet zone. Democracy was being established, industry was promoted, religion was tolerated, and dissent was allowed.

257   SCHALK, ADOLPH. *The Germans.* Englewood Cliffs, N.J.: Prentice-Hall, 1971. 521 p.
      A broad-ranging group of chapters informally discussing many aspects of German life. The author spent several years in Germany after the war collecting personal impressions.

258   SCHIMANSKY, STEFAN. *Vain Victory.* London: Gollancz, 1946. 172 p.
      After a visit to Germany in 1946, the author concludes that the defeated country will not be able to rebuild itself with-out help from the war's victors.

259   SCHÖNKE, ADOLF, ed. "Postwar Reconstruction in Western Germany." *Annals of the American Academy of Political and Social Science* 260 (November 1948).
      The entire volume is devoted to different aspects of postwar reconstruction. The writers are Germans who were recruited to provide essays on topics such as politics, constitutional law, justice, denazification, finance and currency reform, agriculture, transportation, refugees, social welfare, education, and labor.

Foreign Observers

260 SETTEL, ARTHUR. *This Is Germany*. New York: Sloane, 1950. 429 p.

Essays by American journalists who recount their experiences and conclusions about Germany with frankness and honesty.

261 _____, ed. *A Year of Potsdam: The German Economy Since the Surrender*. N.p.: Office of Military Government, U.S., Economic Division, 1946. 217 p.

A comprehensive study of the occupation in Germany, including basic objectives, Potsdam agreements, reparations policies, and four-power cooperative rule. Includes details of industrial production, fuel resources, building materials, consumer goods, price controls, etc.

262 SEVRUK, V., ed. *How Wars End: Eyewitness Accounts of the Fall of Berlin*. Translated from Russian. Moscow: Progress Publishers, 1969. 336 p.

Personal accounts from a number of Russians who were in Berlin at the end of the war. The contributors include a Soviet marshall, a journalist writing for a frontline newspaper, a journalist who kept a diary, a woman interpreter who wrote a book afterward, and the military council notes of a Soviet officer.

263 SHIRER, WILLIAM L. *End of a Berlin Diary*. New York: Knopf, 1947. 369 p.

Chronicles the last year of the war and Shirer's return to Berlin when the war was over. He senses no repentance and urges caution in helping Germany to recover from the defeat.

264 SIMMONS, KENNETH W. *Kriegie*. New York: Nelson & Sons, 1960. 256 p.

Recounts his experiences as an imprisoned airman in Luft IV in eastern Germany. The forced march westward covered 480 miles in thirteen days. The prisoners had daily contact with German civilians.

265 SIMONS, DOLPH. *Germany and Austria in May-June 1947*. Lawrence, Kans., 1947. 63 p.

Chatty newspaper articles written by the publisher of the *Lawrence Journal-World*. His sympathetic observations of daily life in Germany and Austria were always accompanied by the qualifier that "of course they deserve all they got." Nevertheless the author encouraged his readers to recognize that German economic self-sufficiency meant less drain on American pockets.

266 SINGTON, DERRICK. *Belsen Uncovered*. London: Duckworth, 1946. 208 p.

An eyewitness report of the discovery of the Bergen-Belsen concentration camp by the British army as it moved into northern Germany. Sington worked there for five months after liberation, helping the inmates.

267 SKRIABINA, ELENA. *The Allies on the Rhine, 1945-1950*. Translated from Russian. Carbondale: Southern Illinois University, 1980. 158 p.

A Russian emigré, Skriabina happened to be in western Germany doing forced labor when the war ended. Her friendship with French workers during the war paid off. When all Russians were to be repatriated in the summer of 1945, the French protected her and allowed her to stay in the French zone until she was able to immigrate to the United States. This is volume 3 of her memoirs.

268 SMITH, MARCUS J. *Dachau: The Harrowing of Hell*. Albuquerque: University of New Mexico Press, 1972. 291 p.

Smith was the medical officer in the team of American servicemen who handled the liberation and subsequent caring for the inmates of Dachau concentration camp. His personal account of his experiences includes valuable source materials on prisoner committees.

269 SNYDER, HAROLD E., ed. *Responsibilities of Voluntary Agencies in Occupied Countries: Second National Conference on the Occupied Countries*. Washington, D.C.: American Council on Education, 1950. 125 p.

The papers from the conference discuss general concerns and directives concerning both Germany and Japan.

270 SNYDER, HAROLD E., and MARGRETTA S. AUSTIN, eds. *Cultural Relations with the Occupied Countries: First National Conference on the Occupied Countries*. Washington, D.C.: American Council on Education, 1949. 107 p.

The speakers either worked for American educational organizations or were Germans. The conference was primarily on education issues and educational exchanges.

271 SNYDER, HAROLD E., and GEORGE E. BEAUCHAMP. *An Experiment in International Cultural Relations: A Report of the Staff of the Commission on Occupied Areas, American Council on*

Education. Washington, D.C.: American Council on Education, 1951. 112 p.

The Commission was begun in 1948 to conduct field studies, coordinate the efforts of voluntary agencies, and encourage educational exchanges between Germany, Austria, and the United States.

272 SOLZHENITSYN, ALEXANDER. *Prussian Nights: A Poem*. Translated from Russian. New York: Farrar, Straus and Giroux, 1977. 113 p.

Tells of his experiences in the second Byelorussian front as the Soviet army invaded East Prussia from the south in January 1945. The troops were encouraged to take revenge on the civilian population for the actions of the German army as it had moved into Russia. Looting, raping, killing, and burning were therefore common actions.

273 SPEIER, HANS. *From the Ashes of Disgrace: A Journal from Germany, 1945-1955*. Amherst: University of Massachusetts Press, 1981. 314 p.

Served with the U.S. military government supervising the establishment of newspapers and radio stations. In his journal Speier notes sensitive and perceptive observations of Germans.

274 SPENDER, STEPHEN. *European Witness*. New York: Reynal & Hitchcock, 1946. 246 p. Reprint. Westport, Conn.: Greenwood Press, 1971.

British poet sent to the British zone in the fall of 1945 to check on the conditions of libraries. As he had spent time in Germany before the war, he had many intellectual acquaintances to try to find.

275 SPIVEY, DELMAR T. *POW Odyssey: Recollections of Center Compound, Stalag Luft III: German Peace Mission in World War II*. N.p., 1984. 180 p.

Spivey was one of the high-ranking Allied officers in German prison camps. He was evacuated with the rest of the prisoners when the Soviets drew near. He was sent to Berlin on a mission in March and then was smuggled out of Germany into Switzerland in April.

276 SPRING, HENRY p. *A Nation's Gethsemane*. Winter Park, Fla.: Orange Press, 1945. 143 p.

Urges fair and humane treatment for the Germans when the war is over. They were led astray by evil leaders and have had no real freedom since 1933. The Nazis could have come to power anywhere.

Foreign Observers

277 ———. *The Road to Chaos.* Winter Park, Fla.: Orange Press, 1947. 259 p.

Because of the harsh treatment of the Germans by the victors, the people are suffering subhuman conditions and the country is sliding into chaos. It is wrong to punish an entire nation for the actions of a particular group.

278 STANKÉ, ALAIN. *So Much to Forget: A Child's Vision of Hell.* Translated from French. Agincourt, Ont.: Gage Publishers, 1977. 164 p.

Narrates the wartime nightmare of his family's deportation from Lithuania to a labor camp in Germany. Shortly before the end of the war they were moved to a camp near Würtzburg where they stayed until they were liberated by the U.S. army.

279 STARR, JOSEPH R. *Denazification, Occupation and Control of Germany, March-July 1945.* Salisbury, N.C.: Documentary Publications, 1977. 179 p.

Originally written in 1950 for the Historical Division of the Office of Military Government and classified for many years, this report contains useful data on the early occupation period.

280 *Stars and Stripes.*

Unofficial newspaper of the U.S. occupation forces in Germany. Began publishing as soon as American troops moved into Germany and continued to be published in several regional editions.

281 STERN, JAMES A. *The Hidden Damage.* New York: Harcourt, Brace, 1947. 406 p.

Was hired by the U.S. army as part of a strategic bombing survey team which was sent into Bavaria in the summer of 1945 to interview Germans about the effects of Allied bombing during the war. Tells of interviews and of finding old friends.

282 STERNBERGER, ADOLF. *Research in Germany on Pressing Social Problems: A Social Science Survey of German Social Issues.* Washington, D.C.: Library of Congress, European Affairs Division, 1951. 31 p.

Raises many questions about German postwar social issues that need pursuing. One of a series of surveys of intellectual life in western Germany and sponsored by the Oberländer Trust, Philadelphia.

283 STOLPER, GUSTAV. *German Realities*. New York: Reynal & Hitchcock, 1948. 341 p.

A defense of Germans by a former German national who is not surprised that the people have little interest in politics, democracy, and philosophical ideas. They are so hungry and poorly housed that they are unable to concentrate on anything except personal survival.

284 STOUFFER, SAMUEL A., ed. *The American Soldier*. Vol. 2, *Combat and Its Aftermath*. Studies in Social Psychology in World War II, vol. 2. Princeton, N.J.: Princeton University Press, 1949. 634 p.

Results of an official survey of approximately three thousand GIs in April and August 1945, seeking their opinions about Germans, fraternizing, the point system, being sent home, etc.

285 STRINGER, ANN, and HENRY RIES. *German Faces*. New York: W. Sloane Associates, 1950. 114 p.

Presents interviews conducted from 1947 to 1949 with Germans from all classes and prewar occupations. Many were still in desperate situations, unemployed, and living in terrible housing.

286 *Studies of Undernutrition, Wuppertal, 1946-49*. By Members of the Department of Experimental Medicine, Cambridge University. Medical Research Council Special Report Series, no. 275. London: H.M. Stationery Office, 1951. 404 p.

Not reviewed.

287 THAYER, CHARLES W. *The Unquiet Germans*. New York: Harper, 1957. 275 p.

Gives his personal reflections on Germany since the war. The author was a low-level U.S. foreign service officer in the Federal Republic after 1949.

288 UTLEY, FREDA. *The High Cost of Vengeance*. Chicago: Regnery, 1949. 310 p.

With concern for the suffering of the Germans and fear of the influence of the Soviet Union, Utley is critical of the occupation and its methods for handling postwar Germany.

289 VALLANCE, UTE. *A Girl Survives*. London: McGibbon & Kee, 1958. 298 p.

Imprisoned by the Nazis, the author develops tuberculosis and is sent to a hospital. She escapes and manages to avoid capture until liberated by Canadian troops.

290 VANSITTART, ROBERT G. *Bones of Contention*. New York: Knopf, 1945. 157 p.

Lord Vansittart cautions the world to beware of the Germans when the war is over. Watch out for Christian "do-gooders" who will urge compassion and fairness. The Germans are depraved and savage and cannot be redeemed.

291 VASSILTCHIKOV, MARIE. *Berlin Diaries, 1940-1945*. New York: Vintage Books, 1988. 324 p.

The daughter of a White Russian emigre family, the author lived and worked in Berlin until the last year of the war. She was secretly allied with the German aristocrats who were involved in the 20 July plot to assassinate Hitler. After going to Vienna to work as a nurse, Vassiltchikov fled the city just before it fell to the Soviet troops. Her sister's memoirs are also cited: Tatiana Metternich, *Purgatory of Fools*.

292 VERRINA, pseud. *The German Mentality*. Rev. and enl. ed. London: Allen & Unwin, 1946. 344 p.

After some historical background, the author expresses opinions on how to treat the Germans in the postwar period. The Poles' acquisition of East Prussia is just, though there are reservations about Silesia and Pomerania. Germany should receive fair treatment.

293 VIETOR, JOHN A. *Time Out: American Airmen at Stalag Luft I*. Fallbrook, Calif.: Aero Publishers, 1984. 192 p.

Stalag Luft I was located near Stralsund north of Berlin. Vietor's account is unusual because he could speak Russian and was able to communicate with the Russian troops that overran the camp at the end of the war. Reprint of a 1951 ed.

294 WAHLE, ANNE. *Ordeal by Fire: An American Woman's Terror-Filled Trek through War-Torn Germany*. New York: Dell, 1967. 159 p.

Married and mother of three children, Wahle was in Dresden when it was bombed in February of 1945. She got her children and maid out of the city, and they started walking southwest toward the Austrian Alps where the maid's family lived.

295 WANN, MARIE D. *Dependent Baggage: Destination Germany.* New York: Macmillan, 1955. 248 p.

American woman accompanied her civilian husband to an educational assignment in Germany after the war. She was not impressed with the Germans who hung around Americans looking for handouts, though she admitted that she had few opportunities to meet self-respecting, independent Germans.

296 WARBURG, JAMES p. *Germany, Bridge or Battleground.* New York: Harcourt, Brace, 1947. 386 p.

After visiting all four occupation zones in the summer of 1946, the author sets forward his personal assessments of the German occupation. He presents his proposals for dealing with the problems Germany faces.

297 _____. *Germany, Nation or No-Man's Land.* Headline Series, no. 60. New York: Foreign Policy Association, Nov. 1946. 64 p.

Contents include chapters on Germany's economic importance to Europe, the suffering of the German people, descriptions of the four occupation zones, and an explanation of Allied occupation policy.

298 WHITE, THEODORE H. *Fire in the Ashes: Europe in Mid-Century.* New York: W. Sloane Associates, 1953. 405 p.

Included in this general, journalistic assessment of Europe are two chapters on postwar Germany. White traveled around interviewing politicians, intellectuals, and working people.

299 WHITE, WILLIAM L. *Report on the Germans.* New York: Harcourt, Brace, 1947. 260 p.

A return visit to Berlin after the war prompted these personal observations of an American journalist. He has visited with many Germans and is sympathetic to their problems of survival.

300 WOLFERS, ARNOLD. *United States Policy toward Germany.* New Haven: Yale University, Institute of International Studies, 1947. 29 p.

A perceptive analysis of why American occupation plans had to be modified in the face of realities that had not been anticipated.

Foreign Observers

301 WOLFF, KURT H. *German Attempts at Picturing Germany, Texts.* Studies In German-American Postwar Problems, no. 3. Columbus: Ohio State University, 1955. 136 p.

An institute at the University of Frankfurt held discussions among small groups of Germans, surveying their opinions about the Americans, the Soviets, and themselves. Wolff has chosen the most interesting of the opinions to translate into English.

302 ZBLINDEN, HANS. *Whither Germany: Reflections of a Swiss on the Future of Germany and Europe.* Translated from German. Hinsdale, Ill.: Regnery, 1948. 90 p.

A Swiss gives his opinion of the four-power occupation, the successes and failures, and what still needs to be accomplished in Germany.

303 ZINK, HAROLD. *American Military Government in Germany.* New York: Macmillan, 1947. 272 p.

Having served in several capacities in the U.S. military government, the author feels competent to make judgments on the early handling of the occupation by U.S. officials. He criticizes the military for making plans that were not implemented.

304 _____. *United States in Germany, 1944-1955.* Princeton, N.J.: Van Nostrand, 1957. 374 p.

This second book presents a valuable general account of the American occupation of Germany. While Zink criticizes some policies, he believes that, overall, the occupation was a success.

CHAPTER 3

Civilian Relief Efforts

Civilian relief workers followed the Allied troops into Germany in the summer and fall of 1945. After the initial attempts by the armies to deal with released foreign laborers, German refugees from bombed cities, and survivors from concentration camps, there were efforts to coordinate the relief work under the United Nations Relief and Rehabilitation Administration. British and American Catholic and Protestant church agencies sent representatives on fact-finding missions and organized denominational relief programs to be implemented as soon as allowed to do so.

Because of a quirk of circumstances the international relief agencies, UNRRA and its successor, the International Refugee Organization, were not permitted to aid Germans who had been expelled from eastern Europe or who had sought political asylum in the western zones from the Soviet zone. Consequently the major responsibility for helping these people fell to private agencies in Britain and the United States, to groups affiliated with the World Council of Churches, and to the German church agencies: Caritas (Roman Catholic) and the Hilfswerk of the Evangelical Churches (Protestant).

The citations in this chapter consist of memoirs of civilians who entered Germany after the war, histories of international relief organizations, official reports of these organizations, and publications of German and Allied relief agencies.

305 AMERICAN FRIENDS SERVICE COMMITTEE. *Report on Conditions in Central Europe.* Philadelphia: American Friends Service Committee, 1946-194?

A series of pamphlets published irregularly on aspects of occupied Germany, such as public health and expellees.

306 BARTON, BETTY. *The Problem of 12 Million German Refugees in Today's Germany.* Philadelphia: American Friends Service Committee, 1949. 39 p.
Not reviewed.

307 BIGELOW, KARL W. *The Role of American Voluntary Agencies in Germany and Austria.* Washington, D.C.: American Council on Education, Commission on the Occupied Areas, 1951. 22 p.

The report of a team of inquiry that visited Germany and Austria in Oct.-Nov. 1950, at the request of U.S. Department of State.

308 BODER, DAVID P. *I Did Not Interview the Dead.* Urbana: University of Illinois Press, 1949. 220 p.

Transcribed interviews with eight displaced persons in UNRRA camps in 1946. Boder interviewed seventy people all together and the transcription of the interviews is available on microfilm with the title: *Topical Autobiographies of Displaced People.*

309 DARTON, LAURENCE. *An Account of the Work of the Friends Committee for Refugees and Aliens, First Known as the German Emergency Committee of the Society of Friends, 1933-1950.* [London?]: Friends Committee for Refugees and Aliens, 1954. 170 p.
Not reviewed.

310 EGAN, EILEEN M., and ELIZABETH C. REISS. *Transfigured Night: The CRALOG Experience.* Philadelphia: Livingston, 1964. 185 p.

CRALOG coordinated the relief efforts of the U.S. civilian agencies that poured clothing, food, and medical supplies into postwar Germany from March 1946 to 1962.

311 EVANGELISCHE KIRCHE IN DEUTSCHLAND. *Living Conditions in Germany in 1947, a Survey.* Translated from German. Stuttgart: Evangelisches Hilfswerk, 1947. 74 p.
Not reviewed.

312 _____. *Questions and Answers Relative to the German Refugee Problem.* Translated from German. Stuttgart: Evangelisches Hilfswerk, 1949. 18 p.
Not reviewed.

313 _____. *Resumé on the Development of the European Refugee Problem from 1918 to 1948.* Stuttgart: Quell-Verlag der Evangelische Gesellschaft, 1948. 41 p.
Prepared for the World Council of Churches assembly in Amsterdam, the report discusses the assimilation of German refugees and expellees into German society.

314 FLOORE, FRANCES B. *The Bread of the Oppressed: An American Woman's Experiences in War-Disrupted Countries, from the Journal and Letters of Frances Berkeley Floore, 1944-1949.* Hicksville, N.Y.: Exposition Press, 1975. 292 p.
Recounts experiences working as a dietitian for UNRRA and IRO in Germany and elsewhere. She spent some time in an international children's village in Gauting, six miles from Munich.

315 HOEHLER, FRED K. *Europe's Homeless Millions.* Headline Series, no. 54. New York: Foreign Policy Association, Nov.-Dec. 1945. 96 p.
Briefly describes the planning and training that were undertaken by UNRRA prior to the end of the war. It assumed responsibility for displaced persons when the war was over.

316 HOLBORN, LOUISE W. *The International Refugee Organization: A Specialized Agency of the United Nations: Its History and Its Work, 1946-1952.* London: Oxford University Press, 1956. 805 p.
An official history of the work and accomplishments of the IRO. It includes a good bibliography.

317 HOWARD, ELIZABETH F. *Barriers Down: Notes on Postwar Germany.* London: Friends Home Service Committee, 1950.
Not reviewed.

318 HULME, KATHRYN. *The Wild Place.* Boston: Little, Brown, 1953. 275 p.
A personal account of five years as an UNRRA worker in the displaced persons camps in Germany. One of the camps was Wildflecken, a former nazi training center where Polish displaced persons were housed.

319 INTERNATIONAL COMMITTEE OF THE RED CROSS. *Health Conditions Among the Civilian Population of Certain European Countries Affected by the War, August 1947-June 1948.* Geneva: International Committee of the Red Cross, [1948?].
Not reviewed.

320 _____. *Report of the International Committee of the Red Cross on Its Activities during the Second World War, September 1, 1939-June 30, 1947.* 4 vols. Geneva: International Committee of the Red Cross, 1948-50.
The official record of the Red Cross in Europe. The volumes include descriptions of general activities, relief activities, the Central Agency for POWs, and appendixes.

321 INTERNATIONAL REFUGEE ORGANIZATION. *Report of the Director General to the General Council of the International Refugee Organization, July 1948-30 June 1949.* Geneva: International Refugee Organization, [1949?].
Summarizes the year's accomplishments, including the efforts to resettle refugees, provide medical help and vocational training, and to give language instruction.

322 KLEMME, MARVIN. *Inside Story of UNRRA: An Experience in Internationalism: A First Hand Report on the Displaced People of Europe.* New York: Lifetime Editions, 1949. 307 p.
Klemme, a U.S. forester, volunteered his expertise to UNRRA and worked in displaced persons camps in Germany until June 1947. Although he voices dislike of eastern Europeans in general, he is sympathetic to the plight of the German expellees.

323 McNEILL, MARGARET. *By the Rivers of Babylon: A Story of Relief Work among the Displaced Persons of Europe.* London: Bannisdale Press, 1950. 231 p.
Draws on her journals, letters, and personal experiences to tell about going to Germany in June 1946 with a team of Quakers to work in displaced persons camps.

324 McSWEENEY, EDWARD. *American Voluntary Aid for Germany, 1945-1950.* Frieburgh, FRG: Caritas, 1950. 141 p.
Describes the many agencies that contributed food, clothing, medicines, and technical help to Germany. McSweeney cites examples of how the aid was used and what it accomplished.

Civilian Relief Efforts

325 MASER, CLIFFORD. *After Seven Years: World War II Refugees in Germany and Austria Today.* Philadelphia: American Friends Service Committee, 1952. 40 p.
Not reviewed.

326 SWANSTROM, EDWARD E. *Pilgrims of the Night: A Study of Expelled People.* New York: Sheed & Ward, 1950. 114 p.
A Catholic priest who worked in expellee camps at Salzgitte and elsewhere tells of the help of the Protestant and Catholic relief agencies. He describes the experiences of many people.

327 UNITED NATIONS RELIEF AND REHABILITATION ADMINISTRATION. *Displaced Persons Operations: Report of Central Headquarters for Germany, April 1946.* Washington, D.C.: UNRRA, 1946. 148 p.
Summarizes the activities in Germany. Many Poles refused to return to occupied Poland despite the strong encouragement of UNRRA officials. Jews and Balts on the other hand were expected to stay in the west or to emigrate elsewhere.

328 ———. *Economic Recovery in the Countries Assisted by UNRRA: Report Presented by the Director General of UNRRA to the Secretary General of the United Nations.* Prepared by the Economic Advisor of UNRRA. Washington, D.C.: UNRRA, 1946. 182 p.
An official report of the agency's activities.

329 ———. *In the Wake of the Armies: Raw Material for Writers, Directors, Producers, Story-Editors.* Washington, D.C.: UNRRA, May 1945-13 April 1946.
Each weekly issue includes vivid descriptions of displaced persons, their care in centers, and their repatriation.

330 ———. *Operational Analysis Papers.* London: European Regional Office, no. 1 (1946)-no. 53 (1948).
Topical papers describing relief work all over Europe. Three of particular interest are: no. 12, *UNRRA Procurement of US Military Surpluses in Europe* (December 1946); no. 41, *The Food Situation in Continental Europe* (April 1947); and no. 49, *UNRRA in Europe, 1945-1947* (June 1947).

331 _____. *The Story of U.N.R.R.A.* Washington, D.C.: UNRRA, 1948. 47 p.

Issued by its Office of Public Information, this is one of several pamphlets designed to inform the public about UNRRA. Other titles include *UNRRA: Organization, Aims, Progress* (1945), and *50 Facts about UNRRA* (1946).

332 _____. *Summary of D.P. Population, UNRRA Assembly Centers in U.S. Zone, 24 August 1946.* Berlin: UNRRA, 1946. 32 p.

An official report of displaced persons in the American zone.

333 _____. *UNRRA Monthly Review*, no. 1 (August 1944)-no. 26 (October 1946).

Covers all phases of relief work in several countries. After October 1946 the name was changed to *UNRRA Review* and was issued irregularly.

334 _____. *UNRRA Program of Relief and Rehabilitation Supplies: Summary Report.* Washington, D.C.: UNRRA, 1947. 75 p.

Not reviewed.

335 _____. *U.N.R.R.A., the History.* Prepared by a special staff under direction of George Woodbridge. 3 vols. New York: Columbia University Press, 1950.

An official history of the international agency, with statistics and appendixes.

336 *What We Saw in Germany: A Report by British Churchwomen to the Control Commission for Germany.* London: S.P.C.K., Sword of the Spirit, 1948. 30 p.

Eight women toured the British zone in October 1947 to gather information on the nature, scope, and problems of women's church work in Germany after the war. They include recommendations in the report.

337 WILSON, FRANCESCA M. *Aftermath: 1945-1946.* New York: Penguin, 1947. 253 p.

Describes in detail the work of UNRRA in Bavaria at the war's end. Headquartered at Feldafing on a lake near Munich, Wilson helped to find and bring in to the center Polish workers who had been forced to come to Germany to work during the war.

Civilian Relief Efforts

338   WILSON, ROGER C. *Quaker Relief: An Account of the Relief Work of the Society of Friends, 1940-1948*. London: Allen & Unwin, 1952. 373 p.

A general history of the relief work carried on by the Quakers in Britain and in Europe both during and after the war.

339   WORLD COUNCIL OF CHURCHES. REFUGEE DIVISION. *Report from Hamburg: A Survey of the German Refugee Problem in 1949*. Geneva: World Council of Churches, 1949. 32 p.

A paper written for a conference in Hamburg on the efforts of the Hilfswerk of the Evangelical Church in Germany to help expellees become integrated in western German society.

Chapter 4

Journal Articles

The articles cited in this chapter are principally from popular magazines published in Great Britain and the United States during the immediate postwar period. They are representative of the information given to those citizens about their former enemies, the conquered country, and the hometown troops stationed there. Because scholarly journals are predisposed to publish articles that are analytical, historical, and reflective in nature, these often are less concerned with the daily lives of people who lived in the occupied zones and, therefore, are less suitable for this bibliography.

Generally the authors cited in this chapter were journalists who traveled in Germany on assignment for news agencies, newspapers, and magazines. Citations also include articles by persons who were sent to the occupied zones on investigative missions for governmental bodies and private organizations, because such groups wanted concrete information on which to base their decisions to send aid. Journalists on assignment for a magazine often submitted articles on Germany at regular intervals. When these are cited they appear chronologically rather than alphabetically. Also some articles are grouped together when they deal briefly with the same topic in the same journal.

340 ALVAREZ del VAYO, JULIO. "Intermezzo in Berlin." *Nation* 163 (31 August 1946): 232-35.
   Describes life in occupied Berlin in the summer of 1946, the renewal of politics, and the treatment of Germans.

341 "Army Rule for the German Church?" *Christian Century* 63 (24 April 1946): 518-20.
   Pastor Niemoller suggests in a speech before university students at Erlangen that the denazification process of the U.S. military government should not be applied to churchmen.

342 ARNOLD-FORSTER, W. "U.N.R.R.A.'s Work for Displaced Persons in Germany." *International Affairs* 22 (January 1946): 1-13.
   In an address given in October 1945, the author cited the most current statistics of the number of displaced persons in UNRRA camps in Germany. He described the work being done, the groups that were being repatriated, and what the camps were like.

343 BACH, JULIAN S. "America's Germany." *Life* 20 (13 May 1946): 104-14.
   In excerpts from his forthcoming book, the author describes the behavior of Germans and U.S. soldiers in the American occupation zone. Cigarettes function as currency and hunger is a problem everywhere.

344 BACHMANN, E. THEODORE. "Wilderness of Want." *Christian Century* 64 (3 December 1947): 1482-83; "Self-help in German Churches" 64 (31 December 1947): 1609-10.
   Serving as a special representative for the World Council of Churches in Germany, Bachmann writes of the reality of postwar conditions. German churches are making valiant efforts to help their own citizens through the Evangelische Hilfswerk, Caritas, the Workers' Welfare Association, and the German Red Cross.

345 BALLANTYNE, JESSE. "Should We Feed Germany?" *Canadian Forum* 26 (May 1946): 32-34.
   Describing the shortage of food in Germany, the writer suggests that Canadians should join Britain in sending food to the British zone.

346 "Banned German Pastoral." *Commonweal* 44 (7 June 1946): 180-81.
   The Easter pastoral letter issued by German Catholic bishops was banned in the French and American zones but was read in the

British zone. It was a plea for peace through justice, and it should not have been forbidden.

347 BARDENS, DENNIS. "Czechs and Germans." *Spectator* 175 (14 December 1945): 564-65.

The reasons for the Czechs to expel the ethnic Germans from the Sudetenland are understandable. Although it is a harsh experience, it is nothing compared to the German occupation of Czechoslovakia. Bardens personally visited prisons and detention camps to check on alleged mistreatment of Germans.

348 BARTH, KARL. "How My Mind Changed." *Christian Century* 66 (9 March 1949): 298-300; 66 (16 March 1949): 333-34.

This Protestant German theologian had gone into exile in Switzerland during the Hitler years and had become a Swiss citizen. He traveled extensively in postwar Germany, however his views on the role of German churches in the nazi period and his opinion of the responsibility for the war were not well received by Germans.

349 BENTWICH, NORMAN, and VERA DANIEL. "German Snapshots." *Contemporary Review* 172 (November 1947): 275-80.

Although there have been physical changes in Germany since the war, e.g., bridges rebuilt, roads cleared and repaired, and communications reestablished, the Germans feel the lack of a positive policy on the part of the occupation governments. Germans see no hope for the future and only isolation and despair in the present.

350 BERRY, LELAH, as told to ANN STRINGER. "An Army Wife Lives Very Soft in Germany." *Saturday Evening Post* 219 (15 February 1947).

A U.S. army dependent lives in a large requisitioned house with a maid and a cook. Cigarettes are used to buy carpets and furniture that could not be afforded at home. Although there is no chance to meet ordinary Germans, Berry is glad to be in Germany helping to educate them and to show how Americans live well.

351 BESS, DEMAREE. [U.S. occupation of Germany.] *Saturday Evening Post* 217 (26 January 1946); 217 (2 February 1946).

Describes the evolution of JCS 1067, the policy statement that is the basis for the American occupation of Germany. Some aspects of the proposed Morgenthau Plan are included in JCS 1067. Allies need to cooperate more in order to resolve the problems of caring for the expellees, displaced persons, and Germans.

Journal Articles

352   BETTANY, A. G. "With the Americans in Germany." *World Affairs* (London), n.s. 1 (October 1947): 409-18.

    After visiting the American zone, Bettany describes its military government as bureaucratic but generous. The people appear to be well-fed and well-dressed. They seem to like the Americans.

353   BIDWELL, PERCY W. "What Is Happening in Germany?" *Harper's* 196 (February 1948): 173-79.

    The German economy is stagnant, and Germans are still not able to provide enough food, industrial products, and coal for themselves. This is due in part to lack of Soviet cooperation in governing Germany.

354   BINGHAM, BARRY. "The United States Job in Germany." *Freedom and Union* 3, no. 2 (February 1948): 12-15.

    The reeducation and democratization programs are hampered by shortages of books, newsprint, and lack of decent school and university buildings. Cooperation with the Soviets has proved impossible.

355   "Black Market Stalls German Recovery." *World Report* 2 (3 June 1947): 10-11.

    Goods are withheld from regular marketing channels to be bartered on the black market because their prices are fixed so low that the money is almost worthless. Farmers exchange their produce on the black market. This is a bad cycle that must be broken.

356   BLANKFORT, ALICE. "They Live as Conquerors in Occupied Germany." *Survey* 86 (September 1950): 408-11.

    American army dependents live well in Germany, having access to better housing, food, and consumer goods than Germans. Some Germans are resentful.

357   BLOW, JONATHAN. "Germany Approaches the Crossroads." *Quarterly Review* 285 (January 1947): 152-67.

    Life in Germany is still precarious after eighteen months of occupation. Maintenance is costing the British and Americans millions. The western zones must become self-sufficient but avoid Soviet domination.

Journal Articles

358　BOEKER, ALEXANDER. "Agricultural Dilemma in Germany." *Forum* 105 (May 1946): 792-96.

　　The Potsdam agreements, which decreed that Germany must reduce its level of industrialization, makes it impossible for the country to provide a decent standard of living for itself. The success of modern agriculture depends on availability of industrial products.

359　_____. "The Atrocity of Mass Expulsions." *Christian Century* 64 (9 April 1947): 461-63.

　　The author is shocked at the indifference of the Christian world to "one of the most barbarous atrocities of the past two years," that is, the plight of the millions of expellees from the eastern Reich.

360　BOLLINGER, H. D. "This is Mass Starvation." *Christian Century* 63 (30 October 1946): 1310-11.

　　Calls for more effort to prevent the starvation of the German people, including more federal money allocated to the U.S. occupation forces for food. Church people should send food parcels and contribute to private agencies working in Germany.

361　BORNEMAN, ERNEST. "Back to Berlin, the Diary of a Native's Return." *Harpers* 197 (August 1948): 58-66.

　　Returning to Berlin for the first time since 1933, the author searched for his father and for friends. He tells of his emotions upon seeing the ruins of Berlin.

362　BORNOFF, JACQUES. "Musical Life in Germany Today." *Nineteenth Century and After* 140 (December 1946): 339-42.

　　Both the Allies and the Germans are anxious to revive musical events, and halls have been repaired as quickly as possible. Some musicians are forbidden to participate because of their activities in the Third Reich.

363　BOULTON, S. MILES. "Our Mistakes in Germany." *American Mercury* 67 (August 1948): 156-63.

　　Lists several problems with the American occupation of Germany, including carrying dismantling too far, inequities in the denazification process, not using the available work force in factories that had raw materials on hand, and letting Jewish educators direct the reeducation of Germany. American policies are motivated by a desire for revenge.

Journal Articles

364   BOYLE, KAY. "Monument to Hitler." *Nation* 164 (12 April 1947): 417-19.

        Describes a visit to a Polish displaced persons camp, with crowded living conditions and lack of medical supplies and personnel.

365   BRAILSFORD, H. N. "Impressions of Hamburg." *New Statesman and Nation* 34 (4 October 1947): 266-67.

        Describes the ruined city with people still living in cellars and collapsed buildings. The docks are demolished, and there are no building materials to repair them with. The people are deeply resentful of the living conditions and ample food of the British occupiers.

366   _____. "From Morgenthau to Marshall." *New Statesman and Nation* 34 (29 November 1947): 425-26.

        States that it is time to give up the appearance of following the never-implemented Morgenthau Plan. It is vengeful lunacy. Instead the Marshall Plan should be adopted as soon as possible.

367   BRAMALL, ASHLEY. "British Zone." *New Statesman and Nation* 32 (28 December 1946): 476.

        Germans no longer believe that Britain is sincerely trying to help them recover. They now think that Britain is purposely keeping them unindustrialized and starving.

368   BRANDT, KARL. "Inside Russian Occupied Territory." *Commercial and Financial Chronicle* 164 (25 July 1946).

        After four months in Germany, Brandt concludes that the Soviet Union has no intention of cooperating with the other Allies. It has established communistic principles in the eastern zone. It continues to dismantle German factories and ship them eastward, along with manufactured products.

369   _____. "Can Germany Ever Feed Its People?" *Saturday Evening Post* 219 (16 November 1946).

        As an agricultural advisor to the U.S. military government, Brandt is concerned with the recovery of Europe as well as Germany, and with the reduction of occupation costs. Germany's problems are multiplied by the stream of refugees and expellees that cross the Soviet zone into the west.

Journal Articles

370 BRATTER, HERBERT M. "An Economy Based on Cigarettes." *Nation's Business* (June 1947).

The American troops stationed in Germany have managed to bilk the United States out of millions of dollars by playing the black market with their cigarette allotments. Every time the federal government tries to correct the situation, the soldiers find another loophole.

371 BROWN, IRVING J. [Report on Germany.] *American Federationist* 53 (May 1946); 55 (July 1947).

Encourages a change of occupation policy that would give the Germans some hope for the future. Their present state of desperation and misery finds them in a daily struggle for food and shelter. Includes specific details on the condition of German unions, their attempts to organize, elect officials, etc.

372 BURCK, GILBERT. "Ruhr." *Fortune* 34 (December 1946).

Photographs and narrative describe the current state of German industry in the Ruhr district. It is difficult to persuade miners to work because their wages do not buy enough food for their families. They acquire more by bartering things on the black market.

373 _____. "Business in Bizonia." *Fortune* 38 (September 1948).

Before the currency, reform manufacturers traded most of their products on a "compensation basis," working through a series of involved and improvised private deals. After currency reform, almost overnight the shops are well-stocked with goods.

374 BUTLER, HAROLD. "Journey in Europe, II." *Spectator* 177 (6 December 1946): 602-03.

Vividly describes the ruins of Hamburg, Kiel, Berlin, and the Rhineland. People are too dazed, beaten, and hungry to think about politics.

375 CAREY, JANE P. C. "Germany's New People." *Survey* 85 (March 1949): 145-48.

Expellees from the eastern parts of the Reich, Hungary, Czechoslovakia, and Poland are crowding into the western zones of Germany, making additional demands on rationed food and overcrowded shelters.

376 CARMICHAEL, JOEL. [Germany, Berlin, and the Soviet zone.] *Nation* 164 (4 January 1947): 9-11; 164 (1 February 1947): 120-21.

After a trip to the Soviet zone, Carmichael advises that the Russians will not leave Germany because they have reinstituted V-2 rocket manufacturing in underground factories east of Kassel. They will never leave with the factories in working order. Germans in Berlin are suspicious of the Soviets and imagine that living conditions are worse in the Soviet Union than in the east zone.

377 CAVERT, SAMUEL M. "What Hope for Germany?" *Christian Century* 63 (23 October 1946): 1274-76.

After spending several weeks in Germany, Cavert calls for support of a constructive policy of humane and considerate treatment of Germans.

378 *Christian Century* 62 (3 October 1945): 1115; 62 (14 November 1945): 1247-49; 62 (28 November 1945): 1311; 62 (12 December 1945): 1377-79; 62 (19 December 1945): 1403; 62 (26 December 1945): 1439-41; 63 (23 January 1946): 102-4; 63 (20 February 1946): 230; 63 (3 July 1946): 829.

Articles urging Americans to realize that millions of Germans are starving and that it is the responsibility of Christians to insist that U.S. policies be changed to allow private aid to be sent to Germany.

379 CIVIS GERMANICUS. "A German Exile Returns." *Contemporary Review* 171 (April 1947): 217-20.

Pleads with the Allies to consolidate the occupation zones, reintroduce free trade and free movement, and give the Germans a chance to govern themselves democratically.

380 COHN, DAVID L. "First in War, Last in Peace." *Atlantic* 177 (January 1946): 58-61.

Deplores the actions of the U.S. military government. They are too nice to the Germans, who dazzle the soldiers with their work ethic, their pretty girls, and their servility. Americans act "intellectually adolescent."

381 "Conversations with Germans." By the Dean of St. Paul's. *Spectator* 175 (28 December 1945): 613-14.

The dean visited Germany for three weeks to talk with German church leaders and ordinary citizens. Religious leaders acknowledged guilt, but the ordinary Germans seemed only to think about finding enough food, fuel, and shelter.

Journal Articles

382   COSER, LEWIS A. "Germany 1948." *Commonweal* 48 (11 June 1948): 208-11.

Still in the first half of 1948 life in Germany revolves around the black market. People must barter and trade goods or starve to death. Ordinary morality does not enter into the picture.

383   COTTRELL, DONALD P. "University in Germany Today." *School & Society* 66 (27 December 1947): 481-84.

Universities in Germany are in bad shape. Buildings are lacking, professors are scarce, and too many students are enrolled. Everyone is hungry, and morale is low.

384   COUSINS, NORMAN. "Dinner for 26 in Berlin." *Saturday Review* 31 (18 December 1948).

Having invited Germans for dinner, Cousins had to be creative in obtaining enough food from the American military government to feed them all. He was violating U.S. occupation policies to do that.

385   "Crop Waste in Germany: A Problem of Transport." *World Report* 3 (30 September 1947): 14.

The large harvest is spoiling on the farms because there are not enough trucks with tires to collect it. The Germans have avoided producing trucks because they might be considered militaristic.

386   CROSSMAN, R. H. S. "A Voice from Berlin." *New Statesman and Nation* 29 (9 June 1945): 370.

From the Berlin Soviet sector a radio station is broadcasting in German. This seems symbolic of the Russians' determination to push forward with a positive policy for Germany. On the other hand, the western Allies have policies that are negative.

387   _____. "Why Germany Matters." *New Statesman and Nation* 30 (23 September 1945): 188.

Laments the flow of expelled ethnic Germans from Poland and Czechoslovakia into the Soviet zone. The Potsdam agreements are not being followed.

388   _____. "Germany Revisited: Berlin." *New Statesman and Nation* 30 (13 October 1945): 240.

Observed four-power control of Berlin under the nervous eyes of the Soviets who occupied the city first. It was very difficult for the four Allies to agree on policies.

389 _____. "Dismantling or Loot?" *New Statesman and Nation* 36 (28 August 1948): 167-68.

At this late date, the French are still dismantling clock and watchmaking factories in the Swabian region of their zone. These factory breakups leave whole towns out of work. This is bad for the long-range economy of Germany.

390 "A Cry from Germany." *Christian Century* 64 (26 February 1947): 273-74.

A letter from a German pastor explains that Germans have received little help from the United States. The people have lost faith in expecting peace to bring favorable changes.

391 "Czechs and Germans." *New Statesman and Nation* 30 (11 August 1948): 90-91.

In Czechoslovakia, Germans are being rounded up for eventual expulsion. Those who tell them to bear their fate with fortitude and resignation are not helpful.

392 DANIELL, RAYMOND. [The Germans and the occupation.] *New York Times Magazine* (16 March 1947); (14 December 1947).

Although Germany has the potential to rebuild, it is not doing so. It is living on the charity of the Allies. People feel sorry for themselves and dwell on their own misery.

393 DAVENPORT, JOHN. "Der Papierkrieg--the War of Paper Work." *Fortune* 36 (July 1947).

Talks with German businessmen reveal that the economy is bankrupt. Germany is effectively a country without a currency, trying to conduct twentieth-century business with an eighth-century bartering system.

394 DAVIS, JEROME. "Russian Germany--a Dissenting Report." *Christian Century* 65 (28 January 1948): 108-10.

After traveling for two months in the Soviet zone, Davis finds the conditions to be better than western rumors describe them. The Soviet plan to reunite the zones should be given encouragement.

Journal Articles

395 "Denazification: A Letter from a German Anti-Nazi Lawyer to His Friend, an American Scholar." *Social Research* 14 (March 1947): 59-74.
Summarizes his personal experiences with denazification in the American zone. The procedures regard every German as an enemy and are applied unequally from place to place.

396 DERRICK, MICHAEL. "The Task in Germany: Impressions of the British Zone." *Soundings* (May 1949): 27-37.
For British civilians life in their zone is often out of touch with reality. They are governed by an official agency that has its own police, courts, and prisons. The civilians have little contact with Germans.

397 DICKSON, ALEC. "Displaced Persons." *National Review* 129 (November 1947: 382-92; 129 (December 1947): 490-93.
Among major responsibilities of the British occupation troops are the various displaced persons groups still in the zone. These include Poles, Jews, Balts, Romanians, and ethnic Germans expelled from eastern Europe.

398 DIMONT, CHARLES. "The Autobahn." *New Statesman and Nation* 31 (1 June 1946): 391-92.
A British officer who one day walked to the next town noticed Allied personnel in vehicles, while German civilians walked, pulling or pushing carts with their belongings.

399 "Dismantling Dementia." *Christian Century* 65 (6 October 1948): 1028-29.
Urges an immediate halt to the dismantling of factories in the western zones. It has been proved that the factories usually do not work once they are reassembled. In addition, the Germans need the industrial plants to revive their own economy.

400 "Displaced Germans." *Life* 19 (15 October 1945): 107-15.
A photographic essay showing the destitute German expellees from the eastern Reich who flood into Berlin seeking food, shelter, and safety. Berliners cannot absorb them and they must move on to the British and American zones.

Journal Articles

401 "Displaced Persons in Germany: Observations Made by a Delegation of the Polish American Congress, Inc." *Polish Review* (12 December 1946).

　　The delegation charges that, despite the Poles' reluctance to return to their homeland while it is occupied by the Soviets, UNRRA has tried to force repatriation by several tactics, including lies, confiscation of recreational equipment, denial of access to Catholic priests, poor food and housing, etc. The Congress was especially angered by the offer of a year's worth of food to anyone who would return to Poland.

402 DOBIE, J. FRANK. "What I Saw across the Rhine." *National Geographic Magazine* 91 (January 1947): 57-86.

　　Dobie traveled in the American zone as a lecturer in the U.S. army's education program. He describes the ruined cities, the people, the cigarette economy, attitudes of U.S. troops, and the shortage of decent housing for Germans.

403 DÖBLIN, ALFRED. "Germany Is No More: Life among the Ruins." *Commentary* 2 (September 1946): 227-32.

　　After the war Döblin returned to Germany to work with an educational mission in the French zone. He observes that the country is now broken into four parts, each separate from the other, with its own laws, newspapers, officials, etc. There is hardly any travel between zones.

404 DREHER, CARL. "Close-Up of Democracy." *Virginia Quarterly Review* 23 (Winter 1947): 89-107.

　　The officers in the American military government find it difficult to teach democracy to a defeated country. The occupation is imposed upon Germans in an autocratic way.

405 "Drive for Quick Aid to Germans." *United States News* 22 (7 March 1947): 24-25.

　　Former President Hoover recommends to the president in his recent report on Germany that trade should be encouraged by the Allies and that the Germans need to have more food.

406 "East of the Elbe." *Economist* 149 (27 October 1945): 591-92.

　　The German people's first encounters with the Soviets were terrifying because many soldiers were intent on revenge and violence. After the war the Communists began to have the rubble cleared and the utilities reconnected. Large estates were broken up with land reforms.

407   ECKARDT, WOLFGANG. "Germany: East or West?" *Forum* 106 (July 1946): 7-14.

Germans in the western zones have lost all hope for the future. There are no signs of economic recovery, of jobs for skilled workers, of forgiveness for past deeds, or of decent food and housing. The Soviets, on the other hand, are rewarding those who work for the good of the state and are starting political and cultural activities.

408   "Expellees, the Flight and Expulsion of German Minorities in Eastern Europe." *Social Service Review* 20 (December 1946): 567-69.

Excerpts from an American Friends Service Committee pamphlet, report no. 4 (September 1946), describing the terrible consequences of the Potsdam agreements, which the United States was partly responsible for. The Germans and Allies are not only trying to absorb and care for the expellees, but also for the hundred of thousands of displaced persons and returning prisoners of war.

409   FALL, CYRIL. [Visiting the British zone.] *Illustrated London News* 207 (21 July 1945): 66-67; 208 (23 March 1946): 314; 208 (30 March 1946): 342.

Photographs of British soldiers serving as occupation troops in Germany. Most are anxious to return home but are trying to meet their responsibilities of providing food and shelter for needy Germans.

410   FAY, SIDNEY B. [Germany, the expellees, and the occupation.] *Current History* 11 (December 1946): 500-06; 12 (April 1947): 321-28; 15 (August 1948); 65-71; 15 (December 1948): 321-28.

A permanent peace treaty should be signed by the Allies. Germany needs free trade among the zones, more agricultural products from the eastern zone, and a reduction of reparation payments. Refugees of all kinds are waiting for permanent homes.

411   "The Feeding of Western Germany." *World Today* 4 (January 1948): 25-40.

Comparing the current ability of the western zones to produce food with the statistics of the 1930s results in the conclusion that Germany will have to continue to import food and agricultural supplies.

Journal Articles

412 FEY, HAROLD E. "Inside the German Prison." *Christian Century* 65 (8 September 1948): 902-04.

Relays information about the Soviet prisoner-of-war camps that he gained by interviewing returning Germans. Describes also how the currency reform hurt old people, students, and charitable groups.

413 FISCHER, ALFRED J. "Russian Zone in Germany." *Contemporary Review* 174 (September 1948): 142-47.

After a visit to the Soviet zone, Fischer describes politics, food supplies, restored factories, land reform, workers' councils, and cultural affairs. He finds the zone better off than western Germans have been saying.

414 "Forced Migration." *Time* 46 (13 August 1945).

At least ten million Germans are being uprooted from their ancestral homes in East Prussia, Pomerania, Silesia, the Sudetenland, and other places. Because they became refugees after the war, they do not qualify for UNRRA help.

415 FRAENKEL, HEINRICH. "Education in Germany." *New Statesman and Nation* 31 (11 May 1946): 334.

Fraenkel has traveled around the western zones evaluating the educational plans that are being made. Some teachers are working, but there is a terrible shortage of school rooms and texts.

416 _____. [In the Russian zone.] *New Statesman and Nation* 34 (30 August 1947): 166-67; 36 (11 September 1948): 210.

The Soviet zone is rebuilding at a more rapid rate than the western zones. People are happy with socialist educational changes and land reform; however, the farmers are suffering from high prices and shortages of farming equipment.

417 _____. "Berlin and the Russian Zone." *Political Quarterly* 18 (October 1947): 323-30.

Daily life in Berlin is full of shortages, and people attempt to escape their misery with cultural entertainment and newspaper and periodical reading. There are no longer any reserves to draw on, and people are existing from day to day.

418 "From a European Colleague." *Survey Midmonthly* 84 (July 1948): 226.

Addressing an open letter to fellow social workers, a German woman explains some of the difficulties that she encounters. She asks for sympathy, encouragement, and some food in order to believe in Germany's rehabilitation.

419   GARDINER, GERALD. "Migration of Death." *Spectator* 175 (26 October 1945): 378-79.

   Describes the terrible condition of the Germans who are coming into Berlin on foot from the east, driven by Polish militia. Individuals are robbed, raped, and murdered while trying to get to Berlin. The situation will be much worse when winter comes.

420   GARTEN, HUGO F. "Books and Theatres in Germany." *Contemporary Review* 173 (January 1948): 27-31.

   Despite the shortage of paper, books and journals are flourishing in the western zones of Germany. People are flocking to plays by Shakespeare, O'Neill, Wilder, Brecht, and the ancient Greeks.

421   GASKILL, GORDON. [Patrolling the Soviet border, interviewing a military governor.] *American Magazine* 142 (December 1946): 14-19; 143 (January 1947). 32-33, 108-11.

   Details about the U.S. constabulary, which keeps the peace in the American zone and along the border with the Soviet zone. A military governor describes daily experiences.

422   GENET. [Descriptions of Germany.] *New Yorker* 21 (17 November 1945): 71-74; 24 (30 October 1948), 98-101; 24 (6 November 1948): 116-21.

   Visiting several ruined cities in the Rhineland gave the author an opportunity to talk with Germans and describe what he saw. Displaced persons are still not settled in permanent homes.

423   "Germania Deserta, Account of a German Doctor's Wife Describing the Polish Administration Area of Eastern Germany." *Catholic World* 165 (April 1947): 18-25.

   Traveling back to the former eastern part of Germany, a woman encountered Russian and Polish soldiers, roving bands of Polish partisans, deserted and destroyed villages, and empty fields. Food rations were not being allocated to the remaining Germans by Polish officials.

424   "The German Literary Scene." *New Republic* 114 (27 May 1946): 773-74.

   Describes the efforts over the past year to license and publish newspapers and journals.

Journal Articles

425 "Germany: A Year of Defeat." *Business Week* (11 May 1946): 105-06, 108.

Economic recovery is lagging in Germany because there is a shortage of food, raw materials, and coal. In addition, rail and road networks are still disrupted.

426 "Germany Faces the Winter." *Economist* 151 (14 September 1946): 406-10.

In the British zone, conditions continue to deteriorate as winter approaches. Rations have been reduced, and coal mining has slowed down because the miners lack stamina. It is Britain's responsibility to feed the Germans.

427 "Germany in Defeat." *World Today* 2 (February 1946): 66-78.

The author is surprised at the lack of guilt feelings and the callousness of the Germans. They dwell on their own misery, with no concern for others. According to them, their problems are the fault of the displaced persons and the Allies.

428 "Germany Revisited: Some Impressions after Two Years." *World Today* 3 (October 1947): 424-31.

There are few signs of change in two years. Rubble is everywhere, and people look tired, undernourished, and in rags. There have been some political activities, but Germans tend to be suspicious of all politicians.

429 GITTLER, LEWIS F. "Everyday Life in Germany Today." *American Mercury* 61 (October 1945): 400-07.

Survey of hundreds of Germans for the Psychological Warfare Branch of the U.S. army. Gittler found that money is worthless, the black market is thriving, people are hungry, farmers are better off than city dwellers, and everyone is focused on himself and his family.

430 GLASER, DANIEL. "The Sentiments of American Soldiers Abroad toward Europeans." *American Journal of Sociology* 51, no. 5 (March 1946): 433-38.

In addition to seeing European countries at their worst, the American GI quickly picked up on the negative cultural differences that existed between the soldiers and civilians. On the other hand, after the cessation of hostilities, many soldiers were favorably impressed with the friendliness and cleanliness of German women.

431 GOLLANCZ, VICTOR. "The State of Germany." *New Statesman and Nation* 32 (30 November 1946): 392-93.

Laments the failure of the British to be successful as occupiers. Denazification, coal production, encouragement of industries, and reeducation have not gone well. There is no clear policy for the Allies to support because of the uncooperativeness of the Soviet Union.

432 _____. "German Industry." *New Statesman and Nation* 32 (7 December 1946): 414.

The dismantling of German industry for reparations is completely out-of-hand. It proceeds even though the Germans themselves desperately need the factories to get their economy moving again.

433 GOODYKOONTZ, BESS. "Teachers and Children in German Schools." *School Life* 29 (July 1947): 3-6.

As a member of the U.S. Education Mission to Germany, the author visited schools in the zone. The problems were ruined buildings, and shortages of books, paper, and pencils. The children seemed hungry, cold, and frightened.

434 GORDON, SELWYN. "Cologne Revives." *Spectator* 176 (12 April 1946): 372-73.

The center of the city of Cologne is slowly being cleared of the rubble left by the war. Municipal water and sewer pipes are being repaired, and some industrial plants are being permitted to reopen.

435 GORER, GEOFFREY. "The British Zone of Germany." *Fortnightly* 116 (December 1946): 381-87.

Germans are convinced that the inadequate food supplies are the British method of revenge for the war. Denazification is not working very well in practice.

436 GRIFFITHS, ELDON W. "Retrospect on Germany." *Yale Review* 39 (September 1949): 96-107.

After spending part of 1948 in Germany, journalist Griffiths reports that Germans are bitter and full of self-pity. He found little interest in democracy and much discontent with the occupation governments.

Journal Articles

437 GUNNISON, ROYAL A. "The Joneses Move In on the Krauts." *American Magazine* 142, no. 4 (October 1946).

Attitudes of American civilians who go to Berlin to live as dependents with military personnel who are assigned there.

438 GURIAN, WALDEMAR. "Re-educating Germany." *Commonweal* 48 (27 August 1948): 466-69.

Recounts Allied attempts to introduce democracy and culture to the Germans, and finds them unsuccessful. The author suggests that it is time to allow the Germans to rebuild their society, both physically and intellectually.

439 HAGEN, PAUL. [Germany in ruins.] *Survey Graphic* 34 (November 1945); 34 (December 1945).

Drawing on published reports of life in occupied Germany, Hagen describes what has been happening there the past few months. With concern for the possibility of epidemics and rebellion, he urges that the British provide more food and fuel for the Germans.

440 HALE, WILLIAM H. "Germany's Deformed Conscience." *Harper's* 192 (January 1946): 1-9.

After five months in Germany, Hale finds the majority of the population unrepentant and resentful. Denazification is not working well, and Germans are refusing to get involved in politics.

441 HANSER, RICHARD. "German Anti-Semitism Today." *American Mercury* 66 (April 1948): 433-38.

Cites several examples of hatred and abuse directed toward Jewish displaced persons in Germany and Austria. Germans tend to blame the Jews for their misery and for the shortages of food, clothing, and housing.

442 HARKORT, G. "Some Data on the German Standard of Living." *World Affairs* (London), n.s. 2 (July 1948): 271-83.

Writing before the currency reform, the author contrasts production and distribution of food and fuel from 1945 to 1947 with the 1930s. He concludes that Germany needs more food so that people eat better and have more energy to work harder.

443 HARRINGTON, GORDON. "How Berlin Looks." *Spectator* 175 (27 July 1945).

Describes the destruction of the central city and the condition of Grünewald where the British troops are billeted. The Soviets have already opened theaters, and their sector seems more lively. The nonfraternization policy is not working.

444 HAUSER, ERNEST O. [Germans are doubtful.] *Saturday Evening Post* 219 (3 August 1946); 219 (10 August 1946).
The reeducation process is not working in the U.S. zone. People suspect the Allies' form of truth about the Nazis is just propaganda. Hunger is more of a reality to the Germans than the death camps.

445 _____. "The Starving Playground of Power Politics." *Saturday Evening Post* 219 (26 October 1946).
The British are encouraging the rebuilding of heavy industries in the Ruhr, while the Soviets are still demanding more dismantled plants as reparations. Meanwhile, the German miners are having difficulty feeding their families.

446 _____. "A German Family Takes Down Its Hair." *Saturday Evening Post* 220 (27 September 1947).
Hauser visits an ordinary family in Munich. The father is a veteran and was a "small" Nazi. The older son is a prisoner of war in Britain; the younger children were not very involved in the Hitler Youth. The family is poor but trying to get by without trading items on the black market.

447 HAWKINS, THOMAS. [Personal reports from Germany.] *World Report* 1 (20 June 1946): 36; 1 (11 July 1946): 35-36; 1 (22 August 1946): 35-39; 1 (17 December 1946): 36-37; 2 (25 February 1947): 40; 2 (18 March 1947): 39-40; 2 (25 March 1947): 39-40; 2 (1 April 1947): 14-15; 2 (29 April 1947): 22-23; 2 (27 May 1947): 33-34; 2 (3 June 1947): 31-32; 3 (15 July 1947): 32; 3 (22 July 1947): 32; 3 (5 August 1947): 32; 3 (30 July 1947): 31-32; 3 (2 September 1947): 31; 3 (9 September 1947): 8-9; 3 (14 October 1947): 32; 3 (2 December 1947): 31; 3 (9 December 1947): 32; 4 (6 January 1948): 29-30.
During a period of twenty months Hawkins records his impressions of life in occupied Germany. He talks with and observes people in Berlin, the American zone, and the Soviet zone, giving details of rationing, shortages, and black market dealings.

448 "Heirs of Potsdam: The Tragedy of Expelled Germans." *World Today* 4 (October 1948): 446-53.
Dwells on the impact of the ethnic Germans on western Germany rather than on their treatment when they were driven out of

the eastern provinces. The expellees are a terrible drain on the budgets of local governments. Natives resent having them forced on them.

449 HERMANS, FERDINAND A. "Economics of Potsdam." *Review of Politics* 8 (July 1946): 381-403.

The provisions of the Potsdam agreements are too harsh. The results are far more drastic than expected, with low industrial output and reduced agricultural production.

450 HIBBS, BEN. "Journey to a Shattered World." *Saturday Evening Post* 217 (9 June 1945).

Following the U.S. troops into Germany at the war's end, Hibbs is shocked by the concentration camps, destruction in cities, numbers of wandering displaced persons, and hungry children.

451 HILLDRING, JOHN A. "What Is Our Purpose in Germany?" *Annals of the American Academy of Political and Social Science* 255 (January 1948): 77-83.

A former assistant secretary of state tells of the controversy surrounding the concept of a "pastoral policy" for the U.S. occupation in Germany. Although never official policy, it has been discussed for several years.

452 HIRSCH, FELIX E. "What Future for Germany?" *Current History* 13 (October 1947): 204-09.

Describes the physical deprivation the Germans are suffering as well as their need for restored intellectual contacts with the outside world.

453 "Homes and Jobs for Refugees." *Christian Century* 65 (20 October 1948): 1102-03.

A report of the Refugee Commission of the World Council of Churches describes the conditions of various refugee groups in Germany. The worst off are the expellees from the east and the political refugees from the Soviet zone. Neither group qualifies for United Nations assistance.

454 HOMMEN, WILLI. "Letter from Germany." *Fortnightly* 170 (August 1948): 104-09.

Laments the opinions of non-Germans about Germany and urges those who speak out to be knowledgeable. Describes attitudes that are currently held by ordinary Germans.

455 HOPMAN, A. N. "Adult Education in Occupied Germany--U.S. Zone." *School and Society* 66 (27 December 1947): 505-07.

In August 1946 Bremen opened an adult school to train new teachers and rehabilitate dismissed teachers. In other cities, trade unions and industrial groups have also sponsored adult high schools.

456 HUTCHINSON, PAUL. "Notes on the German Churches." *Christian Century* 63 (28 August 1946): 1031-33.

Discusses German Protestantism after traveling around talking with religious leaders and lay people. There seems to be "a widespread religious hunger" among the people.

457 HUTCHISON, KEITH. "Does This Make Sense?" *Nation* 165 (29 November 1947): 586.

Questions the continued dismantling of German factories when the German economy is so closely tied to the recovery of the rest of Europe. Germany should not become a slum supported by the Allies.

458 *Illustrated London News* 206 (9 June 1945): 621; 207 (11 August 1945): 156-58; 207 (13 October 1945): 396-97; 207 (3 November 1945): 487; 207 (10 November 1945): 512-13; 207 (17 November 1945): 536-37; 207 (22 December 1945): 684; 208 (5 January 1946): 8-9; 208 (16 March 1946): 280-81; 210 (12 April 1947): 373; 210 (17 May 1947): 521; 211 (13 December 1947): 657.

Photographs of occupied Germany showing the condition of the people and the destruction of the cities and countryside.

459 "In the Russian Zone." *New Statesman and Nation* 29 (26 May 1945): 334-35.

An early visit to the Soviet zone gives little evidence of supposed atrocities. The streets are busy, and the rubble is being cleared. The Four-Power Control Commission needs to work at resolving the differences of the Allies and to establish a good working relationship.

460 JANOWITZ, MORRIS. "German Reactions to Nazi Atrocities." *American Journal of Sociology* 52, no. 2 (September 1946): 141-46.

Surveyed a sample of German civilians in June 1945 to find out what they had known about the concentration camps prior to the end of the war. He also asked them about the concept of collective responsibility.

Journal Articles

461 JOESTEN, JOACHIM. "The Strange Ways of German Democracy." *Antioch Review* 7 (March 1947): 17-22.

Germans are confused because there are five different kinds of democracy being preached in their country: the American, British, French, Soviet, and the coalition kind in Berlin.

462 JORDAN, PHILIP. "Life in a Vacuum." *Nation* 161 (1 September 1945): 204-05.

In the British zone, the military personnel are not suited for occupation duty. They are half-trained, undirected, and in an information vacuum.

463 JORDY, WILLIAM H. "Germans and the Occupation." *Commonweal* 43 (8 March 1946): 521-24.

Concludes after interviewing Germans that few are interested in politics and many have doubts that democracy will be embraced by their fellow Germans.

464 "Journey to the Rhine." *Canadian Forum* 25 (June 1945): 64-65.

Traveling into Germany with Canadian troops at the end of the war, the reporter describes what they find and regrets that the troops have not been prepared for dealing with civilians. He doubts that the nonfraternization policy will work.

465 KANAAR, A. C. "Land Reform in Germany." *Nineteenth Century and After* 139 (June 1946): 283-86.

The Communists are directing the arbitrary land reform being imposed on the Soviet zone. Junker estates are being broken up, and the landowners imprisoned or killed, with no regard for their anti-nazi pasts. The separation of the east and west zones is so severe that Kanaar fears it will be permanent.

466 KELBER, MAGDA. "Germany--British Zone: From a Relief Worker's Diary." *World Affairs* (London), n.s. 1 (April 1947): 155-62.

As part of the Friends Relief Service in the British zone, Kelber reports conversations with Germans about issues of daily life.

467 _____. "Bizonia after Currency Reform." *World Affairs* (London), n.s. 2 (October 1948): 366-72.

Since the reform, consumer goods have appeared in the shops and the farmers have produce to sell. Germans should govern themselves. Many people still have little understanding of what happened in nazi Germany.

468 KELLY, MATTHEW A. "Allied Policy on Wages in Occupied Germany." *International Labour Review* 55 (May 1947): 351-71.

Details the complex and confusing zonal policies on frozen prices, wages, and real costs of merchandise. Two pages of charts compare costs of living and wages in the British and U.S. zones.

469 KERN, HARRY. "Signposts in the German Rubble: Famine, Cold, Disease, Trouble." *Newsweek* 26 (13 August 1945).

Describes the difficulties facing the military in provisioning and governing the American zone.

470 KESSELL, MARY. "German Diary, August-October, 1945 Excerpts." *Cornhill Magazine* 162 (April 1946): 58-66.

Provides sketches of life in occupied Germany: Yugoslavian forced laborers going home, a Jewish engagement party, people trying to find living quarters in the bombed cities, and the smell and emptiness of Berlin.

471 KEYSERLINGK, ROBERT W. "The German Situation Today." *International Journal* 2 (Winter 1946-47): 26-36.

After a period of endorsing the concepts of justified revenge, punishment of aggressors, and unconditional surrender, the Allies have come to realize that the recovery of Europe is keyed to the recovery of Germany.

472 KIRKPATRICK, CLIFFORD. "Reactions of Educated Germans to Defeat." *American Journal of Sociology* 54, no. 1 (July 1948): 36-47.

In the summer of 1945 the author asked ninety-one well-educated Germans to fill out a questionnaire regarding their opinions on the war, the bombing, nazism, and the occupation.

473 KIRSTEIN, LINCOLN "Monuments of Old Germany." *Nation* 161 (1 September 1945): 206-07.

Some efforts were made during the war by Reich officials to protect and preserve art works. The removal of such treasure was, however, often viewed as defeatist and was discouraged until the last minute.

Journal Articles

474   KNAUTH, PERCY. "Occupied Germany." *Life* 23 (10 February 1947): 85-93.

   The American civilians and soldiers live well, often with their families present. Germans still suffer shortages of food and consumer goods. There needs to be more commerce between zones.

475   _____. "No Road Back?" *Time* 50 (28 July 1947): 23-24.

   Germans are bitter, cynical, and have lost hope that life can ever be normal again. Their good feelings for Americans have evaporated in the misery of the occupation.

476   _____. "Anna on the Autobahn." *Life* 24 (14 June 1948): 5-11.

   Follows the expedition of a young city woman who takes an old wool dress, a pair of shoes, and cigarettes out to the country to barter them for potatoes. The weather is cold and rainy, and Anna has to spend a night in a barn. After being turned away at several farms, she finally is able to trade her things and starts back to the city. She is almost killed on the train trip back.

477   KNOP, WERNER. "I Prowled Russia's Forbidden Zone." *Saturday Evening Post* 221 (11 December 1948); 221 (18 December 1948): 221 (25 December 1948); 221 (1 January 1949).

   Crossing the border illegally, Knop traveled around the Soviet zone talking with Germans and checking out the reopening of industrial plants. People seemed worse off than a year before, and there were food riots.

478   KUEHNELT-LEDDIHN, ERICK von. "What They Are Doing to Germany." *Catholic world* 163 (May 1946): 107-14.

   The Allied agreements at Potsdam have resulted in millions of expellees being forced into postwar Germany. The natives resent having the foreigners thrust upon them to feed and shelter.

479   KUNZIG, ROBERT L. "360,000 P.W.s--the Hope of Germany." *American Magazine* 142, no. 5 (November 1946): 23, 132-37.

   Thousands of German prisoners of war in American camps have been taught the principles of democracy and then are sent home to spread the ideas among their friends and coworkers.

480 LANIA, LEO. "Time Out from Terror: Germany." *Saturday Review* 30 (26 July 1947): 28-30.

Surveys the literary scene in Germany, discussing the writers who stayed there during the nazi period and the current status of book publishing in the western zones.

481 LARSON, RUTH. "Postwar Germany As I Saw It." *Education* 70 (February 1950): 370-75.

After spending two years in Germany in 1947 and 1948, Larson does not like the Hessians. She found them deceitful, arrogant, obdurate, and resentful. They were not good workers.

482 "Letter from Germany." *American Mercury* 61 (August 1945): 155-59.

This early report from the U.S. zone describes the complete breakdown of civilization, including communications and transportation networks. The GIs are less worried about military government than are the British. Fraternization is impossible to prevent because the people are friendly and the children are appealing.

483 "Letter from Germany." *New Statesman and Nation* 33 (1 February 1947): 92.

An exiled German and his family returned to a small town after the war. He writes of his concern for his children who are losing weight because rations are erratic and insufficient. He is thankful for food parcels from friends in the United States. Germans face slow starvation and dangerously incompetent occupation officials.

484 "Letters from Berlin." *Catholic World* 162 (November 1945): 135-42.

A U.S. army officer writes letters to his wife describing the city, German civilians, and the Allied soldiers quartered there.

485 LINDEMAN, EDUARD C. "Death of a German Generation." *New Republic* 113 (26 November 1945): 705-07.

Returning from occupied Germany, the author observes that Germans seem to be putting on an act for the occupiers. No one admits to being responsible for nazi actions.

486 LOGAN, ANDY. [Descriptions of Germany.] *New Yorker* 22 (28 December 1946); 22 (3 May 1947); 24 (29 March 1948); 24 (8 May 1948).

Americans in the military government are so focused on their own problems that they give very little attention to the Germans.

Although the wildness of the occupation has been curbed by allowing families to join personnel, Americans seldom make the effort to get to know Germans. On the other hand, Germans resent the Americans imposing the American way of life on them. They quote Abraham Lincoln and compare Americans to carpetbaggers.

487 _____. "Reporter at Large: Hof Refugee Exchange Camp." *New Yorker* 24 (17 July 1948): 48-56.

The U.S. civilian commander of the camp on the Soviet zonal border used to worry about where people came from and how they would survive. After three years, he simply tries to figure out where to send them next. It seems as if every nationality has passed through the camp. "Had a couple Samoans in here a few weeks ago, and I give you my word nobody even twitched an eyebrow. They wanted to go over east, incidentally."

488 LOUCHEIM, KATIE. "The D.P. Summer." *Virginia Quarterly Review* 61 (Autumn 1985): 691-707.

The author traveled to displaced persons camps in the American zone in the summer of 1945 to collect information for a report to the UNRRA council meeting in London in the fall.

489 MCCORMICK, ANNE O. "Germany, Weak, Is Still a Problem." *New York Times Magazine* (16 December 1945).

On the streets people are silent and sullen, and one cannot guess what they are thinking. Meanwhile, there needs to be a solution to the economic division of the country so that the rest of Europe can also recover.

490 MACKENZIE, NORMAN. "A German Diary." *New Statesman and Nation* 33 (8 March 1947): 149.

Life is difficult in Germany because the winter has been cold, and there are still shortages of food and fuel. Everyone complains. Although the universities are open and overcrowded with students, Germans still lack contact with the outside world.

491 MARCUSE, LUDWIG. "German Ideology, 1946." *Books Abroad* 21, no. 3 (1947): 274-78.

Analyzes East German writers, finding that they minimize social problems and proclaim the ideas of communism, while promoting German virtues and encouraging land reform.

492 MARTIN, KINGSLEY. [Visiting Germany.] *New Statesman and Nation* 31 (20 April 1946): 277; 31 (27 April 1946): 297.

In Berlin, the Germans wonder how long the western Allies will stay. The British treat their zone like a colony, and Germans have no civil rights. There are signs of famine in the zone. Notes that in Dortmund alone the Swedish Red Cross is feeding 15,000 children.

493 MAYER, ARTHUR L. "Winter of Discontent." *New Republic* 116 (10 March 1947): 17-19.

The constant search by city dwellers to find enough to eat leaves little time or energy for politics. Only farm families seem to have enough to eat.

494 _____. "Disquiet on the Western Front." *Theatre Arts* 34 (May 1950): 47-50.

As head of the Motion Picture Branch of the U.S. military government, Mayer directed the production of weekly newsreels to be distributed to German theaters in the zone. The branch also censored foreign films and licensed German movie companies in the zone.

495 MENCK, CLARA. "Germany Today." Translated from German. *Review of Politics* 8 (July 1946): 354-80.

Explains the political and intellectual thinking of Germans since the war. Finds dangers in the theories of German writer Ernst Jünger.

496 MENDE, TIBOR. "Public Opinion in Germany." *Fortnightly* (July 1946): 34-41.

Some of the common denominators among the four zones are the concerns of Germans for food, shelter, and the erratic application of denazification policies, and their attitudes toward their occupiers. Up to the spring of 1946, the British and American zones were seen as the better places to live.

497 MICHELFELDER, SYLVESTER C. "O Come, Sweet Death." *Christian Century* 63 (16 January 1946): 79-80.

Having talked with hundreds of German expellees who are in desperate need of help, the author urges readers to let public officials know that American people want their government to aid the Germans.

498 "Military Occupation Can't Succeed." *Harper's* 191 (November 1945): 385-90.

   A member of the RAF urges a hard line be taken in Germany. Since Germans will hate the occupiers and will form underground resistance units, the Allies should have a highly trained, highly mobile force ready to strike at suspected groups and other targets. Keep the occupiers untainted by enforcing nonfraternization.

499 MILLER, DOUGLAS. "Sidelights on Germany: How Life Progresses in Occupied Territory." *Nations Business* 33 (September 1945).

   Normal activities are beginning again in Germany with banks opening, shops being stocked, and want ads appearing in licensed newspapers. The four zones can learn from each other in governing Germany.

500 MUHLEN, NORBERT. "America and American Occupation in German Eyes." *Annals of the American Academy of Political and Social Science* 295 (September 1954): 52-61.

   A useful summary of German opinion, stated a few years after the military occupation had ended. Although Germans had little respect for the United States as a whole, they often came to like individual soldiers and civilians.

501 MUIR, MALCOLM. "Europe: This Side of the Iron Curtain." *Newsweek* 27 (3 June 1946): 34-35.

   Reports on a journalists' tour of the American zone, sponsored by the U.S. army. Germans need raw materials to get their industries started again. The Soviets are not cooperating in the administration of the four zones.

502 NAPOLI, JOSEPH F. "Denazification from an American's Point of View." *Annals of the American Academy of Political and Social Science* 264 (July 1949): 115-23.

   Having served in the occupation in Bremen, Napoli feels knowledgeable about the inconsistencies and failures of the denazification attempts in the U.S. zone.

503 NELSON, SAUL. "Daily Life in Occupied Germany." *Duns Review* 55 (April 1947).

   Describes life as an American military government official in Berlin. His family is with him, and he reports that Americans do not trade on the black market very much. Although he likes Germans, he

Journal Articles

thinks they feel very sorry for themselves, and everyone complains about the Soviet troops.

504 NETTLE, PETER. [The Soviet zone.] *New Republic* 119 (2 August 1948): 14-16; 119 (9 August 1948): 17-20; 119 (16 August 1948): 17-20.

After a visit to the Soviet zone the author describes the political climate of the zone, the relations between Germans and Russians, and the official opinions of Soviet occupation officials. The Soviets have a firm hold on the zone and will not consider merging zones unless they can dominate the subsequent central government.

505 "The Occupation--It's Got to Work." *Time* 45 (25 June 1945): 21-24.

Describes the conditions found in Germany immediately after the cessation of fighting, including the disruption of communications, public utilities, and transportation networks. Food supplies are low, and the country is teeming with displaced persons and refugees from the eastern provinces.

506 O'DONNELL, JAMES P. "GI Legacy in Germany." *Newsweek* 29 (16 June 1947): 48-50.

As a result of two years of occupation, there are possibly thirty to forty thousand new German-American babies. Although many soldiers want to marry German women, the regulations and obstacles make it difficult. Americans cannot adopt German children either. Some American organizations have opened orphanages to help care for the children in Germany.

507 "Old, Meager, and Ugly." *Commonweal* 43 (11 January 1946): 326-29.

In a letter from a German woman to an American friend, she describes her life during and after the war, and tells of the fate of her family.

508 "Orders Is Orders." *New Statesman and Nation* 30 (7 July 1945): 6-7.

A British soldier relates how he felt at being ordered to evict a German family from their home so the British could be billeted in it. He cannot hate the whole nation despite the stories of the concentration camps.

Journal Articles

509   PADOVER, SAUL K. "What Happened in Bavaria." *Nation* 161 (20 October 1945): 397-99.

The American military government personnel are doing a poor job of denazification in Bavaria. Padover quotes from German concentration camp returnees who feel discriminated against in the housing situation in Munich.

510   _____. "German Grave Digger." *American Mercury* 62 (January 1946): 55-63.

In Wuerselen three Germans a day were being killed by mines and booby traps buried by the German army. The German who volunteered to disconnect the mines happened to be a Communist. In an interview he reveals himself to be well informed and sensitive. He is disgusted with his fellow Germans.

511   _____. "German Bishop." *American Mercury* 62 (March 1946): 306-11.

An interview with the bishop of Aachen early in the occupation period examines politics, youth, German guilt, and Catholic nonresistance.

512   PARGIELLO, JAN S. "I Saw Polish D.P. Camps in Germany." *Polish Review* (7 March 1946).

Poles who were forced into the Reich as slave laborers are refusing to return to Poland while it is in Soviet control. Meanwhile, they are reviving their cultural and religious customs while they seek food, clothing, and jobs.

513   PEISS, REUBEN. "Report from Leipzig." *Library Journal* 71 (October 1946).

In August Peiss undertook a mission for the U.S. Library of Congress. He went to the Soviet zone to make arrangements for two freight carloads of books and periodicals to be sent to the American zone. These were the materials that German book dealers had accumulated from American prewar orders. The Soviets were courteous and helpful.

514   PETERSON, THEODORE C. "From behind the Iron Curtain." *Catholic World* 163 (April 1946): 11-19.

The author relates the experiences of a Catholic priest who lived in the Soviet zone. The priest was especially concerned with the suffering of the expellees there.

Journal Articles

515 PICK, F. W. "The German Problem." *Contemporary Review* 172 (December 1947): 336-39.
Time is desperately short to save the Germans from a worse winter than the previous year's. Food and fuel shortages are caused by the withholding of supplies for use on the black market.

516 PIPER, OTTO A. "Behind the Population Transfers." *Christian Century* 62 (14 November 1945): 1250-52.
Explains the background of the agreements made at Potsdam and how Christian moral laws are being violated by those countries who are expelling the ethnic Germans.

517 POWELL, ROBERT. "The German-Polish Frontier." *Fortnightly* 165 (April 1946): 237-42.
The author has traveled in the area between the Oder and Neisse rivers and the old Polish border that had been given by the Potsdam agreements to Poland to administrate. He has found the farms deserted and the fields unplanted. Amidst the Soviet soldiers and Polish militia are a few Polish farm families who have been moved into the area to settle on the deserted farms.

518 "Prospect for Germany." *Commonweal* 43 (25 January 1946): 371-72.
An editorial regrets that letters and food parcels cannot be sent to the Germans, who are isolated and hungry. At least private U.S. relief agencies should be allowed to operate in the zone.

519 "Reich: Hungry Herrenvolk." *Newsweek* 29 (11 November 1946): 49-51.
In the British and American zones, industrial stagnation and food shortages will likely cause riots this winter. Germans are too weak to put in a full day's work.

520 REINHOLD, H. A. "Mail from the Enemy Defeated." *Commonweal* 46 (23 May 1947): 134-37.
A Catholic priest describes the letters that he has received from friends in Germany. The people find life very unfair. Some have been caught dealing on the black market and are resentful because they are only trying to stay alive. Denazification has been enforced unevenly. Everyone knows a former Nazi who is still in a position of importance and someone who has been charged unjustly.

Journal Articles

521 "Relief Work with Displaced Persons in Germany." *World Today* n.s. 1 (September 1945): 135-44.

In their zone in the summer of 1945 the British used teams from voluntary agencies to work in the displaced persons camps. Many teams were Friends ambulance units.

522 "Reunion in Berlin." *Life* 22 (3 March 1947): 36-37.

The Eyewitness, an organization for locating missing persons, uses newsreels in movie theaters to show children who are seeking parents or other relatives. Many families have been reunited by this method.

523 REYNOLDS, J. LACEY. "Germany Is Our Peace Frontier." *Nations Business* (March 1947).

Germans in the spring of 1947 are hostile toward Americans and afraid of the Soviets. The occupation has been a messy business, but the United States should not give up. Germany needs to be reunited for real economic recovery.

524 REYNOLDS, QUENTIN. "They've Had It: This Is Defeat." *Colliers* 116 (1 December 1945).

In talking with American military commanders, all agree that Germany is thoroughly beaten. Reynolds observes that the Germans have no right to complain about their treatment. They deserve all the misery they have, and no one cares if they are hungry and cold.

525 ROBINSON, DONALD R. "Why Denazification Is Lagging." *American Mercury* 62 (May 1946): 563-70.

Charges that the U.S. military government is less than enthusiastic about uncovering Nazis because these former officials and businessmen are efficient at getting things done in the postwar period.

526 RÖPKE, WILHELM. "Germany Economy in State of Pernicious Anaemia." *Commercial and Financial Chronicle* 165 (27 February 1947).

Gives many examples of economic paralysis and disorder that affect all segments of German society. Currency is worthless so people refuse to work for it. Meanwhile, it costs more and more for the Allies to feed the Germans.

Journal Articles

527   ROSE, BEN L. "As Niemoeller Sees Germany's Future." *Christian Century* 62 (3 October 1945): 1155-57.
   Chaplain Rose interviewed Martin Niemoeller, seeking to find out his relationship with the nazi government, his opposition to it, and the position of the Confessional Church both during and after the war.

528   ROSS, ALAN. "Books in Germany." *Spectator* 178 (16 May 1947): 554-55.
   German publishers are publishing books as fast as the availability of supplies will allow. The people are anxious to end their intellectual isolation of the nazi years.

529   "Ruhr Miner." *Life* 22 (9 June 1947): 17-24.
   A photographic essay of a miner and his family. He gets extra monthly food allotments as well as a daily meal at the mine site. He considers himself lucky to have part of a damaged house for his family to live in.

530   "Russia Milks Its German Zone." *Business Week* (6 March 1948): 109-10.
   Describes the dismantled industries and the newly produced goods that are sent east into the Soviet Union.

531   "Russian Zone of Germany." *Fortnightly* 169 (January 1948): 19-23.
   Despite Soviet efforts to control information, people in Berlin know some things about the eastern zone. They hear that land reform was not very successful and that the Silesian coal being mined is shipped to the Soviet Union. Skilled technicians are still being forcibly moved to Russia also.

532   SALTZMAN, CHARLES E. "The Problem of German Recovery." *Annals of the American Academy of Political and Social Science* 258 (July 1948): 74-78.
   As assistant secretary of state, Saltzman reflects American policy when he states the three objectives of the occupation in 1948: to eliminate war potential, to introduce democracy, and to restore the German economy to self-sufficiency.

533   "Scandal in Germany." *New Statesman and Nation* 32 (9 November 1946): 331-32.
   Evaluates the British zone administration and concludes that it is not very successful. Industry has not revived sufficiently, and there is

too much bureaucracy. Many soldiers have been corrupted by the black market and desperate women.

534 SCHAFFER, GORDON. "Inside the Soviet Zone: Who Kidnapped the Scientists, an Untold Story." *Soviet Russia Today* (July 1947).
    Not reviewed.

535 SCHECHTMAN, JOSEPH B. "Resettlement of Transferred Volksdeutsche in Germany." *Journal of Central European Affairs* 7 (October 1947): 262-84.
    Describes the impact of the ethnic Germans on the areas of Germany into which they were expelled. Neither the expellees nor the natives accepted the transfer of the eastern provinces to Poland. Some politicians in the western zones encourage the expellees to believe they will eventually return to their homelands.

536 SCHEPSES, ERWIN. "Juvenile Vagrancy in Germany." *Social Service Review* 22 (March 1948): 40-45.
    As a result of the war and the expulsion of ethnic Germans into the remnant of Germany, there are thousands of children and adolescents roaming the western zones without supervision or homes. They live off the black market and help to spread sexually transmitted diseases.

537 SCHMID, RICHARD. "Denazification: A German Critique." *American Perspective* 2 (October 1948): 231-42.
    After describing the three phases of U.S. denazification, the writer finds all to be ineffective, discriminatory, and arbitrary. Germans are becoming more openly obstinate.

538 SCHMIDT, DANA A. "Land of Questions without Answers." *New York Times Magazine* (26 May 1946).
    Talking with ordinary Germans, Schmidt finds that they do not have time to think about politics, but they do want occupation policies that are clear and consistent. They believe they have suffered enough for the war, even though they were not personally responsible for the war crimes.

539 SCHOONMAKER, FRANK. "Letter from Germany." *New Yorker* 22 (23 November 1946).
    Expresses the concerns of vintners in the wine region of Germany. The wartime bombing destroyed many wineries and

vineyards. The vintners want to be able to bottle and market the wines they make.

540 SCHÜTZ, W. W. "Germany Revisited." *Contemporary Review* 168 (December 1945): 339-43.

Describes the Ruhr, Kassel, Berlin, and the condition of the people. They walk along the roads looking hungry and poorly dressed.

541 SCHWARTZ, HARRY. "Rural Conditions in Postwar Germany." *Rural Sociology* 11 (December 1946): 330-39.

The author traveled in the American and Soviet zones to form his opinions of rural life. People told him they moved around during the war to escape the bombing. He describes the land reform in the eastern zone.

542 SCHWARZENBERGER, SUSE. "Trends of Thought in Germany." *World Affairs* (London), n.s. 2 (January 1948): 40-48.

Germans see too much hypocrisy and mismanagement in the Allied occupation governments. They are sure the Allies are starving them intentionally. They do not admit mistakes or guilt and are certain that they have paid by their postwar suffering whatever debt was owed.

543 SHIRER, WILLIAM L. "End of a Berlin Diary." *Atlantic* 179, no. 5 (May 1947): 107-22; 179, no. 6 (June 1947): 93-106; 180, no. 1 (July 1947): 89-100.

Excerpts from his book *End of a Berlin Diary* describing his return to the city after the war, his impressions of conditions there, and the lives of the people.

544 SIBERT, EDWIN L. "The German Mind: Our Biggest Problem." *New York Times Magazine* (17 February 1946).

Lumps all Germans together and finds them all guilty of war crimes. The American military government must be tough. We must impose our will on Germany, control it tightly, and expect the worst in response.

545 "Sins of the Fathers." *Time* 46 (22 October 1945): 26-27.

Describes the flight of the ethnic Germans who were expelled from the eastern territories into the remnant of Germany. The misery of the displaced persons and expellees would have been intolerable before the war. Now their condition seems a routine part of the postwar world.

Journal Articles

546   SLATOFF, WALTER J. "GI Morals in Germany." *New Republic* 114 (13 May 1946): 686-87.

         GIs in Germany are being corrupted by the black market, the availability of women, and the possibilities of making money illegally. Ninety percent of the soldiers are involved.

547   SMALLWOOD, RUSSELL. "Our Changing Approach to the Germans." *Contemporary Review* 170 (September 1946): 138-41.

         In one year the attitudes of Allied troops have changed from vindictiveness to tolerance. Although there is little contact with civilians outside of official work, the Germans in the British zone are generally friendly and agreeable.

548   SMITH, RENNIE. "Concerning Germany." *Quarterly Review* 284 (October 1946): 504-20.

         Draws some conclusions about German problems after conversations with some ordinary Germans. One major issue is maintaining a supply of labor for the industries in the Ruhr valley.

549   SOMMERS, MARTIN. "Looting with Consent." *Saturday Evening Post* 220 (13 March 1948): 12.

         Describes the U.S. army's barter centers in Frankfurt and Berlin where Germans bring in household goods to be evaluated and traded. The Germans receive the equivalent worth in barter points that can be exchanged for surplus American foods.

550   SORIO, GEORGES. "Through the Iron Curtain." *Soviet Russia Today* (January 1947).

         Not reviewed.

551   SPENDER, STEPHEN. "Germany in Europe." *Fortnightly* 165 (June 1946): 401-07.

         After a visit to occupied Germany, Spender urges the Allies to end German isolation from the rest of Europe and to pursue joint policies fairly and uniformly. The Germans need to have some hope for the future.

552   STERNBERG, FRITZ. "Cancer Spot of Europe: Diagnosis of the German Problem." *Nation* 164 (8 February 1947): 146-50.

         Reviews current economic conditions in Germany, including the shortages of food and the lack of household goods. Sternberg guesses that forty percent of the population is destitute.

Journal Articles

553 STONBOROUGH, JOHN. "Can Germany be Re-educated?" *National Review* 128 (February 1947): 125-37.

Sees the need for group education, focusing on groups that have the possibility of becoming important in communities. Suspicious persons should be monitored to be sure they are not employed in postwar government or industry.

554 STONE, SHEPARD. [Denazification and Germans' mood.] *New York Times Magazine* (15 December 1946): 12-13; (26 January 1947).

Describes the denazification process, with photographs. The mood is somber. Germans focus on their need for food and shelter. They feel they have suffered more than enough for their country's war crimes, because of the treatment they have endured in the hands of Allied occupation troops.

555 STONE, VERNON W. "German Baby Crop Left by Negro GIs." *Survey* 85 (November 1949): 579-83.

In the summer of 1947 Stone surveyed more than three thousand people to compile his statistics. He estimates that about 2,100 children in Germany have German mothers and Negro fathers. Most mothers keep their children.

556 STRIKE, CLIFFORD S. "Revenge Is Expensive." *American Magazine* 144, no. 3 (September 1947): 50-51, 82-84.

Calls for an official change of policy in the occupation of Germany and Japan. Each country needs to become self-sufficient because their care is an enormous drain on the American taxpayer.

557 TAPER, BERNARD. "Report from Frankfurt." *Nation* 166 (1 May 1948): 464-65.

Germans are critical of occupation policies and the denazification process. They resent taking charity, and they resent the food distribution questionnaires they are required to fill out.

558 TAYLOR, J. E. "Back to the Reich." *Blackwell's Magazine* 259 (February 1946): 81-90.

Touring the British zone in the fall of 1945, Taylor describes the people, the destroyed cities and harbors, and the general atmosphere. He senses that servility has replaced arrogance.

559 TESCHNER, RICHARD. "Germany Currency Reform." *Canadian Forum* 28 (December 1948): 200.

Describes the impact of the currency reform on the average German who has lost his savings but has found consumer goods in shops after three years.

560 "This Is Germany." *Spectator* 174 (20 July 1945): 54-55.

Views the defeated country from a plane. One can see ruins everywhere. Streams of refugees, former slave laborers, and released German soldiers are on the roads. Some fields are being tilled.

561 THOMPSON, DOROTHY. "Last Time I Saw Berlin." *Saturday Review of Literature* 30 (15 March 1947): 9-10.

Returning to Berlin after thirteen years, Thompson sought old friends. They had suffered during the nazi period and had found resistance to be ineffective. They only learned the full story of the death camps after the war.

562 TREVOR-ROPER, HUGH. "The Strange Vacuum That Is Germany." *New York Times Magazine* (6 July 1947).

After two years of peace, the Germans have exhausted their reserves of clothes, shoes, food, etc. They have lost the will to survive and all hope for the future. In addition there is a political vacuum in Germany that needs to be filled.

563 TRIAL, GEORGE T. and M. K. GOLDSMITH. "Rebuilding Germany's Schools." *Current History* 11 (August 1946): 101-08.

After the war, Germany suffered a shortage of denazified teachers, approved textbooks, supplies, and buildings in good repair. The United States intended that German cultural and educational institutions would help shape a democratic Germany.

564 TURNER, EWART E. [German churches.] *Christian Century* 63 (6 February 1946): 173-74; 63 (20 February 1946): 237-39.

Reveals conversations with church pastors and lay people during four months of travel in Germany. Many church leaders report that they clung to "otherworldliness" during the nazi period.

565 TURNER, PHILIP. "Report on Germany: First-Hand Report on Conditions in Germany Today." *Parliament* (December 1946): 7-8.
Not reviewed.

566 VALENTIN, VEIT. "Germany after Twelve Years." *Contemporary Review* 169 (January 1946): 10-14.

Makes a plea for fair treatment of the Germans. They need more food and good will. Children should not be punished for criminal acts of the Nazis.

567 VIATOR. "German Balance Sheet." *Spectator* 177 (18 October 1946): 37-38.

Weighs the pluses and minuses of British occupational administration. A lot of rubble has been cleared, and canals, bridges, and railroads have been repaired. There are, however, still coal and food shortages.

568 VOIGHT, F. A. [Articles about expellees.] *Nineteenth Century and After* 138 (November 1945): 193-205; 138 (December 1945): 263-69; 139 (February 1946): 49-66; 139 (March 1946): 97-101.

The brutal expelling of ethnic Germans from their homes in Poland and Czechoslovakia has not been humane. The mandate from the Potsdam agreements that the population transfers be orderly has been impossible to enforce. In the Soviet zone the Germans are suffering, and western journalists do not always give sensible descriptions. Land reform is a catastrophe, and men are still being seized and sent eastward to labor camps in the Soviet Union.

569 WALN, NORA. [Return to Germany.] *Atlantic* 176 (October 1945): 43-45; 176 (November 1945): 45-49; 176 (December 1945): 52-54; 177 (January 1946): 43-47.

Traveling to Germany in August 1945 to look up old friends, the author finds destroyed cities, untouched countryside, and people in a state of shock. She visited Heidelberg, an UNRRA children's camp, and a German home. She also attended the Nuremberg trials.

570 WALSTON, H. D. "Demoralized Germany." *Spectator* 179 (4-11 July 1947): 9-10.

Everyone in Germany is forced to barter on the black market to have enough food to feed their families. The necessity of breaking the law to survive lowers the morale of the country and sets a terrible example for children.

Journal Articles

571 WALT, H. P. van. [Occupied Germany.] *Knickerbocker Weekly* (16 September 1946): 4-7; (23 September 1946): 4-7; (30 September 1946): 5-7; (7 October 1946): 4-7; (14 October 1946): 10-12; (21 October 1946): 10-11.
Not reviewed.

572 WARBURG, JAMES P. "Report on Germany--I, II." *New Statesman and Nation* 32 (10 August 1946): 92; 32 (17 August 1946): 114.
Describes conditions in the Soviet and French zones. In the east, land reform has been accomplished and there is no unemployment. The French have the Saar mines in operation, but the occupation government is very oppressive and the Germans are sullen. In the British and American zones, Germans are disappointed in the governments. They had expected better treatment from them.

573 WEISKOPF, F. C. "German Publishers Have Their Problems." *Books Abroad* 21, no. 1 (1947): 9-13.
Describes the difficulties that Germans have getting reading materials. Issues of licensed German magazines are limited because of the paper shortage.

574 WERNER, ALFRED. "A German Explains." *Journal of Central European Affairs* 9 (July 1949): 159-66.
Reviews the writings of Röpke and Hauser on the occupation of Germany. Werner does not agree with the opinion of some Germans that since the war they have suffered more than the Jews suffered during the war.

575 "Why Germany Is Failing As Producer." *World Report* 3 (18 November 1947): 15-17.
German heavy industries and manufacturing plants are still hampered by the lack of raw materials, the constant hunger of workers, and the fact that wages have no buying power.

576 WILLIAMS, FREDERICK W. "German Opinion and American Isolationism." *Public Opinion Quarterly* 11 (Summer 1947): 179-88.
Reports the results of a public opinion survey made among Germans. The survey focused on political and economic affairs.

Journal Articles

577　WILSON, IAIN. "German Churches Fail Youth." *Christian Century* 66 (30 March 1949): 397-98.

　　The German churches have not aggressively sought to reach young people who are inactive in religious groups. This is principally due to the lack of physical equipment and buildings.

578　_____. "Human Explosives in Germany." *Christian Century* 66 (14 December 1949): 1486-87.

　　Expellees from the eastern territories support the idea of another war to regain their lost homelands. They see no future for themselves in Germany. The only international agency that has aided them is the World Council of Churches through its refugee division.

579　"Winter's Tale." *Spectator* 175 (28 September 1945): 284.

　　A captain in the British Army of the Rhine reports that British soldiers in their occupied zone are bored and indifferent to what happens there. They drink heavily to fill the time. The Germans are worse off, of course. The captain senses a pending tragedy as people battle to stay alive in the coming winter.

580　WOLFSON, IRVING. "The AMG Mess in Germany." *New Republic* 114 (4 March 1946): 310-13.

　　Explains that the American military government has not been successful. The personnel are mediocre and the black market continues to flourish. Denazification is not applied uniformly.

581　WOOD, JUNIUS B. "Four Cooks Spoil the German Broth." *Nations Business* 34 (April 1946).

　　The occupation carried out by four countries is not working. There is not enough cooperation among Allies. In the U.S. zone people are starving, there is a shortage of housing and fuel, and denazification has made it almost impossible to find qualified people for jobs.

582　WORSLEY, R. H. M. "Mass Expulsions." *Nineteenth Century and After* 138 (December 1945): 270-74; 139 (February 1946): 90-96.

　　Uses statistics to explain where the expellees originated and where they have ultimately settled. The conditions in the areas where they settled is so terrible, with housing, food, and fuel shortages, that the western Allies have called for a halt to the expulsions so that procedures can be drawn up.

Journal Articles

583 WYLIE, I. A. R. "Germany, Nation of Nazis Still." *Ladies Home Journal* 63 (November 1946).

   Germans refuse to accept blame for the war and the war crimes. Instead they are sullen and angry at the Allies whom they think dropped bombs randomly during the war and are starving the Germans since the war.

584 ZINK, HAROLD. "The American Denazification Program in Germany." *Journal of Central European Affairs* 6 (October 1946): 227-40.

   From personal experience Zink testifies that the denazification regulations are implemented a little differently by each military government officer in the American zone.

585 ZUCKMAYER, CARL. "Germany's Lost Youth." *Life* 23 (15 September 1947): 124-38.

   Young people all over the British and American zones are dealing on the black market because they cannot earn enough to feed themselves with a regular job. They have no homes, no families, and no morals. They are determined not to be regimented again.

Chapter 5

Fiction by Germans

One method of coming to terms with one's experiences is to write about them. Some persons can tell their stories directly, others rely on the device of fictionalizing their tales. Writing a novel allows an author to tailor experiences to a fast-paced narrative and to protect friends and relatives by assigning composite personalities to the characters. Other authors tell the experiences of someone else or want to explain to their readers the moods of people, their disillusionment with German leaders, the horrors of war, and the despair and misery of defeat.

Only a few German fictional works from the postwar period have been translated into English because British and American readers have had very little interest in German experiences. In fact, only the most unusual, literary, or sensational novels and short stories have been translated. Works originally written for children and young adults are also cited because they relate experiences in a straightforward manner, with a minimum of embellishment.

One must search for historical fiction in general bibliographies, fiction indexes, and book review indexes, although subject headings are usually nonspecific. In addition, the books themselves are hard to locate because public libraries weed old fiction as their readers lose interest, and academic libraries seldom buy popular fiction at all. Consequently, most of the annotations are based on index citations and reviews rather than on personal examination.

Fiction by Germans

586   ALBRAND, MARTHA, pseud. [HEIDE H. LOEWENGARD]. *Desperate Moment*. Translated from German. New York: Random House, 1951. 242 p.

A German is accused of murdering an American military policeman. With the help of a young woman he clears his name.

587   ANDERSCH, ALFRED. *My Disappearance in Providence, and Other Stories*. Translated from German. Garden City, N.Y.: Doubleday, 1978. 231 p.

Short stories that describe the effect of the war and and Germany's defeat on the young adults of the period.

588   _____. *Winterspelt*. Translated from German. Garden City, N.Y.: Doubleday, 1978. 480 p.

Describes a nazi officer's attempts to have his unit captured by approaching American troops as the war draws to an end.

589   BAER, FRANK. *Max's Gang*. Translated from German. Boston: Little, Brown, 1983. 298 p.

At the end of the war, a group of children who had been evacuated to Czechoslovakia make their way back to their homes in Berlin. Survival is difficult in the chaos of the postwar period.

590   BEMELMANS, LUDWIG. *Are You Hungry, Are You Cold*. Cleveland, Ohio: World, 1960. 245 p.

The daughter of a German general grows up in occupied Germany, exposed to the desolation and deprivation of her country. Her personality is shaped by her environment.

591   BENARY-ISBERT, MARGOT. *The Ark*. Translated from German. New York: Harcourt, Brace, 1953. 246 p.

A woman and her children, refugees of the war, settle in a ruined city and try to rebuild their lives.

592   _____. *Castle on the Border*. Translated from German. New York: Harcourt, Brace, 1956. 277 p.

A young German girl finds refuge and support with a group of actors who have found shelter in a ruined castle. She achieves her dream of becoming an actress.

Fiction by Germans

593 _____. *Dangerous Spring*. Translated from German. New York: Harcourt, Brace and World, 1961. 252 p.

The dangerous spring is that of 1945, which forms the background for a love story.

594 _____. *A Long Way Home*. Translated from German. New York: Harcourt, Brace, 1959. 280 p.

A young East German refugee seeks a new life and family in the United States. He has to make many adjustments when he finds a home in California.

595 _____. *Rowan Farm*. Translated from German. New York: Harcourt, Brace, 1954. 277 p.

In a sequel to *The Ark*, Rowan farm becomes the rural home of the Lechow family when they move out of Frankfurt to help with the farm and the dog kennels there. The husband and father returns from imprisonment in Russia to find his family on the farm.

596 BENN, GOTTFRIED. *Primal Vision: Selected Writings*. Translated from German. Norfolk, Conn.: New Directions, 1958. 291 p.

Benn was a physician in Berlin during and after the war. Some of these short stories were written in this period.

597 BIELER, MANFRED. *The Sailor in the Bottle*. Translated from German. New York: Dutton, 1966. 221 p.

A disillusioned young man travels through the ruined cities and countryside of occupied Germany.

598 BIENEK, HORST. *Earth and Fire*. Translated from German. New York: Atheneum, 1988. 257 p.

Explores the lives of German and Polish families in the border region of Upper Silesia during the last months of the war. This is the last novel in Bienek's *Gleiwitz Suite*.

599 BÖLL, HEINRICH. *Acquainted with the Night*. Translated from German. New York: Holt, 1954. 200 p.

A man in the industrial Ruhr Valley leads a depressing postwar life of too little income and too much liquor.

600 _____. *And Never Said a Word*. Translated from German. New York: McGraw Hill, 1978. 197 p.

Describes the lives of a family from the end of the war to the 1970s.

Fiction by Germans

601 _____. *The Bread of Those Early Years*. Translated from German. New York: McGraw Hill, 1976. 134 p.
A love story set in postwar Germany.

602 _____. *Children Are Civilians Too*. Translated from German. New York: Penguin, 1976. 184 p.
Short stories focused on the occupation period.

603 _____. *The Clown*. Translated from German. New York: McGraw Hill, 1965. 247 p.
Through flashbacks, a clown's relationship to German society during and after the war is revealed. He comes to question politics, religion, and relationships.

604 _____. *Group Portrait with Lady*. Translated from German. New York: McGraw Hill, 1973. 405 p.
A woman's personality is revealed by witnesses from the past who recreate the events in her life, during and after the war.

605 _____. *Tomorrow and Yesterday*. Translated from German. New York: Criterion Books, 1957. 250 p.
Two boys whose fathers were killed in the war become companions as they struggle to survive the devastation of their surroundings.

606 BORCHERT, WOLFGANG. *Man Outside: The Prose Works*. Translated from German. Norfolk, Conn.: New Directions, 1952. 259 p.
A young German's despair over the war and its effects is reflected in his short stories. He died of war injuries in 1947.

607 BRÜCKNER, CHRISTINE. *Flight of Cranes*. Translated from German. New York: Fromm Publishing Corp., 1982. 372 p.
Maximiliane and her children flee from their Pomeranian estate ahead of the Soviet advance in the spring of 1945. She struggles to survive and make a life for her children in western Germany. This is a sequel to *Gillyflower Kid*, a novel of Maximiliane's childhood and adolescence in Pomerania.

608 CONTE, MANFRED. *Jeopardy*. Translated from German. New York: W. Sloane Associates, 1956. 214 p. English title: *Cassia*.
A Viennese artist becomes a counterfeiter after the war and is entangled with a woman and more than one police department.

Fiction by Germans

609 DEGENS, T. *Transport 7-41-R*. New York: Viking, 1974. 171 p.

   A young German girl is sent by her family from eastern Germany to Cologne after the war. She is bitter and angry at the necessity and is determined not to become involved in other people's problems. Nevertheless, she ends up helping an elderly couple.

610 DOUTINÉ, HEIKE. *German Requiem*. Translated from German. New York: Scribner's Sons, 1975. 307 p.

   Set in postwar Germany amid repressed guilt and lost values.

611 ECKE, WOLFGANG. *Flight towards Home*. Translated from German. New York: Macmillan, 1970. 116 p.

   A young orphan is stranded in the east zone, and his grandmother is in the west. He determines to try to cross the border to be with her.

612 FAECKE, PETER. *The Firebugs*. Translated from German. New York: Knopf, 1966. 140 p.

   Immediately after the war, a Polish-German man seeks to father a son who is "racially pure."

613 FÄHRMANN, WILLI. *The Year of the Wolves: The Story of an Exodus*. Translated from German. London: Oxford University Press, 1973. 195 p.

   The novel is centered around a family who flees their home in East Prussia to escape the revenge of the Soviet army. Companions freeze to death, starve, fall through the ice, and are overrun by first one army and then the other.

614 FANGER, HORST. *A Life for a Life*. Translated from German. New York: Ballantine, 1954. 171 p.

   German survivors of a prison camp decide to hunt down the former camp leader, now living in the Soviet zone.

615 FISCHER, BERTHA. *Right to Love*. New York: Harper, 1956. 280 p.

   Three love stories set in occupied Berlin.

616 GAISER, GERD. *The Final Ball*. Translated from German. New York: Pantheon Books, 1960. 254 p.

   A novel of postwar Germany and the corruption that accompanies the destitution of the early years and the prosperity of those that follow.

Fiction by Germans

617 GEISSLER, CHRISTIAN. *The Sins of the Fathers*. Translated from German. New York: Random House, 1962. 266 p.

In the postwar period, a man becomes curious about the fate of the Jewish family in whose home he is living. He also tries to discover who arrested them and sent them away.

618 GLAESER, ERNST. *The Shady Miracle*. Translated from German. London: Secker & Warburg, 1963. 287 p.

Set in Germany during the occupation and into the 1950s.

619 GRASS, GÜNTER. *Dog Years*. Translated from German. New York: Harcourt, Brace & World, 1965. 570 p.

A satire set in the Danzig area of Germany from the period of the Third Reich to the 1950s. The narrators are a Jewish maker of scarecrows, an Aryan who writes love letters to his cousin, and a blood brother to a Jew.

620 _____. *Local Anaesthetic*. Translated from German. New York: Harcourt, Brace & World, 1969. 284 p.

While sitting in a dentist's chair, the narrator imagines his life as a teacher of older adolescents, telling them of Germany during the war when he himself was seventeen.

621 GREGOR, MANFRED. *The Bridge*. Translated from German. New York: Random House, 1960. 215 p.

At the end of the war, boys are drafted into the army, given weapons, and told to defend a bridge for the honor of the fatherland.

622 GRUND, JOSEF C. *Beyond the Bridge*. Translated from German. Boston: Little, Brown, 1968. 143 p.

Fritz and his father belatedly come to discuss his father's role as a pilot in the war. Dying, Fritz's father admits his feelings of guilt.

623 HÄRTLING, PETER. *Crutches*. New York: Lothrop, Lee & Sheppard Books, 1988. 163 p.

In postwar Vienna, a man on crutches befriends a young boy who is searching for his mother. The two become friends and begin to look ahead.

Fiction by Germans

624 HEINRICH, WILLI. *The Lonely Conqueror*. Translated from German. New York: Dial Press, 1962. 379 p.

An American sergeant falls in love with a German woman during the occupation. His problems are compounded by the fact that he is black.

625 _____. *Mark of Shame*. Translated from German. New York: Bantam Books, 1960. 277 p.

In occupied Nuremberg, a man is threatened with blackmail because of his past. The plot moves back and forth among zones.

626 JAEGER, HENRY. *The Fortress*. Translated from German. New York: Harper & Row, 1967. 250 p.

Postwar Germany is a shattered country with no redeeming virtues. Amid the ruins life is grim, and people lose their sense of values.

627 KAUFMANN, RICHARD. *Heaven Pays No Dividends*. Translated from German. New York: Viking, 1952. 310 p.

A German soldier who drifted into the war is in the same purposeless mood after the war ends. He has no foundations or goals.

628 KIRST, HANS H. *Return of Gunner Asch*. Translated from German. Boston: Little, Brown, 1957. 310 p.

One of a series of novels about an average German soldier whom Kirst follows through the war and into the postwar period. This episode finds Asch and two friends tracking down the army officer who ordered their unit to make a suicidal stand during the war.

629 KLAUSSNER, WOLF. *Survive the Storm*. Translated from German. London: Methuen, 1984. 156 p.

An ordinary German family suffered under the Nazis, and, when the war ended, they discover that some of the American conquerors are just as vicious. Life is as precarious after the war as during it.

630 KOEHN, ILSE. *Tilla*. New York: Greenwillow, 1981. 240 p.

A young girl seeks her aunt in Berlin and together they survive the Soviet assault and occupation of the city. When calm returns, she enrolls in art school.

Fiction by Germans

631 KOEPPEN, WOLFGANG. *Death in Rome*. Translated from German. New York: Vanguard Press, 1956. 217 p.

After the war ex-nazi Germans meet in Rome. Their unrepentant but guilt-ridden personalities lead to strange and spiteful behavior.

632 KÖRNER, WOLFGANG. *The Green Frontier*. Translated from German. New York: Morrow, 1977. 190 p.

In the postwar period, a young boy reluctantly accompanies his parents in an illegal move to western Germany from the eastern zone.

633 KRÜSS, JAMES. *Coming Home from the War: An Idyll*. Translated from German. Garden City, N.Y.: Doubleday, 1970. 133 p.

A young soldier returns home from the war as the country is occupied by the Allies. He discovers that the interim of lawlessness between nazism and the rule of the conquerors is a period of independence for him. He is freed from the blind obedience of a soldier and is not yet under the control of the occupiers.

634 KÜPPER, HEINZ. *Simplicus 45, a Novel*. Translated from German. London: Secker & Warburg, 1966. 251 p.

A story of Germany at the end of the war and the beginning of the occupation.

635 LANGGÄSSER, ELISABETH. *The Quest*. Translated from German. New York: Knopf, 1953. 370 p.

Seven people, all affected by the war, set out in August of 1945 to travel to a Benedictine monastery in the eastern zone.

636 LENZ, SIEGFRIED. *The German Lesson*. Translated from German. New York: Hill & Wang, 1972. 470 p.

In the postwar period, a family is split between the son and the father by their attitudes toward duty and conscience.

637 _____. *The Heritage*. Translated from German. New York: Hill & Wang, 1981. 458 p.

In the eastern zone is a German patriarch with a family museum. His difficulties coping with the postwar period and with rising Polish fortunes are played out in the novel.

Fiction by Germans

638   LIND, JAKOV. *Landscape in Concrete, a Novel*. Translated from German. New York: Grove Press, 1966. 190 p.

    At the end of the war, a German soldier travels across Europe in search of his sanity. Lawlessness and anarchy blur his perception of reality.

639   LUNDHOLM, ANJA. *Rainbow in the Night*. Translated from German. London: Spearman, 1975. 380 p.

    Released from a concentration camp by the Soviets, a group of women decides to travel to the western zones of postwar Germany rather than stay under communist control.

640   MOOSDORF, JOHANNA. *Next Door*. Translated from German. New York: Knopf, 1963. 224 p.

    Atrocities committed during the war continue to haunt Germans who escaped being held responsible. A doctor who is uneasy with his wife's questions of his wartime life ultimately has her declared insane. After a second marriage, his new wife begins to ask the same questions.

641   NEUMANN, ROBERT. *Children of Vienna*. Translated from German. New York: Dutton, 1947. 223 p.

    A realistic description of a group of abandoned children who survive the war in Vienna. They create a make-shift home for themselves in a cellar under the ruins and look out for one another. They are befriended by a black chaplain attached to a U.S. army unit.

642   NÖSTLINGER, CHRISTINE. *Fly Away Home*. Translated from German. New York: Watts, 1975. 135 p.

    A young girl's family survives the end of the war in Vienna. Her experiences with the Soviet soldiers are not colored by the attitudes of most adults, who fear them as barbarians. Instead Christal is able to perceive them as men who react to soldiering in many different ways.

643   OPITZ, KARLLUDWIG. *The General*. Translated from German. New York: J. Day Co., 1956. 191 p.

    Traces the lives of a German general and his personal soldier from the end of the war through captivity, release, and eventual spiraling downward into madness.

Fiction by Germans

644 PLIEVIER, THEODOR. *Berlin, a Novel.* Translated from German. Garden City, N.Y.: Doubleday, 1957. 446 p.
   Describes the saga of the siege of Berlin, the end of the war, and the occupation.

645 RINSER, LUISE. *Nina.* Chicago: Regnery, 1956. 284 p.
   Follows the life of Nina from the nazi period and the war through the immediate postwar chaos and occupation.

646 ———. *Rings of Glass.* Translated from German. Chicago: Regnery, 1958. 176 p.
   Set in occupied Germany.

647 SCHAPER, EDZARD H. *The Dancing Bear.* Translated from German. New York: J. Day, 1961. 224 p.
   Caught in the Russian advance through the Baltic states and eastern Germany near the end of the war, Oscar ends up in the Soviet zone and is forced to fight for his survival.

648 SCHIRMBECK, HEINRICH. *If Thine Eye Offend Thee.* Translated from German. New York: Simon and Schuster, 1961. 405 p. British title: *The Blinding Light.*
   Traces the career of the main character from before the war to the postwar period. His idealism is tested.

649 SCHOLZ, HANS. *Through the Night.* Translated from German. New York: Crowell, 1959. 350 p.
   A group of friends entertains itself at a Berlin hotel by each member relating an event during or after the war that affected him strongly.

650 SCHROBSDORFF, ANGELIKA. *The Men.* Translated from German. New York: Putnam, 1964. 382 p.
   In the aftermath of the war, a Jewish-German refugee tries to survive in Bulgaria and occupied Germany.

651 SPÄTH, GEROLD. *A Prelude to the Long Happy Life of Maximilian Goodman.* Translated from German. Boston: Little, Brown, 1975. 435 p.
   Goodman is shaped by the events in Germany both during and after the war.

Fiction by Germans

652 STALMANN, REINHART. *Rise Up in Anger*. Translated from German. New York: Putnam, 1963. 384 p.

Boysen, an independent thinker, got into trouble while in the German army. He was sent first to a concentration camp and then to the eastern front. Surviving the war, he becomes rich and seeks revenge on the officers who had him arrested earlier.

653 WERLBERGER, HANS. *Without Sanction*. Translated from German. New York: Criterion Books, 1955. 348 p.

A German doctor tries to practice his profession in occupied Bavaria. The living conditions and the American occupation make it difficult to be a good doctor.

654 WIECHERT, ERNST E. *Tidings*. Translated from German. New York: Macmillan, 1959. 302 p. British title: *Misse Sine Nomine*.

A nobleman returns to his ancestral home after a long stay in a prison camp to discover that it is full of American soldiers. Though at first he reacts with anger and bitterness, he is able to come to terms with the new residents.

655 WOLF, CHRISTA. *A Model Childhood*. Translated from German. New York: Farrar, Straus & Giroux, 1980. 407 p.

An autobiographical novel built on flashbacks between a present day visit to her former home, now in Poland, and her life in the 1940s.

656 _____. *The Quest for Christa T*. Translated from German. New York: Farrar, Straus & Giroux, 1971. 185 p.

A retelling of the life of a young woman who tried but failed to adapt and conform to the new order in the Soviet zone of Germany.

657 ZIMNIK, REINER. *The Crane*. Translated from German. New York: Harper & Row, 1970. 92 p.

A children's story about a blue-capped man who operates a crane. He is so attached to it that he never leaves it, despite a war and the peace that follows.

658 ZWERENZ, GERHARD. *Remembrance Day: Thirteen Attempts in Prose to Adopt an Attitude of Respect*. Translated from German. New York: Dutton, 1966. 167 p.

Short stories set in occupied Germany.

Chapter 6

Non-German Fiction

Most of the fiction written about the occupation period is derived from personal experiences of the authors as military personnel, civilian relief workers, military dependents, and journalists who spent time in Germany at the end of the war and during the occupation period. Although a few works express a sensitive and perceptive understanding of Germans and their lives, many appear to be superficial, stereotypical stories of spies, soldiers, ingenues, whores, and thugs.

As with fiction that has been translated from German, books that deal with this specific period in history are difficult to locate. Generally their availability is dependent upon the continuing interest of readers, so only the most unusual or captivating novels outlive the period. Most annotations, therefore, are based on book reviews rather than personal examination.

659   ARCHER, JANE. *Let Not Your Flight Be in Winter*. N.p., n.d.
A one-act play based on the author's experiences of fleeing from eastern Germany ahead of the advancing Soviet troops.

Non-German Fiction

660 ARNOLD, ELLIOTT. *Forests of the Night*. New York: Scribner's Sons, 1971. 344 p.

After the war, Peter Bauer returns to Germany to try to discover how his mother died. He tangles with neo-Nazis and is almost killed.

661 BACHMANN, LAWRENCE P. *Phoenix*. London: Collins, 1955. 319 p.

Six bomb-disposal workers in postwar Berlin make a pact. Their high-risk job leads them to agree that the last one of them to be alive will get the common savings. Suspicion and greed rule the group.

662 _____. *Ten Seconds to Hell*. Greenwich, Conn.: Fawcett Pub., 1958. 222 p.

Takes place in postwar Berlin.

663 BAKER, W. HOWARD. *The Rape of Berlin*. New York: Prestige Books, 1967. 144 p.

Near the end of the war, a British secret agent is sent into Berlin to find and snatch the top-secret plans for a new weapon that the Nazis were developing. It is imperative that the plans not fall into Soviet hands.

664 BARRETT, WILLIAM E. *A Woman in the House*. Garden City, N.Y.: Doubleday, 1971. 227 p.

In the chaos of the postwar period, Konrad finds peace living with Russian monks and restoring works of art. He befriends a Czech girl, and they fall in love.

665 BAYLEY, JOHN. *In Another Country*. New York: Coward-McCann, 1955. 283 p. Reprint. New York: Oxford University Press, 1986.

The occupation from the British point of view.

666 BERCKMAN, EVELYN. *Evil of Time*. New York: Dodd, Mead, 1954. 197 p.

A mystery story set in postwar Germany.

667 BERGER, THOMAS. *Crazy in Berlin*. New York: Scribner's Sons, 1958. 438 p.

An American GI with knowledge of German has run-ins with Germans, Jews, black marketeers, Communists, etc.

Non-German Fiction

668 BEYMER, WILLIAM G. *Middle of Midnight.* New York: McGraw, 1947. 242 p.

An American occupation unit is stationed in a small Bavarian village where peace and quiet exists on the surface only.

669 BLOCH, MARIE H. *Displaced Person.* New York: Lothrop, Lee, & Shepard, 1978. 191 p.

A German teenager from the Ukraine struggles to survive after the war when his family is expelled from their ancestral home.

670 BOTSFORD, KEITH. *Master Race.* London: Wingate, 1955. 245 p.

Takes place in occupied Germany.

671 BOYLE, KAY. *Generation without Farewell.* New York: Knopf, 1960. 300 p.

A love story involving a German American journalist and the wife of an occupation officer. The story also explores relations between conquered and conquerors.

672 ———. *The Smoking Mountain: Stories of Germany during the Occupation.* New York: McGraw-Hill, 1951. 273 p.

Many of these stories were first published in American journals. Boyle is puzzled by the enigma of a Germany that created the Holocaust but was unwilling to accept responsibility for it.

673 BUCKNER, ROBERT H. *Sigrid and the Sergeant.* New York: Appleton, Century, Croft, 1957. 246 p.

Slap-stick comedy with no basis in reality.

674 BURKE, JAMES W. *Big Rape.* New York: Farrar, Straus, 1952. 282 p.

Berlin in 1945 when the Russians captured the city and were out of control.

675 CARLETON, VERNA B. *Back to Berlin: An Exile Returns.* Boston: Little, Brown, 1959. 309 p.

A German who sought refuge in Britain during the Third Reich returns to Berlin after the war. It is based on a true story.

Non-German Fiction

676 COTTERELL, GEOFFREY. *Randle in Springtime*. London: Eyre & Spottiswoode, 1949. 287 p.

When the British army occupies Hamburg after the war, Randle gets mixed up in the German black market.

677 CROSS, JAMES, pseud. [H. J. PARRY]. *The Dark Road*. New York: Messner, 1959. 191 p.

An American lawyer in Germany is trapped by circumstances into becoming an undercover agent between the Soviet and American zones.

678 DAVIDSON, DAVID A. *Steeper Cliff*. New York: Random House, 1947. 340 p.

An American seeks the whereabouts of an anti-nazi journalist in Bavaria after the war. In the process of becoming familiar with the journalist's background and family, the American falls in love with the man's wife.

679 DIBNER, MARTIN. *A God for Tomorrow*. New York: Doubleday, 1961. 263 p.

Set in postwar Germany. A rumor that Hitler left a son causes a reporter to pursue the story.

680 EDMONDS, HENRY M. *Clockmaker of Heidelberg*. New York: Nelson, 1949. 240 p.

Takes place in postwar Germany.

681 EDMONDSON, PAUL. *Spoils of the Victors*. New York: Simon & Schuster, 1964. 379 p.

An officer of the occupying forces acquires many luxuries for himself as commander of a prison camp. He then further degrades himself by trying to hang on to his luxuries.

682 EDWARDS, JULIA. *The Occupiers*. New York: Fleet Publishers, 1967. 304 p.

Reveals the prevailing lack of morals that affected both the Germans and the Allies in the immediate postwar period.

683 FAVIELL, FRANCES, pseud. [OLIVIA PARKER]. *A House on the Rhine*. New York: Farrar, Straus & Cudahy, 1956. 255 p.

In postwar Cologne, a large, disorderly working-class family has degenerated into crime, with the implication that it was a common occurrence in the ruined country.

Non-German Fiction

684 FIELDING, GABRIEL, pseud. [ALAN G. BARNSLEY]. *The Birthday King.* New York: Morrow, 1962. 320 p. Reprint. University of Chicago Press, 1985.

    The moral dilemmas of the last years of the war and the first years of peace are demonstrated in the history of a German industrialist's family divided by nazism and war guilt.

685 FORMAN, JAMES. *Horses of Anger.* New York: Farrar, Straus & Giroux, 1967. 249 p.

    A young German gunner encounters two prevalent attitudes toward the end of the war. His favorite uncle has become disillusioned with the Nazis, while his good friend has become more fanatical.

686 FRIEDRICH, OTTO. *Poor in Spirit.* Boston: Little, Brown, 1952. 246 p.

    In Berlin, an American who happened to be a Jew falls in love temporarily with a German girl he met at a concert.

687 GAINHAM, SARAH. *Private Worlds.* New York: Holt, 1971. 321 p.

    This is the third book about twentieth-century Vienna. The heroine, a classical actress, returns to the city after the war with a new husband. Shadows of their earlier lives during the nazi occupation threaten their current tranquillity.

688 GIBBS, PHILIP H. *Thine Enemy.* New York: M. McBride, 1950. 316 p.

    Reproduces the frantic flight of ethnic Germans from the eastern territories in front of the advancing Soviet armies.

689 GREENE, HARRIS. *The "Mozart" Leaves at Nine.* Garden City, N.Y.: Doubleday, 1961. 452 p.

    The security officer of the U.S. army's military government in Salzburg faces many problems, including a defecting Soviet officer.

690 GROUSSARD, SERGE. *German Officer.* Translated from French. New York: Putnam, 1955. 218 p.

    In a war crimes trial in postwar Germany, a German officer justifies his actions by claiming to be a tool of evil men rather than evil himself. Nevertheless, he receives eventual retribution.

Non-German Fiction

691   HABE, HANS, pseud. [JEAN BEKESSY]. *Aftermath*. Translated from German. New York: Viking, 1947. 345 p.

   The stylized theme of this novel is a debate between two American army officers regarding the relative merits of German women and American women. The American is found lacking, and the European is idealized.

692   ———. *Off Limits*. Translated from German. New York: Fell, 1957. 466 p.

   Follows the lives of Germans and Americans in occupied Germany, making effective use of reality to form the backdrop for fictional events.

693   ———. *Walk in Darkness*. Translated from German. New York: Putnam, 1948. 314 p.

   A disillusioned black man reenlists in the army to return to Germany where he hopes he will escape discrimination. He marries a German girl, deserts from the army, becomes involved with black marketeers, and kills a soldier. Eventually he is caught and hanged.

694   HALL, ADAM, pseud. *The Quiller Memorandum*. New York: Simon & Schuster, 1965. 224 p.

   In Berlin after the war, British and Germans work together to track down nazi leaders who were not arrested at the end of the war.

695   HAWKES, JOHN. *The Cannibal*. New York: New Directions, 1950. 223 p.

   A ruined village in postwar Germany is the setting for this novel of disjointed images and sketches.

696   HOLM, ANNE. *North to Freedom*. New York: Harcourt, Brace & World, 1965. 190 p. Reprint. Peter Smith, 1984.

   Having been released from a concentration camp, a teenage boy sets out to make his way north to Denmark. He encounters all kinds of people on his journey, some of whom take advantage of his naiveté.

697   HUTCHINSON, RAY C. *March the Ninth*. New York: Rinehart, 1957. 371 p.

   An American traveling in Germany becomes accidently involved in the hiding of a German officer who fears being charged with war crimes.

Non-German Fiction

698 JAMESON, STORM. *Black Laurel*. New York: Macmillan, 1948. 338 p.
Set in Berlin in the early days of the occupation, the plot concerns survival in the ruins of the city.

699 KAYE, MARY M. *Death in Berlin*. New York: St. Martin's Press, 1983. 254 p. British title: *Death Walked in Berlin* (1955).
Visiting Berlin with her relatives, a young woman is an unwilling witness to a murder that has strange connections with her own past.

700 KEEFE, FREDERICK L. *The Investigating Officer*. New York: Delacorte Press, 1966. 406 p.
In the summer of 1945, an American officer in Vienna becomes a suspect when two nazi SS men are murdered.

701 KELLOGG, VIRGINIA. *Verboten*. N.p., 1960.
Set in postwar Berlin.

702 KLAAS, JOE. *Maybe I'm Dead*. New York: Macmillan, 1955. 408 p.
Allied prisoners of war in German camps are forced to march westward away from the oncoming Soviet troops. They are put on the road in January 1945 without adequate food or clothing. Many die on the march.

703 KRUGER, RAYNE. *My Name is Celia*. London: Longmans, Green, 1954. 227 p.
In Berlin after the war, a middle-class British woman is pulled into the lives of black marketeers. After a dead-end affair, she finally realizes how low her life has sunk.

704 LAQUEUR, WALTER. *Farewell to Europe*. Boston: Little, Brown, 1981. 336 p.
In postwar Berlin, the plot follows the lives of a Jew who escaped death during the war and his two sons. One seeks a new life in Israel, and the other immigrates to America with his father.

705 LITVINOFF, EMANUEL. *The Lost Europeans*. New York: Vanguard Press, 1959. 282 p.
Two surviving Jews return to Berlin after the war to trace friends and relatives, apply for restitution, and search for those who betrayed them.

Non-German Fiction

706 MABLEY, EDWARD, and LEONARD MINS. *Temper the Wind*. N.p., n.d.

A play about the U.S. occupation. A review appeared in an article entitled "Watch on the Rhine," *Saturday Review* 30 (18 January 1947): 20-22.

707 McGOVERN, JAMES W. *The Berlin Couriers*. New York: Abelard-Schuman, 1960. 175 p.

This spy thriller takes place in postwar Berlin across the Soviet and western zones. A German scientist is snatched by East German agents and has to be rescued. Spies, couriers, and government agents are involved.

708 ———. *Fräulein*. New York: Crown, 1956. 312 p. Also published with title: *Erika*. New York: Popular Library, 1957.

A young German woman leaves Dresden for Berlin in the postwar period, hoping to find a job to support herself. Life is very difficult, and starvation is a reality in the ruined city.

709 ———. *No Ruined Castles*. New York: Putnam, 1957. 287 p.

An American foreign service officer is stationed in a small German town where he has to deal with the many problems of the local population. He falls in love with a German woman.

710 MacINNES, COLIN. *To the Victors the Spoils*. London: MacGibbon & Kee, 1950. 350 p.

Set in occupied Germany.

711 McMAHON, FINN. *Post Bellum Blues: A Novel about a Soldier in Trouble*. New York: New American Library, 1965. 168 p.

A fictionalized story about the author's army life in occupied Germany.

712 MALCOLM, JEAN. *Discourse with Shadows*. New York: Doubleday, 1958. 215 p.

A man returns to Frankfurt after the war. He finds a group of people who are trying to find housing, food, and work. The stresses of survival in the ruined city erupt into chaos.

Non-German Fiction

713 MANNIN, ETHEL E. *Bavarian Story*. New York: Appleton-Century-Croft, 1950. 314 p.

A novel in U.S. occupied Bavaria has as characters a German woman, her American soldier suitor, and a choirmaster who has returned from Dachau.

714 MARCUS, ALAN. *Straw to Make Brick*. Boston: Little, Brown, 1948. 435 p.

The author draws upon his experiences as a member of the U.S. military government to write this novel of rural Bavaria. A Jewish-American soldier falls in love with a German woman. When a crisis arises, the woman clings to her long-standing loyalties, and the soldier breaks off the relationship.

715 MARSHALL, BRUCE. *Vespers in Vienna*. Boston: Houghton Mifflin, 1947. 279 p.

The Allied occupation in Vienna has a unit headquartered in a convent. The lives of the men and the nuns converge in unusual ways.

716 MILLAR, GEORGE R. *My Past Was an Evil River*. New York: Doubleday, 1946. 306 p.

A French forced laborer becomes the protector of a German woman in the days just before American troops move into Austria. When an important German official seeks refuge with the woman, the two men have an inevitable conflict.

717 NASSAUER, RUDOLF. *Reparations*. London: J. Cape, 1981. 254 p.

A family returns to Frankfurt after the war from exile in Britain. Old acquaintances and old politics have significance as the characters pick up the pieces of their lives.

718 NEWELL, BERGEN F. *Naked before My Captors*. New York: F. Fell, 1959. 222 p.

Set in occupied Germany.

719 NOWAKOWSKI, TADEUSZ. *Camp of All Saints*. New York: St. Martin's Press, 1962. 314 p.

Released from a concentration camp, a Pole stays in postwar Germany and marries a German woman. Her past and his are linked in an unusual way.

720 POPKIN, ZELDA. *Small Victory.* Philadelphia: Lippincott, 1947. 280 p.

    In response to the need for civilians to serve in the American occupation government, a college professor volunteers to go to Germany. He becomes involved in the lives of German friends.

721 PREBBLE, JOHN. *Edge of Night.* New York: W. Sloane Associates, 1948. 325 p. British title: *Edge of Darkness.*

    The experiences of a British soldier in the last months of the war are the foundations of this novel. He stays in Germany as part of the British occupation forces when the war ends.

722 PUZO, MARIO. *The Dark Arena.* New York: Random House, 1955. 308 p.

    A realistic portrayal of life in the American zone. An ex-soldier returns to his mistress in Germany as soon as he gets out of the army, but he unintentionally contributes to her death.

723 SARTRE, JEAN-PAUL. *The Condemned of Altona: A Play in Five Acts.* Translated from French. New York: Knopf, 1961. 182 p.

    The existential novel is about assuming responsibility for the war and the crimes that were committed in the name of the German people. A man stays in a room for thirteen years after the war. Various members of his family become involved in his life in the room.

724 SHAPIRO, LIONEL. *Sealed Verdict.* Garden City, N.Y.: Doubleday, 1947. 278 p.

    Six Nazis are tried by a court in the American zone of occupied Germany. The various participants in the trial are the characters in the novel.

725 SMITH, WILLIAM G. *Last of the Conquerors.* New York: Farrar, Straus, 1948. 262 p.

    A black American GI stationed in occupied Germany falls in love with a German woman. The problems associated with the presence of black soldiers in Germany are apparent in the relationship between the two people.

726 STILES, MARTHA B. *Darkness over the Land.* New York: Dial, 1966. 269 p.

    A Polish orphan who was reared as a German in Munich comes to realize the true significance of Germany being defeated in the war. He has to eventually decide if he will stay in Germany or immigrate to the United States.

727 URIS, LEON. *Armageddon: A Novel of Berlin*. Garden City, N.Y.: Doubleday, 1964. 632 p.

An American officer in the occupation government of the U.S. sector in Berlin is filled with hatred for the defeated Germans. When he unintentionally falls in love with a German woman, his harsh opinions are modified after coming to understand the Germans' struggle to earn respect.

728 VALTIN, JAN, pseud. [RICHARD J. H. KREBS]. *Wintertime*. New York: Rinehart, 1950. 439 p.

A Latvian girl seeks refuge with a German ship captain in the period immediately after the war. He falls in love with her, and together they attempt to build a new life.

729 WEITZ, JOHN. *Friends in High Places*. New York: Macmillan, 1982. 387 p.

A former German soldier is sent to the United States as a representative of his employer, a German car company. He finds that he is continually challenged by coworkers and business associates to prove that he was not a Nazi.

730 WELT, ELLY. *Berlin Wild*. New York: Viking, 1986. 368 p.

Josef Bernhardt, half-Jewish, barely escaped being killed during the war, although most of his mother's family was deported and murdered. Years afterward, Josef is haunted by the guilt of having survived.

731 WHITING, CHARLES. *The Frat Wagon*. London: J. Cape, 1954. 220 p.

Set in occupied Germany.

732 ———. *Lest I Fall*. London: J. Cape, 1956. 176 p.

After failing as a teacher in civilian life, a man returns to Germany, marries the daughter of a successful industrialist, and receives a soft job from his father-in-law.

Non-German Fiction

733 WISEMAN, THOMAS. *The Day before Sunrise.* New York: Holt, Rinehart & Winston, 1976. 347 p.
   As the Allied armies push into Germany, there are secret deals being arranged for the surrender of German officers and the obtaining of files on certain Nazis.

734 WYLIE, IDA A. *Where No Birds Sing.* New York: Random House, 1947. 252 p.
   A love story of an American soldier and a German woman, complicated by the involvement of a fanatical Nazi who disguises himself as a Jewish displaced person.

CHAPTER 7

Films about Germany

Cited in this chapter are motion pictures produced in the occupied zones of Germany from 1945 to 1948, as well as educational, documentary, and entertainment films and filmstrips concerning the period produced in the United States by the federal government and by civilian companies. The films from Germany had to be licensed by the occupation government in whose zone they were made. A few of these were eventually released in the United States with English subtitles, although most were not.

A few films made in postwar Germany dealt directly with the struggle to come to terms with nazism and life in the ruins. Others focused on the rise of national socialism and the period of World War II. Nevertheless, whatever the subjects, all films produced during this time were indirectly influenced by the difficulties filmmakers had in obtaining film and other supplies, feeding crews, and finding suitable filming locations. Germans called films from this early postwar period "Trümmerfilme" (films of the rubble). For this reason, the citations in this chapter include all the German-made films that could be found rather than just those that deal directly with the period or have been released in Great Britain or the United States. When there is one, the English title is also given. Since motion pictures are not readily available for reviewing, the descriptions are taken from written sources. These sources are cited in the last chapter, on consulted bibliographic works. Commercial film distributors in the United States often

Films about Germany

market a product several times with few changes, so only one release is listed if the name and description of later releases are substantially the same.

735   *Affäre Blum* = *Blum Affair*. Production: DEFA, Berlin. Director: Erich Engel. Soviet license. Released 1948.

   Explores the anti-Semitism of the 1920s, during the Weimar Republic. A Jewish industrialist narrowly escapes false charges of murder.

736   *Der Apfel Ist Ab*. Production: Camera-Film, Hamburg. Director: Helmut Käutner. British license. Released 1948.

   A man is drawn to two women, one representing good and one, evil. As he tries to choose between them, they fuse into one person.

737   *Arche Nora* = *Nora's Ark*. Production: Real-Film, Hamburg. Director: Werner Klingler. British license. Released 1948.

   A comedy about a young couple who, lacking a place to live, finds a derelict boat that will furnish shelter.

738   *Assignment Germany*. Production: United States Army. Released 1950. 14 min., 16 mm.

   A documentary describing the U.S. occupation, the denazification and reeducation of Germans, and the revival of politics.

739   *Beate*. Production: Tova-Filmproduktion, Berlin. Director: Carl Boese. British license. Released 1948.

   Optimistically portraying postwar life, the film follows identical twin sisters, one of whom falls in love with a soldier. When he returns from the war, the other sister pretends to be his lover.

740   *Berliner Ballade* = *The Berliner*. Production: Comedia-Film, Berlin/Munich. Director: Robert A. Stemmle. Joint license. Released 1948. Released in the U.S. by Joseph Burstyn, Inc., 1952.

   Satirizes life in Berlin after the war. The black market, bureaucracy, political issues, and the hardships of daily life are attacked.

741   *Berlin Express*. Production: RKO Radio, U.S.A. Director: Jacques Tourneur. Released 1948.

   The postwar nazi underground wants to kill a German statesman who is promoting a unified Germany. Scenes of Frankfurt and Berlin ruins.

Films about Germany

742   *Berlin--Kaiser to Khrushchev*. Production: Encyclopedia Britannica, Chicago. Released 1964. 52 min.

   The history of Berlin is illustrated using rare footage of newsreels, propaganda films, and military films.

743   *Berlin Powderkeg*. Production: RKO Pathe. Director: William Deeke. This Is America, no. 3. Released 1949. 19 min., 35 mm.

   A documentary about life in postwar Berlin and the effects of the cold war and the Berlin airlift on the city.

744   *Blockierte Signale*. Production: Ondia-Film, Berlin. Director: Johannes Meyer. British license. Released 1948.

   Explores the criminal side of life in Germany after the war, when racketeers and black marketeers were flaunting the laws and conventional moral codes.

745   *Bombing of Germany*. Production: Anargyros Film Library. Released 1974. 4 min., super 8.

   Documentary footage of Allied aerial bombings of Germany in World War II.

746   *Die Brücke = The Bridge*. Production: DEFA, Berlin. Director: Arthur Pohl. Soviet license. Released [1949?].

   Explores the ways that expelled Germans found new homes in the Soviet zone. Their presence was resented by the original Germans.

747   *Die Brücke = The Bridge*. Production: Fono-Film and Jochen Severin. Director: Bernhard Wicki. Released 1959. Released in the U.S. by Allied Artists Pictures Corp., 1960.

   Young boys are ordered to defend a bridge in the last days of the war. This has been called a classic antiwar film of West Germany.

748   *Chemie Und Liebe*. Production: DEFA, Berlin. Director: Arthur M. Rabenalt. Soviet license. Released 1948.

   The theme of capitalist business versus socialist progress is illustrated with humor and satire.

749   *Comeback for Germany*. [Filmstrip.] Production: New York Times. Released 1955. 60 frames, 35 mm.

   After briefly tracing the history of the Third Reich, the war, and the four zones of occupation, it describes the amazing revival of the West German economy and the place of West Germany in the defense network of Europe.

Films about Germany

750   *A Divided Germany.* [Filmstrip.] Production: Current Affairs Films. Released 1958. 41 frames, 35 mm.

   Describes the evolution of East and West Germany since the war. Their politics, economy, and social conditions are compared.

751   *Die Ehe der Maria Braun = The Marriage of Maria Braun.* Production: Michael Fengler for Albatros Film/Trio Film/Westdeutscher Rundfunk. Director: Rainer W. Fassbinder. Released 1978. Released in the U.S., 1979.

   The life of Maria Braun reflects the recovery of Germany in the first nine years after the war. The devastation of Berlin is accurately portrayed in the first third of the film.

752   *Ehe im Schatten = Marriage in the Shadow.* Production: DEFA, Berlin. Director: Kurt Maetzig. Soviet license. Released 1947.

   An important film that allowed the Germans to reflect on their immediate past history. It describes the ill-fated mixed marriage of a couple in the 1930s.

753   *1-2-3 [Eins-Zwei-Drei] Corona.* Production: DEFA, Berlin. Director: Hans Müller. Soviet license. Released 1948.

   An upbeat description of life in Berlin right after the war. Young people in desperate straits become circus workers to earn a living legitimately.

754   *Es Liegt an Dir = It's Up to You.* Production: U.S. Office of Military Government. Director: Wolfgang Kiepenheuer. Licensed by U.S. Released [1948?].

   A documentary that follows the evolution of German thought from 1919 to 1948, to show the Germans how their country accepted the Nazis and their principles.

755   *Film ohne Titel = Film without Name.* Production: Camera-Film, Hamburg. Director: Rudolph Jugert. British license. Released 1948.

   The making of a film within a film, with movie people sitting around discussing how to make a comedy that will not distress German audiences.

Films about Germany

756   *Finale*. Production: Real-Film, Hamburg. Director: Ulrich Erfurth. British license. Released 1948.

   In Hamburg after the war, a former pianist and his wife try to resume their marriage. War injuries prevent the husband from playing, yet he can not find other employment.

757   *A Foreign Affair*. Production: Paramount Pictures. Director: Billy Wilder. Released 1948.

   A romantic comedy featuring an American congresswoman who visits Berlin to check on the morale of U.S. troops stationed there. The exteriors are filmed in Berlin.

758   *Freies Land = Free Land*. Production: DEFA, Berlin. Director: Milo Harbich. Soviet license. Released 1946.

   Illustrates the value of land reform and redistribution from the Soviet point-of-view. The peasants who are given the lands of an aristocrat learn to work together collectively.

759   *German Children*. Production: Swank Films. Released 1953. 13 min., 16 mm.

   Follows a typical day in the life of a German child to show how similar his life is when compared to American children, in spite of his different clothes and surroundings.

760   *Germania, Anno Zero = Germany, Year Zero*. Production: Tevere Film in collaboration with Salvo d'Angelo Productions. Director: Robert Rossellini. Released 1947. Released in the U.S., 1949.

   Life in the ruins of Berlin after the war is desperate. A young boy tries to support his family by stealing and dealing on the black market. His disillusionment, hunger, and exhaustion lead him to suicide. Rossellini is praised for filming the reality of the destroyed city.

761   *Germany*. Production: U.S. Army. Released 1950. 9 min., 16 mm.

   Describes the purpose of the occupation of Germany and the recovery of the western zones. Produced for U.S. armed forces personnel.

762   *Germany*. Production: March of Time. Released 1952. 29 min., 16 mm.

   Shows the economic revival of western Germany since the war and contrasts life in East and West Germany.

Films about Germany

763 *Germany.* Production: Dudley Pictures, released by Republic Pictures. This World of Ours. Released 1953. 1 reel, 35 mm.

A tour of western Germany showing the restoration and new building that have occurred since the war.

764 *Germany after the Fall.* Production: National Educational Television, released by Indiana University Audio Visual Center. Released 1970. 58 min., 16 mm.

Thilo Koch presents his interpretation of western German social, political, and economic reconstruction, 1945-49.

765 *Germany Divided.* [Filmstrip]. Production: Training Films, released by New York Times. Released 1952. 53 frames, 35 mm.

Describes the four zones of occupation, the establishment of the Federal Republic and the Democratic Republic, and the problems they currently face.

766 *Germany--Handle with Care*! Production: March of Time, released by 20th Century-Fox. Released 1946?

Describes the occupation of Germany and the division of the country into four zones. The occupying troops are helping to denazify and democratize the people as well as to rebuild the country.

767 *Germany, Key to Europe.* Production: National Film Board of Canada, Ottawa. Canada Carries on Series. Released 1953. 21 min., 16 mm.

Shows the importance of West Germany in Europe by tracing the fall of the Third Reich, the military occupation of the postwar years, and the economic recovery of the western zones.

768 *Germany Surrenders.* Production: Filmrite Associates, released by Official Films. Released 1960. 3 min., 16 mm.

Documentary footage of the last days of the war after Hitler's suicide, including the surrender of Dönitz, and the signing of the final documents on 7 May 1945.

769 *Germany Today.* Production: RKO Pathe, in collaboration with the editors of *This Week Magazine.* Director: William Murray. This Is America, no. 2. Released 1946. 16 min., 35 mm.

Describes the defeated country and the chaos that existed when the war ended.

Films about Germany

770 *Grube Morgenrot*. Production: DEFA, Berlin. Director: Wolfgang Schleif, Erich Freund. Soviet license. Released 1948.
Incidents in a mine during the nazi period are the basis for the film.

771 *Hallo Fraülein*. Production: Camera-Film, Hamburg. Director: Rudolf Jugert. Released 1949.
Explores German and American relations in the days of nonfraternization between the conquered and the conquerors.

772 *Here Is Germany*. Production: U.S. Army Pictorial Service, Signal Corps, 1945. Distributed by National AudioVisual Center, [19--?]. 52 min., 16 mm. Also issued as a videocassette.
Using German and American archival materials, the film traces the military power of Germany from Frederick the Great to the end of the Third Reich.

773 *Der Herr vom Andern Stern*. Production: Comedia-Film, Berin/Munich. Director: Heinz Hilpert. Joint license. Released 1948.
A man from another planet lands on earth and tries to make sense out of life here.

774 *Herzkönig*. Production: CCC Film, Berlin. Director: Helmut Weiss. French license. Released 1947.
No description.

775 *Hunger*. Production: U.S. Office of Military Government. Director: Erich Pommer. American license. Released [1946-47?].
Film intended for rural audiences to encourage them to produce more food and ship more to market.

776 *Ich War 19 = I Was 19*. Production: Deutsche F.A.G., East Germany. Director: Konrad Wolf. Released 1968.
Tells the story of the siege of Berlin in April 1945 from the point-of-view of the Soviet troops.

777 *In Jenen Tagen = In Those Days*. Production: Camera-Film, Hamburg. Director: Helmut Käutner. British license. Released 1947.
Illustrates recent German history by describing episodes in the life of an old car: driven by people fleeing persecution, resisting the Nazis, escaping from the eastern provinces, and observing repression by the Gestapo.

Films about Germany

778 *Irgendwo in Berlin = Somewhere in Berlin*. Production: DEFA, Berlin. Director: Gerhard Lamprecht. Soviet license. Released 1946.

In the ruins of Berlin, young children become juvenile delinquents in order to survive. The father of one of the boys returns from the war and intervenes before the children are hopelessly meshed in crime.

779 *Justice Comes to Germany*. Production: The March of Time, released by 20th Century-Fox. Released 1946.

Follows the trial of a German for the murder of an American airman who had been a prisoner of war.

780 *Kein Platz für Liebe = No Place for Love*. Production: DEFA, Berlin. Director: Hans Deppe. Soviet license. Released 1947.

A comedy that features the contemporary housing shortage as the pivotal issue around which the film was created.

781 *Kinder, Mütter, Und ein General = Children, Mothers, And a General*. Production: Erich Pommer/Intercontinental. Director: Laslo Benedek. Released 1955.

Describes the last weeks of World War II in Germany.

782 *Die Kupferne Hochzeit*. Production: Comedia-Film, West Berlin. Director: Heinz Rühmann. Joint license. Released 1948.

No description.

783 *Lang Ist der Weg*. Production: Internationale Film Organization, Munich. Director: Herbert B. Fredersdorf and Marek Goldstein. U.S. license. Released 1948.

A story of Jews in the Warsaw Ghetto, their starvation and their deportation to the death camps. After the war, a few people survived.

784 *Let Us Live*. Production: U.S. Dept. of State, released by the U.S. Office of Education for educational use. Released 1953. Released in 1954 by Lutheran World Action, New York. 19 min., 16 mm.

A documentary of ethnic Germans expelled into the western zones from their ancestral homes in Poland, Czechoslovakia, and other east European countries.

Films about Germany

785 *Liebe '47 = Love '47*. Production: Filmaufbau. Director: Wolfgang Liebeneiner. British license. Released 1949.

   A woman's disillusionment with the war leads to attempted suicide. Her final despair is alleviated by her love for a war-injured soldier.

786 *The Man Between*. Production: London Film Productions. Released in the United States by United Artists Corp. Director: Carol Reed. Released 1953.

   In postwar Berlin, a young Englishwoman becomes involved with an East German who smuggles people out of the eastern zone into West Berlin.

787 *Menschen in Gottes Hand*. Production: Junge Film--Union Rolf Meyer, Hamburg. Director: Rolf Meyer. British license. Released 1948.

   An East Prussian farmer and his family seek refuge with their son in Hamburg after being expelled from their home. Their responsible and dutiful work ethic contrasts sharply with that of their dissolute son.

788 *Die Mörder Sind unter Uns = The Murderers Are among Us*. Production: DEFA, Berlin. Director: Wolfgang Staudte. Soviet license. Released 1946. Released in the U.S., 1947.

   Amid the realities of postwar Berlin, a former soldier comes to terms with his actions during the war. This was the first feature film made in Germany after the war.

789 *Morgen Ist Alles Besser*. Production: Berolina-Filmproduktion, Berlin. Director: Arthur M. Rabenalt. British license. Released 1948.

   A young woman needs money to send her father to a rest home. When she gets the money, she also finds love.

790 *Morituri*. Production: CCC, Berlin. Director: Eugen York. French license. Released 1948.

   An examination of the nazi concentration camps and their functions.

Films about Germany

791   *New German Republic Born.* Production: Filmrite Associates. Released by Official Films. Released 1961. 3 min., 16 mm.

   Documentary footage of the German surrender, the functioning of four occupation zones, and the development of the constitution of the Federal Republic.

792   *Nuremberg = Nürnberg, 1948.* Production: U.S. Office of Military Government. Directors: Pare Lorentz, Stuart Schulberg. Released 1948.

   An informative film about nazi war crimes and the Nuremberg trials. Most of the war film footage was found at the Army Signal Corps Pictorial Center in Astoria, New York. The film was shown only in the U.S. and British zones and was withdrawn from circulation in 1950.

793   *The Nuremberg Trials, a Documentary Record of the Trial of Germany's Top War Criminals.* Production: R. Karmen for Central Documentary Film Studios, U.S.S.R. Released in U.S. by Artkino Pictures. 60 min.

   An informative film that uses official military film and flashbacks to illustrate the charges against the defendants.

794   *Nürnberg Und Seine Lehren.* Released 1947.

   An informative film about the Nuremberg trials, from the Allied point-of-view.

795   *Operation Thunderbolt.* Production: U.S. Dept. of the Army. Released 1947. Released for public educational use by the U.S. Office of Education, 1950.

   An informational film about the United States Constabulary Forces that formed the police force in the American zone.

796   *Razzia = Round-Up.* Production: DEFA, Berlin. Director: Werner Klinger. Soviet license. Released 1947.

   The attempts of the German and occupation authorities to control the black market, with the atmosphere of an adventure film.

797   *Report on the Refugee Situation.* Production: Information Services of the British Control Commission. Released 1949.

   Reveals the hopelessness of the expellees from the eastern provinces. They arrived in the British zone with no belongings, no housing, and no means of earning a living.

Films about Germany

798   *Resettled Heifers for Resettled Refugees.* [Filmstrip.] Production: Commission of World Service of the Evangelical and Reformed Church. Released 1954. 74 frames, 35 mm.

   Individual congregations in the E. & R. church sent cattle to expellees in western Germany. German relief organizations coordinated the efforts.

799   *Der Ruf = The Challenge.* Production: Objectiv Film, West Berlin. Director: Josef von Baky. Released 1949.

   A German-Jewish professor returns to postwar Germany from exile though he is advised against it. He becomes disillusioned.

800   *Sag die Wahrheit = Tell the Truth.* Production: Studio 45, Berlin. Director: Helmut Weiss. British license. Released 1946.

   A comedy about a man who wants to convince his fiancee that it is possible to speak only the truth for twenty-four hours.

801   *Seeds of Destiny.* Production: U.S. Army Pictorial Service, for UNRRA, 1946. Distributed by National Audiovisual Center, 1982. 21 min., 16 mm.

   Shows the plight of refugees and displaced persons in postwar Europe, with descriptions of nazi Germany's wartime program of subjugating the rest of Europe to illustrate the antecedents of the displacement.

802   *Die Seltsamen Abenteuer des Herrn Fridolin B.* Production: DEFA, Berlin. Director: Wolfgang Staudte. Soviet license. Released 1948.

   Satire of bureaucracy and the middle class.

803   *Die Söhne des Herrn Gaspary = The Sons of Herr Gaspary.* Production: Junge Film--Union Rolf Meyer, Hamburg. Director: Rolf Meyer. British license. Released 1948.

   Gaspary sends one son to spend the war years in Switzerland where he grows rich. The second son remains in Germany, suffering hardships and serving in the Luftwaffe. The brothers are reunited in Hamburg after the war.

804   *Strassenbekanntschaft.* Production: DEFA, Berlin. Director: Peter Pewas. Soviet license. Released 1948.

   A dramatization of postwar German society among the class of people who grow rich dealing on the black market.

Films about Germany

805   *Die Todesmühlen.* Production: Allied Occupation Forces. Director: Hans H. Burger. Released 1945, withdrawn from circulation, 1946.
      A documentary of the liberation of the death camps as filmed by military photographers who were present.

806   *Und Finden Dereinst Wir Uns Wieder.* Production: Studio 45-Film, Berlin. Director: Hans Müller. British license. Released 1947.
      Children are evacuated from Berlin in the later years of the war to escape the bombing of the city. Some are taken by their teachers to a castle in Westphalia. They sneak back to the city to take part in its defense.

807   *Und über Uns der Himmel! = The Sky above Us.* Production: Objectiv Film, Berlin. Director: Josef von Baky. American license. Released 1947.
      A former soldier returns to Berlin from the war and is swept into the black market activities of the city. When his blinded son also returns, the son is able to rescue the father from his degenerate life.

808   *Und wieder 48.* Production: DEFA, Berlin. Director: Gustav von Wagenheim. Soviet license. Released 1948.
      No description.

809   *UNRRA Goes into Action.* [Filmstrip.] Production: National Film Board of Canada for UNRRA. Released 1945. 50 frames, 35 mm.
      Illustrates the role of the United Nations Relief and Rehabilitation Administration in helping the displaced persons and refugees of Europe after the war.

810   *U.S. Forces in Europe.* Production: U.S. Dept. of the Army, for the U.S. Dept. of Defense. Released 1951. 17 min., 16 mm.
      Compares and contrasts the work of the U.S. army and the work of Soviet troops in rehabilitating the German people.

811   *United States Occupies Germany.* Production: Filmrite Associates, released by Official Films. Released 1961. 3 min., 16 mm.
      Documents the problems of occupied Germany with the focus on the reeducation of the young people.

Films about Germany

812 *United States Occupation of Germany.* Production: Thorne Films. Released 1971. 4 min., Super 8 mm.

Illustrates numerous aspects of the American occupation of Germany, including supervision of the denazification process, enforcement of health measures, and maintenance of law and order.

813 *Unser Mittwochabend.* Production: Ondia-Filmproduktion, Berlin. Directors: Werner Illing and Georg Krause. British license. Released 1948.

A weekly discussion group among friends is the vehicle for an energetic, frank, yet optimistic view of life in the British zone.

814 *Das Verlorene Gesicht.* Production: Neue Deutsche Filmgesellschaft, Munich. Director: Kurt Hoffman. American license. Released 1947.

A young girl imagines herself to be a person from Tibet.

815 *Vor Uns Liegt das Leben.* Production: Stella-Film, Berlin. Director: Günther Rittau. American license. Released 1948.

Dramatizes the difficulties encountered by ordinary families in finding peace and contentment in postwar Germany.

816 *Wege im Zwielicht.* Production: Junge Film, Hamburg. Director: Gustav Fröhlich. British license. Released 1948.

Three returned prisoners of war find a new home while working on a bridge.

817 *The World in Film.* Production: British and American film-makers. Released summer 1945.

A film designed to reassure German audiences that the occupation troops will act justly and will encourage the development of democratic attitudes.

818 *Wozzeck.* Production: DEFA, Berlin. Director: Georg Klaren. Soviet license. Released 1947.

Based on a play by German poet Georg Büchner about a victimized Prussian soldier.

Films about Germany

819   *Your Job in Germany*. Production: U.S. Army Pictorial Service, Signal Corps, 1945. Distributed by National Audiovisual Center, 1982. Directors: Frank Capra and Theodore Geisel. 15 min., 16 mm.
   Developed immediately after the war to discourage U.S. troops from fraternizing with the hated Germans.

820   *Die Zeit mit Dir*. Production: Camera-Film, Hamburg. Director: Georg Hurdalek. British license. Released 1948.
   After the war an ex-soldier hires an expellee girl to care for his children. Eventually he marries her so the children would have a mother.

821   *Zugvögel = Birds of Migration*. Production: Studio 45, Berlin. Director: Rolf Meyer. British license. Released 1947.
   Dramatizes the situation of German expellees wandering around western Germany seeking a place to settle and begin life again.

822   *Zwischen Gestern Und Morgan = Palace Hotel*. Production: Neue Deutsche Film-gesellschaft, Munich. Director: Harald Braun. American license. Released 1947.
   Filmed in the ruins of Munich, the film describes the nazi party structure and purpose as it developed after World War I.

CHAPTER *8*

Historical Studies

Separating historical studies from works written by contemporary observers is sometimes a matter of interpretation because many reflective and analytical histories have come from persons who also were in Germany during part of the postwar period as observers. Often their participation in the occupation aroused their interest in writing an historical study. In fact, in the case of the Historical Branch of the U.S. Office of Military Government, historians were sent to Germany to collect information to write accounts of specific aspects of the occupation, such as fraternization, denazification, and reeducation.

Historical studies of the imprisonment of German and Allied prisoners of war are included to complement their personal experiences cited in chapters 1 and 2. Of the many histories of the war in Germany that have been written, citations are listed for those that focus particularly on some aspect of the average person's experiences during the last weeks of the war.

823   ABOSCH, HEINZ. *Menace of the Miracle: Germany from Hitler to Adenauer.* Translated from French. New York: Monthly Review Press, 1963. 277 p.
        Traces the political and economic recovery of Germany.

Historical Studies

824 ABZUG, ROBERT H. *Inside the Vicious Heart: Americans and the Concentration Camps.* New York: Oxford University Press, 1985. 192 p.

The American troops that moved into Germany in the spring of 1945 came upon nazi concentration camps. The author gives a description and analysis of their experiences, as recorded in memoirs and related in interviews.

825 ALMOND, GABRIEL, ed. *The Struggle for Democracy in Germany.* Chapel Hill, N.C.: University of North Carolina Press, 1949. 345 p.

The book's second section has four essays dealing with occupation policies in economics, political party development, rebuilding of government, and reeducation.

826 BACKER, JOHN H. *The Decision to Divide Germany: American Foreign Policy in Transition.* Durham, N.C.: Duke University Press, 1978. 212 p.

Discusses the reasons for the eventual division of Germany into east and west by tracing the postwar policy decisions. The last chapter analyzes several interpretations of the division. Backer was an American foreign service officer in the occupation government.

827 _____. *Priming the German Economy: American Occupation Policies, 1945-1948.* Durham, N.C.: Duke University Press, 1971. 212 p.

Traces the achievements and failures of the American military government in rebuilding the German postwar economy.

828 _____. *Winds of History: The German Years of Lucius D. Clay.* New York: Van Nostrand Reinhold, 1983. 323 p.

Clay played an important role in the administration of the U.S. zone and Berlin. He was a vigorous proponent of U.S. occupation policy.

829 BALABKINS, NICHOLAS. *Germany under Direct Controls: Economic Aspects of Industrial Disarmament, 1945-1948.* New Brunswick, N.J.: Rutgers University Press, 1964. 265 p.

Details the economic constraints on occupied Germany. Policies were gradually modified as the United States realized that the European economy was directly tied to the German economy.

830 BALFOUR, MICHAEL L.G., and J. MAIR. *Four-Power Control in Germany and Austria, 1945-1946.* Pt. 1, "Germany"; pt. 2, "Austria."

Issued under the auspices of the Royal Institute of International Affairs. London: Oxford University Press, 1956. 390 p. Reprint. Johnson Reprint, 1972.

Describes the work of the Allied Control Commission in governing Germany. Having served with the British, Balfour gives good details of daily life, food shortages, behavior of Allied troops, etc.

831 BECK, EARL R. *Under the Bombs: The German Home Front, 1942-1945.* Lexington, Ky.: University Press of Kentucky, 1986. 252 p.

Emphasizes the war years; however, it is useful for the inclusion of individual experiences of many people. Beck weaves personal stories with official reports in a chronological manner.

832 BOTTING, DOUGLAS. *From the Ruins of the Reich: Germany 1945-1949.* New York: Crown, 1985. 341 p.

A social history of the immediate postwar years in occupied Germany, with chapters on the end of the war, the siege of Berlin, occupiers and civilians, the black market, the Soviets, and the revival of the economy.

833 BOTZENHART-VIEHE, VERENA. "The German Reaction to the American Occupation, 1944-1947." Ph.D. diss., University of California, Santa Barbara, 1980. 220 p.

Uses German written and oral sources to explain German attitudes toward the Americans and their occupation policies.

834 BOWER, TOM. *The Pledge Betrayed: America and Britain and the Denazification of Postwar Germany.* Garden City, N.Y.: Doubleday, 1982. 462 p. British title: *Blind Eye to Murder: British, America, and the Purging of Nazi Germany: A Pledge Betrayed.*

A recent account of the attempts to purge occupied Germany of active Nazis. The task was overwhelming, and the successes were inconsistent. Many small-fry were punished, while important Nazis were given jobs in the occupation governments.

835 CLARK, PENNY. *Farm Work and Friendship: The German Prisoner of War Camp at Lake Wabaunsee.* Emporia State Research Studies, vol. 36, no. 3. Emporia, Kans.: School of Graduate and Professional Studies, Emporia State University, 1988. 43 p.

Sketches the experience of one hundred German prisoners who were sent to the area to do farm work. In general the men were hard workers, and some friendships developed with local people.

836 CONOVER, DENISE O. "James F. Byrnes, Germany, and the Cold War, 1946." Ph.D. diss., Washington State University, 1978. 190 p.
   Not reviewed.

837 CRAIG, GORDON A. *The Germans*. New York: Putnam, 1982. 350 p.
   History and memoirs are combined in this book about the postwar period. German civilization and culture are also examined.

838 CRAWLEY, AIDAN. *Escape from Germany: The Methods of Escape Used by RAF Airmen during the War*. London: H.M.S.O., 1985. 352 p.
   The expurgated version was first published in 1956. This is the first printing of the complete narrative. Crawley was a prisoner of war in Germany, so he drew upon his own experiences as well as those of many other airmen. Included is the description of the evacuation of ten thousand U.S. and British prisoners who joined the westward exodus from Silesia in January 1945. Conditions were so chaotic that the men kept themselves together and got food from civilians along the route.

839 _____. *The Spoils of War: The Rise of Western Germany, 1945-1972*. Indianapolis, Ind.: Bobbs-Merrill, 1973. 315 p. British title: *The Rise of Western Germany, 1945-1972*.
   In the first third of the book, the author discusses the immediate postwar period. His concern for the German people is obvious in his descriptions of the expellees and their struggles to survive.

840 DASTRUP, BOYD L. *Crusade in Nuremberg: Military Occupation, 1945-1949*. Westport, Conn.: Greenwood Press, 1985. 159 p.
   Factually examines the operation of the military government in Nuremberg and its use of German personnel in the daily business of running the city.

841 DAVIDSON, EUGENE. *The Death and Life of Germany: An Account of the American Occupation*. New York: Knopf, 1959. 422 p.
   Discusses the occupation seriously and comprehensively. Combines a chronological presentation of events with views of various people and a sketch of German social history.

Historical Studies

842 DE ZAYAS, ALFRED M. *Nemesis at Potsdam: The Anglo-Americans and the Expulsion of the Germans: Background, Execution, Consequences.* 2d ed. London: Routledge & Kegan Paul, 1979. 268 p.

Describes in detail how the concept of mass population transfers came to be accepted at Potsdam and how the Allies tried to keep them "orderly and humane," to no avail. Good bibliography.

843 DOBSON, CHRISTOPHER, JOHN MILLER, and RONALD PAYNE. *The Cruelest Night.* Boston: Little, Brown, 1979. 223 p.

A history of the evacuation of over two million soldiers, sailors, and civilians from the northern shore of East Prussia, with the spotlight on the ship, *Wilhelm Gustloff*, which was torpedoed and sunk with over seven thousand people on board.

844 DONNISON, FRANK S. *Civil Affairs and Military Government, North-West Europe, 1944-1946.* History of the Second World War, United Kingdom Military Series. London: H.M.S.O., 1961. 518 p.

An official history of the British Army of the Rhine in northern Germany. Includes detailed descriptions of the work of the soldiers after the end of the war. They assisted in relief operations, found supplies of food and fuel for civilians, and implemented occupation policies.

845 DOYLE, FREDERICK J. "German Prisoners of War in the Southwest United States during World War II: An Oral History." Ph.D. diss., University of Denver, 1978. 202 p.

Not reviewed.

846 DRATH, VIOLA H., ed. *Germany in World Politics.* New York: Cyrco Press, 1979.

A collection of articles on many aspects of postwar Germany, including an essay on the role of German churches in the reconstruction of the country.

847 EDDING, FRIEDRICH. *The Refugees as a Burden, a Stimulus, and a Challenge to the West German Economy.* Publications of the Research Group for European Migration Problems, no. 4. The Hague: M. Nijhoff, 1951. 53 p.

Statistics are cited to explain the numbers, ages, and employability of the expellees. Although there are too many people for West Germany to absorb, the rapid economic recovery of the country is due in part to their desire to make a place for themselves.

Nevertheless, the expellees are a drain on the country's economy because they need medical care, housing, and job training.

848   FARQUHARSON, JOHN E. *The Western Allies and the Politics of Food: Agrarian Management in Postwar Germany*. Dover, N.H.: Berg Publishers, 1985. 279 p.
   Examines the interrelationships of Allied occupation policies, the scarcity of food, and the economic reconstruction of bizonal Germany.

849   FAULK, HENRY. *Group Captives: The Re-education of German Prisoners of War in Britain, 1945-1948*. Atlantic Highlands, N.J.: Humanities Press, 1977. 233 p.
   Studies the experiences of Germans and British when prisoners of war were housed in Britain. Analyzes the attitudes of both groups.

850   FITZGIBBON, CONSTANTINE. *Denazification*. New York: W.W. Norton, 1969. 222 p.
   Detailed study of denazification policies, their zonal differences, and their unsystematic enforcement.

851   FOY, DAVID A. *For You the War Is Over: American Prisoners of War in Nazi Germany*. New York: Stein & Day, 1984. 200 p.
   Describes the capture and imprisonment of American soldiers who fell into German hands. In camps, men formed groups of all kinds for many purposes, including escape. When the Soviet troops approached the camps, the prisoners were marched westward under extremely harsh conditions.

852   FREDERIKSEN, OLIVER J. *The American Military Occupation of Germany, 1945-1953*. [Darmstadt, FRG]: Historical Division, Headquarters, U.S. Army, Europe, 1953. 222 p.
   Records the history of the occupation from the vantage point of being part of the occupation. The author provides details on the problems and successes of American policies.

853   GANSBERG, JUDITH M. *Stalag U.S.A.: The Remarkable Story of German POWs in America*. New York: Crowell, 1977. 233 p.
   Describes the experiences of German prisoners in U.S. facilities. This unique opportunity to reeducate Germans away from fascism was considered successful.

Historical Studies

854 GARDNER, BRIAN. *The Year That Changed the World: 1945*. New York: Coward-McCann, 1964. 356 p.

A straight-forward account of political events throughout the year. No personal reflections on what was happening.

855 GIMBEL, JOHN. *The American Occupation of Germany: Politics and the Military, 1945-1949*. Stanford, Calif.: Stanford University Press, 1968. 335 p.

A broad, factual account of the political and economic aspects of the United States' presence in Germany.

856 _____. *A German Community under American Occupation, Marburg, 1945-1952*. Stanford, Calif.: Stanford University Press, 1961. 259 p.

Analyzes the occupation in one community, using archival sources in the United States and Germany to report details of policy implementation and circumvention.

857 _____. *The Origins of the Marshall Plan*. Stanford, Calif.: Stanford University Press, 1976. 344 p.

Focuses on the importance of Germany's economic recovery within the context of the recovery of the rest of Europe. The occupation costs had continued to escalate, to the distress of the United States. The Marshall Plan was proposed as a solution.

858 GROSSER, ALFRED. *The Colossus Again: Western Germany from Defeat to Rearmament*. Translated from French. New York: Praeger, 1955. 249 p.

One of the standard histories of the recovery of Germany and the beginnings of the Federal Republic. Thorough in scope.

859 _____. *Germany in Our Time: A Political History of the Postwar Years*. Translated from French. New York: Praeger, 1971. 378 p.

A comprehensive history of the first years of the Federal Republic of Germany. Only one chapter deals directly with the occupation period.

Historical Studies

860 GULGOWSKI, PAUL W. *The American Military Government of the United States Occupied Zones of Post World War II Germany in Relation to Policies Expressed by Its Civilian Governmental Authorities at Home, during the Course of 1944/45 through 1949.* Frankfurt am Main: Haag & Herchen, 1983. 438 p.

Examines the relationship between the military government in Germany and the executive and legislative branches of American government at home. In the bibliography there is an excellent description of governmental sources available for research.

861 HEARNDEN, ARTHUR, ed. *The British in Germany: Educational Reconstruction after 1945.* London: Hamilton, 1978. 335 p.

Factual essays on the development of German education in the postwar period.

862 HOCKING, WILLIAM E. *Experiment in Education: What We Can Learn from Teaching Germany.* Chicago: H. Regnery Co., 1954. 303 p.

Teaching democracy to Germans depends on an understanding of its philosophical underpinnings and on the setting of good examples.

863 HOGAN, MICHAEL J. *The Marshall Plan: America, Britain, and the Reconstruction of Western Europe, 1947-1952.* New York: Cambridge University Press, 1987. 482 p.

A recent account of the origins of the Marshall Plan, its purposes, and its accomplishments. Hogan argues that the plan was successful even though Europe was not shaped in the American image.

864 HOLLER, JOANNE E. *The German Expellees: A Problem of Integration.* Washington D.C.: Population Research Project of the George Washington University, 1963. 45 p.

A detailed explanation of the problems faced by the Federal Republic and its citizens in absorbing the millions of ethnic Germans who were driven into the shrunken Reich after the war.

865 JASPERS, KARL. *The Future of Germany.* Translated from German. Chicago: University of Chicago Press, 1967. 173 p.

A philosopher at the University of Basel presents criticisms of western Germany, fearing that it is about to turn its back on parliamentary democracy and embrace dictatorship again.

866 JOHNSEN, JULIA E. *The Dilemma of Postwar Germany*. Reference Shelf, vol. 20, no. 3. New York: H.W. Wilson, 1948. 304 p.

A collection of readings to furnish background material on postwar problems of demilitarization, industrial recovery, denazification, and reeducation in the western zones of Germany.

867 KEE, ROBERT. *1945: The World We Fought For*. London: Hamish Hamilton, 1985. 371 p.

Using newspapers and magazines from 1945, Kee has created a picture of what it was like for the British and Americans to live through the last months of the war and the first months of peace.

868 KELLERMANN, HENRY J. *Cultural Relations as an Instrument of United States Foreign Policy: The Educational Exchange Program Between the United States and Germany, 1945-1954*. Washington, D.C.: Department of State, 1978. 289 p.

An historical study of the origin and development of educational exchanges as a method of developing better relations between Germany and the United States. Also useful as a guide to the documents available from the State Department.

869 KIMBALL, WARREN F. *Swords or Plowshares?, the Morgenthau Plan for Defeated Nazi Germany, 1943-1946*. Philadelphia: Lippincott, 1976. 172 p.

The first third of the book narrates the origin, life, and death of the Morgenthau plan. Documents supporting the development of the plan make up the remainder of the book. Includes a bibliographic essay on postwar planning materials.

870 KOOP, ALLEN V. *Stark Decency: German Prisoners of War in a New England Village*. Hanover, N.H.: University Press of New England, 1988. 136 p.

An old CCC camp in Stark, N.H., was renovated as a camp for German prisoners of war who were to cut pulp wood. Although local relations were strained at first, eventually mutual respect and friendships developed among the prisoners and their guards.

871 KORMANN, JOHN G. *U.S. Denazification Policy in Germany, 1944-1950*. Bad-Godesberg, FRG: Historical Division, Office of the High Commissioner for Germany, 1952. 153 p.

One of several official accounts of specific American policies prepared by the Historical Division of the U.S. military government.

The author gives the historical background, the procedures, and the results of denazification in the U.S. zone.

872 KRAMMER, ARNOLD. *Nazi Prisoners of War in America*. New York: Stein & Day, 1979. 338 p.

Nearly 400,000 Germans were in American prison camps in World War II. Krammer describes their capture, imprisonment, treatment, activities, reeducation methods, impressions of the United States, and their return to Europe and eventually to home.

873 KUBY, ERICH. *The Russians and Berlin, 1945*. Translated from German. New York: Hill & Wang, 1968. 372 p.

A factual, day-by-day account of the battle for Berlin through June 1945. Uses documents, interviews, and eyewitness accounts to substantiate the narrative. Originally published in *Der Spiegel*.

874 KUKLICK, BRUCE. *American Policy and the Division of Germany: The Clash with Russia over Reparations*. Ithaca, N.Y.: Cornell University Press, 1972. 286 p.

Examines the reparations aspect of the Allies' relations after the war. Kuklick suggests that the United States was suspicious of and uncooperative with the Soviet Union and must assume some of the blame for the division of Germany.

875 KURTZ, MICHAEL J. "American Cultural Restitution Policy in Germany during the Occupation, 1945-1949." Ph.D. diss., Georgetown University, 1982. 224 p.

Studies the American diplomatic and administrative policies pursued in returning art objects, libraries, archives, and other cultural property taken by the Germans during the war.

876 LANG, DANIEL. *A Backward Look: Germans Remember*. New York: McGraw-Hill, 1979. 112 p.

Interviews with middle-aged German men who served as teenage anti-aircraft artillery personnel around Aachen during the final years of the war. Gives the opinions of the average man regarding the war, the Third Reich, and the postwar period.

Historical Studies

877 LATTIMORE, BETRAM G. *The Assimilation of German Expellees into the West German Polity and Society since 1945: A Case Study of Eutin, Schleswig-Holstein.* The Hague: M. Nijhoff, 1974. 158 p.

Using city and political party documents, Lattimore traces the assimilation of expellees in a particular city where the strain of absorbing them was severe. Politics are emphasized.

878 LAWSON, ROBERT F. "Reform of the West German School System, 1945-1962." Ph.D. diss., University of Michigan, 1965. 230 p.

Not reviewed.

879 LOWIE, ROBERT H. *Toward Understanding Germany.* Chicago: University of Chicago Press, 1954. 396 p.

Lowie uses diaries, novels, autobiographies, poetry, and history to explain German characteristics and society.

880 McINNIS, EDGAR. *The Shaping of Postwar Germany.* New York: Praeger, 1960. 195 p.

Four Canadian scholars focus on issues important to postwar Germany: its internal division, its role in Europe, the lack of a treaty ending the war, and Berlin's unique position.

881 McKEE, ALEXANDER. *Dresden 1945: The Devil's Tinderbox.* New York: Dutton, 1984. 334 p.

Examines the destruction of Dresden from the viewpoint of the average person. The narrative is based on eyewitness accounts by Dresdeners who survived the bombings and by Allied airmen who carried out the bombing runs. Occurring close to the end of the war, the destruction had postwar repercussions.

882 MARRUS, MICHAEL R. *The Unwanted: European Refugees in the Twentieth Century.* New York: Oxford University Press, 1985. 414 p.

An extended historical study of refugees, with a valuable chapter on the immediate postwar period. Marrus summarizes current research. He states that twelve million ethnic Germans were expelled from eastern Europe in the years following the war.

883 *Memo to America, the DP Story: The Final Report of the U.S. Displaced Persons Commission.* Washington, D.C.: U.S. Displaced Persons Commission, 1952. 376 p.

A history of the work of the commission from 1948 to 1952, during which time the existing barriers to immigration to the United

States were temporarily relaxed, allowing over 400,000 people admittance.

884 MONTGOMERY, JOHN D. *Forced to be Free: The Artificial Revolution in Germany and Japan*. Chicago: University of Chicago Press, 1957. 209 p.

   Looks at the political issues that surround the occupation and the subsequent development of democratic governments in Germany and Japan after the war.

885 MOORE, JOHN H. *The Faustball Tunnel: German P.O.W.s in America and Their Great Escape*. New York: Random House, 1978. 268 p.

   Describes the war experiences and capture of German prisoners, their transportation to Arizona, and their attempts to escape.

886 MORGAN, ROGER. *The United States and West Germany, 1945-1973: A Study in Alliance Politics*. London: Oxford University Press, 1974. 282 p.

   Examines both economic and military issues and seeks to identify the major themes running through the postwar period.

887 MURPHY, HENRY B. M. *Flight and Resettlement*. Paris: UNESCO, 1955. 231 p.

   An international conference discussing the many aspects of refugees and displaced persons. A short chapter on Germany.

888 NETTL, J. P. *The Eastern Zone and Soviet Policy in Germany, 1945-1950*. New York: Oxford University Press, 1951. 324 p.

   A factual, thorough study of the Soviet zone. The book was praised for its value at the time it was published.

889 NEVEN-DU MONT, JÜRGEN. *After Hitler: A Report on Today's West Germans*. Translated from German. New York: Pantheon Books, 1970. 319 p.

   Interviews were conducted with one hundred and twenty-one Heidelbergers in the mid-1960s. They were from every strata of society. Forty-two of the interviews are presented in the book, as examples of how Germans feel about the past and present. Many emphasize the war and immediate postwar period.

Historical Studies

890 PAIKERT, G. C. *The German Exodus: A Selective Study on the Post World War II Expulsion of German Populations and Its Effects.* The Hague: M. Nijhoff, 1962. 97 p.

A factual account of the cause and effect of the expulsion of the ethnic Germans from eastern Europe. Good bibliography.

891 PETERSON, EDWARD N. *The American Occupation of Germany: Retreat to Victory.* Detroit: Wayne State University Press, 1977. 376 p.

Traces the history of military government in the American zone from the U.S. perspective. The last chapter examines the military government in specific cities to illustrate local variations.

892 PHILLIPS, DAVID, ed. *German Universities after the Surrender: British Occupation Policy and the Control of Higher Education.* Oxford: University of Oxford, Dept. of Educational Studies, 1983. 171 p.

Papers prepared for a conference at Oxford. Examines various aspects of the impact of British policies on German universities in their zone.

893 *Postwar Changes in German Education, U.S. Zone and U.S. Sector Berlin.* Frankfurt, FRG: Education Branch, Education and Cultural Relations Division, Office of High Commissioner for Germany, 1951. 294 p.

Analyzes the effects of the U.S. occupation on German education in the American zone.

894 RADSPIELER, TONY. *The Ethnic German in Austria, 1945-1954.* The Hague: M. Nijhoff, 1955. 197 p.

Gives a sympathetic description of the condition of the half-million ethnic Germans who sought asylum in Austria after the war.

895 ROTH, GÜNTHER, and KURT H. WOLFF. *The American Denazification of Germany: A Historical Survey and Appraisal.* Studies in German-American Postwar Problems, no. 1. Columbus: Ohio State University, Dept. of Sociology and Anthropology, 1954. 49 p.

Not reviewed.

896 RUHM von OPPEN, BEATE. *Documents on Germany under Occupation, 1945-1954.* New York: Oxford University Press, 1955. 660 p.

Includes the most important official documents from all four zones of occupation.

897 RUNDELL, WALTER. *Black Market Money: The Collapse of United States Military Currency Control in World War II.* Baton Rouge: Louisiana State University Press, 1964. 125 p.

The military government in the American zone was always one step behind the GIs, who were creative in converting army pay into big money on the German black market.

898 SCHAFFNER, BETRAM H. *Father Land: A Study of Authoritarianism in the German Family.* New York: Columbia University Press, 1948. 203 p.

One of the earlier studies comparing German family traditions with German political traditions.

899 SCHECHTMAN, JOSEPH B. *Postwar Population Transfers in Europe, 1945-1955.* Philadelphia: University of Pennsylvania Press, 1962. 417 p.

An unsympathetic view of the expulsion of ethnic Germans from eastern Europe. Supports the Potsdam agreements and uses official documents to prove that the horror was overstated.

900 SCHMITT, HANS A., ed. *U.S. Occupation in Europe after World War II: Papers and Reminiscences from the April 23-24, 1976, Conference held at the George C. Marshall Research Foundation, Lexington, Virginia.* Lawrence, Kans.: Regents Press of Kansas, 1978. 172 p.

Papers from a conference of scholars and former government officials at which several occupation topics were discussed, including interpretations of Soviet rule in the eastern zone and the issues of the occupation in the American zone of Austria.

901 SCHOENBERG, HANS W. *Germans from the East.* Studies in Social Life, no. 15. The Hague: M. Nijhoff, 1970. 366 p.

Studies the expulsion of the ethnic Germans, their resettlement, and subsequent group history.

Historical Studies

902 SCHWARZ, LEO W. *Refugees in Germany Today.* New York: Twayne, 1957. 172 p.

Analyzes the legal implications of the masses of expellees and assesses the influences on international law.

903 SNELL, JOHN L. *Wartime Origins of the East-West Dilemma over Germany.* New Orleans: Hauser Press, 1959. 268 p.

Examines the wartime planning for the occupation of Germany and follows the evolution of policy changes.

904 SOLBERG, RICHARD W. *God and Caesar in East Germany.* New York: Macmillan, 1962. 294 p.

Traces the postwar deterioration of the relationship of church and state in East Germany. The original neutrality has become open hostility.

905 SORGE, MARTIN K. *The Other Price of Hitler's War: German Military and Civilian Losses Resulting from World War II.* New York: Greenwood Press, 1986. 175 p.

Current estimates of deaths caused by the war, with chapters on regular ground forces, naval, air force, and special troops, civilian losses, damage caused by various partisan groups, and refugees and expellees.

906 STEINERT, MARLIS G. *Hitler's War and the Germans: Public Mood and Attitude during the Second World War.* Translated from German. Athens: Ohio University Press, 1977. 387 p.

During the war, government agents continuously recorded the opinions of German civilians. These records were kept up until the last few weeks of the Reich's existence. Useful for what ordinary people were thinking and for comparison with postwar attitudes.

907 SULLIVAN, MATTHEW B. *Thresholds of Peace: Four Hundred Thousand German Prisoners and the People of Britain, 1944-1948.* London: Hamish Hamilton, 1979. 420 p.

Reconstructs the history of German prisoners in British camps. Through official documents, interviews, and memoirs, Sullivan describes their surrender, transit, interrogation, camp treatment, and return home after the war.

Historical Studies

908 SZAZ, ZOLTAN M. *Germany's Eastern Frontiers: The Problem of the Oder-Neisse Line*. Chicago: H. Regnery, 1960. 256 p.
Attempts to sort through the archival and published materials to present a factual, historical account. Points out that almost every publication has a strong bias. Good bibliography.

909 TAUBER, KURT P. *Beyond Eagle and Swastika: German Nationalism since 1945*. 2 vols. Middletown, Conn.: Wesleyan University Press, 1967.
A comprehensive history of German nationalistic groups that have formed since the war. Describes their interrelationships, their backgrounds, and their connections with prewar groups.

910 TENT, JAMES F. *Mission on the Rhine: Reeducation and Denazification in American-Occupied Germany*. Chicago: University of Chicago Press, 1982. 369 p.
A detailed study of the educational and political aspects of the U.S. occupation.

911 *Transfer of the German Population from Poland: Legend and Reality*. Warsaw: Western Press Agency, 1966. 54 p.
The Polish point of view on the expulsion of the ethnic Germans from the territory now considered western Poland. The transfer was not vindictive but rather was done to ensure peace.

912 TULLY, ANDREW. *Berlin: Story of a Battle*. New York: Simon & Schuster, 1963. Reprint. Westport, Conn.: Greenwood Press, 1977. 304 p.
Describes the end of the war in Berlin using details of people's daily lives to give the personal side of the capture of the city by Soviet troops.

913 *United States and Germany, 1945-1955*. Washington, D.C.: U.S. Department of State, 1955. 55 p.
A brief, straight-forward explanation of major documents and events that shaped American-German relations in the ten years after the war.

914 VERNANT, JACQUES. *The Refugee in the Post-War World*. New Haven: Yale University Press, 1953. 827 p.
Examines the problem of refugees everywhere in the world. Includes statistics and affected legalities.

915 WALLICH, HENRY C. *Mainsprings of German Revival*. New Haven: Yale University Press, 1955. 401 p.

Analyzes Germany's economic revival. It is due less to a miracle and more to successful economic policies practiced by the western Allies and later West German governments.

916 WARBURG, JAMES P. *Germany, Key to Peace*. Cambridge, Mass.: Harvard University Press, 1953. 344 p.

Examines the role of Germany in the political context of postwar Europe.

917 WILLIS, FRANK R. *The French in Germany, 1945-1949*. Stanford, Calif.: Stanford University Press, 1962. 308 p.

A factual, political history of the French zone of occupation. The French worried less about denazification but drained more reparations from their zone than the British or Americans.

918 WINDSOR, PHILLIP. *City on Leave: A History of Berlin, 1945-1962*. New York: Praeger, 1963. 275 p.

An examination of the successive Berlin crises, explaining how each arose out of the postwar situation of four zones of occupation, with four-power rule.

919 WISKEMANN, ELIZABETH. *Germany's Eastern Neighbours: Problems Relating to the Oder-Neisse Line and the Czech Frontier Regions*. London: Oxford University Press, 1956. 309 p.

A balanced, objective study of the disputed borders on Germany's eastern edge, including the Potsdam agreements and the expulsion of the ethnic Germans.

920 WOLFE, ROBERT, ed. *Americans as Proconsuls: United States Military Government in Germany and Japan, 1944-1952*. Carbondale: Southern Illinois University Press, 1984. 563 p.

Papers delivered at a Smithsonian conference in 1977. The participants included experts such as Ziemke, Gimbel, Backer, Clay, McCloy, Backer, and Peterson.

Historical Studies

921 ZIEMKE, EARL F. *The United States Army in the Occupation of Germany, 1944-1946.* Washington, D.C.: U.S. Govt. Printing Office, 1975. 477 p.

Examines the early work of the military government in Germany and traces its evolution from quickly assembled teams left in newly conquered towns to a network of organized units created for the occupation.

CHAPTER *9*

Bibliographies Consulted

This bibliography is based on other bibliographies. From the Library of Congress's extensive subject books to small pamphlets issued by private agencies, each list has contributed to the whole. In a few cases, the bibliographies themselves are so obscure that they are listed but have not been consulted. Other major sources for appropriate citations are to be found in the bibliographies of histories of the period. These cannot be listed separately, of course, but can be deduced from chapter 8.

922 *Audiovisual Materials, 1979-1982.* 4 vols. Washington D.C.: Library of Congress, 1980-1983.
    The latest of several chronological and subject listings of films and filmstrips cataloged by the Library of Congress, starting with 1948, and having several title changes.

923 BAYLISS, G. M., comp. *Bibliographic Guide to the Two World Wars: An Annotated Survey of English Language Reference Material.* New York: Bowker, 1977. 578 p.
    Bibliography of bibliography.

Bibliographies Consulted

924   BETTE, KARL-HEINRICH, comp. *Bibliography of German Sociology, 1945-1977*. Göttingen: O. Schwartz, 1980. 800 p.
   Citations are principally journal articles in German on subjects such as economics, families, relationships, etc.

925   BOSHYK, YURI, and BORIS BALAN, comp. *Political Refugees and "Displaced Persons," 1945-1954: A Selected Bibliography and Guide to Research with Special Reference to Ukranians*.
   Edmonton, Alberta: Canadian Institute of Ukranian Studies of the University of Alberta, 1982. 424 p.

926   BRAY, MAYFIELD S., comp. *Audiovisual Records in the National Archives Relating to World War II*. Washington, D.C.: National Archives, 1971. 41 p.
   Not consulted.

927   BROWN, GENE, ed. *The New York Times Encyclopedia of Film, 1896-1979*. 13 vols. New York: New York Times Books, 1984.

928   CARGAS, HARRY J., comp. *The Holocaust: An Annotated Bibliography*. 2d ed. Chicago: American Library Association, 1985. 196 p.
   The section "Reflections on the Holocaust" was helpful.

929   CONOVER, HELEN F., comp. *The Displaced Persons Analytical Bibliography*. Washington, D.C.: Library of Congress, European Affairs Division, 1950. 82 p.
   Report of a special subcommittee on the Judiciary, House of Representatives.

930   _____, comp. *United States and Europe: A Bibliographical Examination of Thought Expressed in American Publications*. 3 vols. Washington, D.C.: Library of Congress, Reference Dept., European Affairs Division, 1948-53.

931   *Cumulated Fiction Index*. 4 vols. London: Association of Assistant Librarians, 1945-83.
   The subject headings are broad, such as World War II, Germany, and Refugees.

Bibliographies Consulted

932 DEUTSCHE BIBLIOTHEK (FRANKFURT AM MAIN). *Bibliography of German Publications in English Translation, 1972-1976*. Frankfurt am Main: Buchandlen-Vereinigung, 1978. 220 p.

933 ENSER, A. G. S., comp. *A Subject Bibliography of the Second World War: Books in English, 1939-1974*. Boulder, Colo.: Westview, 1977. 592 p.

934 _____, comp. *A Subject Bibliography of the Second World War: Books in English, 1975-1983*. Brookfield, Vt.: Gower, 1985. 225 p.
Both books include all theaters of the war and are arranged by broad subjects. Fiction is omitted, and there are no annotations. The sections "Germany," "Refugees," and "Personal Narratives" were helpful.

935 *Films on UNRRA and Related Subjects*. Washington, D.C.: United Nations Relief and Rehabilitation Administration, Visual Media Branch, 1945.
Not consulted.

936 FUNK, ARTHUR L., comp. *The Second World War, a Bibliography: A Select List of Publications Appearing Since 1968*. Gaines-ville, Fla.: American Committee on the History of the Second World War, 1972. 32 p.

937 _____, comp. *The Second World War: A Select Bibliography of Books in English Published since 1975*. Claremont, Calif.: Regina Books, 1985. 210 p.

938 _____, comp. *A Select Bibliography of Books on World War II Published in the United States, 1966-1975*. [Gainesville, Fla.]: American Committee on History of the Second World War, 1975. 33 p.

939 FUSS, FELICIA, comp. *Displaced Persons: A Selected Bibliography, 1939-1947*. New York: Russell Sage Foundation, 1948. 11 p.

940 HAROLD, JOHN E., comp. *An Annotated Bibliography: The American Military Occupation of Germany, 1945-1949*. Carlisle Barracks, Pa.: Military History Research Collection, 1971. 17 p.
Very helpful.

941 HELT, RICHARD C., and MARIE E. HELT. *West German Cinema since 1945: A Reference Book*. Metuchen, N.J.: Scarecrow Press, 1987. 736 p.

Describes plots and lists producers, directors, casts, and release dates.

942 HERSCH, GISELA, comp. *A Bibliography of German Studies, 1945-1971; Germany under Allied Occupation*. Bloomington: Indiana University Press, 1972. 603 p.

Almost all the citations are in German and the topical divisions are broad.

943 HOTCHKISS, JEANETTE, comp. *European Historical Fiction and Biography for Children and Young People*. 2d ed. Metuchen, N.J.: Scarecrow, 1972. 272 p.

944 *Index to Documents Series of UNRRA, 1943-1949*. United Nations Archives Reference Series, no. 18. N.p., n.d.

Not consulted.

945 KEHR, HELEN, comp. *After Hitler: Germany, 1945-1963*. Prepared for the Wiener Library. London: Vallentine, Mitchell, 1963. 261 p.

Has entries in German, English, and French, with German being the predominent language. When there is a choice, the bibliography usually lists the British imprint only. The citations are grouped by topic. Very helpful.

946 KEHR, HELEN, and JANET LANGMAID. *The Nazi Era, 1919-1945: A Select Bibliography of Books Published, Works from the Early Roots to 1980*. New York: Mansell, 1981. 621 p.

Many citations are in German; the section "After the Fall of the Third Reich" was helpful.

947 LACH, DONALD F. "What They Would Do about Germany." *Journal of Modern History* 17 (September 1945): 227-43.

A survey of the recently published books that gave advice about how to treat Germany when the war was over. The suggested treatment went from taking a hard stance to being generous and forgiving.

Bibliographies Consulted

948 LANDAUER, CARL. "Allies and Germany's Future." *Journal of Modern History* 18 (September 1946): 251-60.

A bibliographical review of recent books about postwar Germany, its political antecedents, and future prospects.

949 _____. "United States Economic Policy Toward Germany." *Journal of Modern History* 19 (September 1947): 239-53.

Examines materials which discuss the changes in policies toward Germany between the Potsdam Conference (July 1945) and the Moscow Conference (March 1947). Considers the changes to be in response to the Soviet policies in the eastern zone.

950 LEE, GUY A. *Guide to Studies of the Historical Division of United States High Commissioner of Germany*. Bad Godesberg-Mehlem: US HICOG, Management and Budget Division, 1954. 131 p.

The U.S. Office of Military Government gave way to the U.S. High Commission when the Federal Republic of Germany was formed. Most of the studies concentrate on aspects of the U.S. High Commission in West Germany after 1948.

951 *Library of Congress Author Catalog: Films, 1948-1952*. Washington, D.C.: Library of Congress, 1953. 410 p.

952 *List of World War II Historical Studies Made by Civilian Agencies of the Federal Government*. Washington, D.C.: National Historical Publications Commission, 1951. 53 p.

Known as the World War II history program, the historical studies concentrate on internal American agencies, not those in Germany.

953 MAGILL, FRANK N., ed. *Magill's Survey of Cinema: Foreign Language Films*. 8 vols. Englewood Cliffs, N.J.: Salem Press, 1985.

954 _____, ed. *Magill's Survey of Contemporary Literature*. 12 vols. Englewood Cliffs, N.J.: Salem Press, 1976.

This set continues as *Magill's Literary Annual*.

955 MERRITT, ANNA J. *Politics, Economics, and Society in the Two Germanies, 1945-1975: A Bibliography of English-Language Works*. Urbana: University of Illinois Press, 1978. 268 p.

Includes citations to journals. The sections "Displaced Persons," "Military Occupation," "Re-education/Post War Views," "Social Conditions," and "Cultural Developments" were helpful.

956 MÖNNING, RICHARD, comp. *Berlin Book List.* 2d ed. Bonn: Inter Nationes, 1963. 15 p.
   Includes fiction as well as nonfiction.

957 _____, comp. *Translations from the German: English, 1948-1964.* 2d rev. ed. Göttingen: Vandenhoeck & Ruprecht, 1968. 509 p.
   Very helpful.

958 MONROE, JAMES L., comp. *Prisoners of War and Political Hostages, a Select Bibliography.* Report A 10-1. Springfield, Va.: Monroe Corp., 1973. 46 p.

959 MORGAN, BAYARD Q., comp. *A Critical Bibliography of German Literature in English Translation.* 2 vols. New York: Scarecrow, 1965.
   Supplements the original, which covered 1928-55. There is no subject approach; arranged by author.

960 *Motion Pictures 1940-1969.* 3 vols. Washington, D.C.: Library of Congress, Copyright Office, 1953-71.

961 MUFFS, JUDITH H., comp. *The Holocaust in Books and Films: A Selected Annotated List.* New York: Center for Studies on the Holocaust, Anti-Defamation League of B'nai B'rith, 1982. 67 p.
   A bibliography of books and films for elementary students through college.

962 *National Union Catalog: Motion Pictures and Film Strips, 1953-1978.* Compiled by the Library of Congress. 17 vols. Ann Arbor, Mich.: J.W. Edwards, 1958-80.

963 PLEYER, PETER. *Deutscher Nachkriegsfilm 1946-48.* Münster: Institut für Publizistik, 1965. 490 p.
   Useful for lists of films licensed by each occupation zone.

964 PRICE, ARNOLD H., comp. *The Federal Republic of Germany: A Select Bibliography of English-Language Publications.* 2d rev. ed. Washington, D.C.: Library of Congress, 1978. 116 p.
   Most citations are for the time period after 1949.

Bibliographies Consulted

965   *Selected Reading List on United Nations Relief and Rehabilitation Administration.* New York: United Nations Information Office, 1945. 10 p.

966   SMITH, MYRON J., comp. *World War II: European and Mediterranean Theatres.* New York: Garland Publishing Co., 1984. 450 p.
      Arranged by subject area, country, and type of service.

967   TAYLOR, PHILIP H., and RALPH J.D. BRAIBANTI. *Administration of Occupied Area: A Study Guide.* Syracuse, N.Y.: Syracuse University Press, 1948. 111 p.
      Citations cover the military occupation from the American point of view.

968   *Union List of UNRRA Films: A Guide to Motion Picture Records Produced by Agencies throughout the World on the Activities of the United Nations Relief and Rehabilitation Administration, 1943-47.* Archives Reference Guide, no. 5. N.p., n.d.
      Not consulted.

969   *World War II from an American Perspective: An Annotated Bibliography.* Santa Barbara, Calif.: ABC-Clio, 1983. 277 p.
      Principally cites articles from American periodicals, not helpful.

970   ZIEGLER, JANET. *World War II: Books in English, 1945-1964.* Stanford, Calif.: Hoover Institution Press, 1971. 223 p.
      Section "Social Impact of the War" was helpful.

Index

Abosch, Heinz, 823
Abzug, Robert H., 824
Account of the Work of the Friends Committee for Refugees, 309
Account Rendered, 66
Acquainted with the Night, 599
Addresses upon the American Road, 180
Adenauer, Konrad, 1
Administration of Occupied Area, 967
Affäre Blum, 735
After Hitler, 889
After Hitler: Germany, 1945-1963, 945
Aftermath, 691
Aftermath: 1945-1946, 337
After Seven Years, 325
After the Flood, 54
Again the Goose Step, 131
Albrand, Martha [pseud.], 596
Alien Years, 134

All Honorable Men, 214
Allied Control Council, Berlin, 152, 235
Allied Military Government of Germany, 160
Allies on the Rhine, 267
Almond, Gabriel, 825
Alvarez del Vayo, Julio, 340
American Association for a Democratic Germany, 154
American Council on Education, 269, 270, 271, 307
"American Cultural Restitution Policy in Germany," 875
American Denazification of Germany, 895
American Experiences in Military Government in World War II, 161
American Federationist, 371

American Friends Service
    Committee, 305, 306, 325
American Journal of Sociology,
    430, 460, 472
American Magazine, 421, 437,
    479, 556
American Mercury, 363, 429,
    441, 482, 510, 511, 525
American Military Government,
    179
*American Military Government
    in Germany*, 303
*American Military Government
    of the United States
    Occupied Zones*, 860
*American Military Occupation
    of Germany*, 852
*American Occupation of
    Germany*, 855, 892
American Perspective, 537
*American Policy and the
    Division of Germany*, 874
American Soldier. Vol. 2,
    *Combat and Its
    Aftermath*, 284
*American Voluntary Aid for
    Germany*, 324
Americans as Proconsuls, 920
America's Germany, 108
*Among the Survivors of the
    Holocaust*, 175
And Call It Peace, 195
And Never Said a Word, 600
Andersch, Alfred, 587, 588
Andersen, Hartvig, 105
Andreas-Friederich, Ruth, 2
Andrews, Stanley, 106
*Annals of the American
    Academy of Political and
    Social Science*, 140, 259,
    451, 500, 502, 532

*Annotated Bibliography: The
    American Military
    Occupation*, 940
Answer of a German, 33
Answers of Ernst von Salomon,
    79
Antioch Review, 461
Apfel Ist Ab, 736
Arche Nora, 737
Archer, Jane, 659
Are You Hungry, Are You Cold,
    590
Ark, 591
Armageddon, 727
Arnold, Elliott, 660
Arnold-Forster, W., 342
*As Far As My Feet Will Carry
    Me*, 21
Assignment Germany, 738
*Assimilation of German
    Expellees into the West
    German Polity and
    Society*, 877
As the Waltz Was Ending, 8
Atlantic, 380, 543, 569
Aubert, Louis, 107
*Audiovisual Materials, 1979-
    1982*, 922
*Audiovisual Records in the
    National Archives*, 926
Austin, Margretta S., 269

Bach, Julian S., 108, 343
Bachmann, E. Theodore, 344
Bachmann, Lawrence P., 661,
    662
Backer, John H., 826, 827, 828
Back to Berlin, 675
Backward Look, 876
Baer, Frank, 589
Bailey, Thomas A., 109
Baker, W. Howard, 663
Balabkins, Nicholas, 829

Index

Balan, Boris, 925
Balfour, Michael L. G., 830
Ballantyne, Jesse, 345
Bannister, Sybil, 110
Bardens, Dennis, 347
Barnsley, Alan G. [pseud., Fielding, Gabriel], 684
Barrett, William E., 664
Barriers Down, 317
Barth, Karl, 3, 348
Barton, Betty, 306
Bauer, Josef M. [pseud., Forell, Clemens], 21
Bavarian Story, 713
Bayley, John, 665
Bayliss, G. M., 923
Beate, 739
Beauchamp, George E., 271
Beck, Earl R., 831
Becker, Hans [pseud.], 4
Beckmann, E., 165
Bekessy, Jean [pseud., Habe, Hans], 172, 691, 692, 693
Belfrage, Cedric, 111
Belgion, Montgomery, 112
Belsen Uncovered, 266
Bemelmans, Ludwig, 590
Benary-Isbert, Margot, 591, 592, 593, 594, 595
Benn, Gottfried, 596
Bentwich, Norman, 349
Berckman, Evelyn, 666
Berger, Thomas, 667
Berlin, 644
Berlin, Beset and Bedeviled, 138
Berlin Book List, 956
Berlin Command, 182
Berlin Couriers, 708
Berlin Diaries, 1940-1945, 291
Berliner. See *Berliner Ballade*
Berliner Ballade, 740
Berlin Express, 741
Berlin '45, the Grey City, 122

Berlin--Kaiser to Khrushchev, 742
Berlin Powderkeg, 743
Berlin Reparations Assignment, 246
Berlin Story, 251
Berlin: Story of a Battle, 912
Berlin Twilight, 129
Berlin Underground, 1938-1945, 2
Berlin Wild, 730
Bernadotte of Wisborg, Folke, 113, 114
Bernhard, Thomas, 5
Berry, Lelah, 350
Bess, Demaree, 351
Betrayal, 190
Bettany, A. G., 352
Bette, Karl-Heinrich, 924
Beveridge, William H., 115
Beymer, William G., 668
Beyond Eagle and Swastika, 909
Beyond the Bridge, 622
Bialek Affair, 92
Bialek, Robert, 92
Bibliographic Guide to the Two World Wars, 923
Bibliography of German Publications in English Translation, 933
Bibliography of German Sociology, 924
Bibliography of German Studies, 942
Bidwell, Percy W., 353
Bielenberg, Christabel, 116
Bieler, Manfred, 597
Bienek, Horst, 598
Bigelow, Karl W., 307
Big Rape, 674
Bingham, Barry, 354
Birds of Migration. See *Zugvögel*
Bitter Harvest, 135

Black Laurel, 698
Black Market Money, 897
Blackwell's Magazine, 558
Blankfort, Alice, 356
Blind Eye to Murder. See *Pledge Betrayed*
Blinding Light. See *If Thine Eye Offend Thee*
Bloch, Marie H., 669
Blockierte Signale, 744
Blow, Jonathan, 357
Blücher von Wahlstatt, Kurt, 6
Blum Affair. See *Affäre Blum*
Boder, David P., 308
Boeker, Alexander, 358, 359
Bohlen, Charles E., 117
Böll, Heinrich, 500, 600, 601, 602, 603, 604, 605
Bollinger, H. D., 360
Bombing of Germany, 745
Bondy, Louis W., 153
Bones of Contention, 290
Books Abroad, 491, 573
Borchert, Wolfgang, 606
Borneman, Ernest, 361
Bornoff, Jacques, 362
Born to Believe, 237
Boshyk, Yuri, 925
Botsford, Keith, 670
Botting, Douglas, 832
Botzenhart-Viehe, Verena, 833
Boulton, S. Miles, 363
Bouman, Pieter J., 118
Bourke-White, Margaret, 119
Bower, Tom, 834
Boy Between, 81
Boyle, Kay, 364, 671, 672
Braibanti, Ralph J. D., 967
Brailsford, H. N., 365, 366
Bramall, Ashley, 367
Brandt, Karl, 120, 121, 368, 369
Bratter, Herbert M., 370
Bray, Mayfield S., 926

Bread of the Oppressed, 314
Bread of Those Early Years, 601
Breaking Down the Barrier, 77
Brett-Smith, Richard, 122
Bridge, 621
Bridge. See *Brücke*
Bridges over the Rhine, 200, 232
British in Germany, 861
British Zone Review, 123
Brockway, Fenner, 124
Brodrick, Alan H., 125
Brown, Gene, 927
Brown, Irving J., 371
Brown, Lewis H., 126
Brown, Liane I., 7
Brücke, 746, 747
Brückner, Christine, 607
Buckham, Robert, 127
Buckner, Robert H., 673
Bundesministerium für Angelegenheiten der Vertriebenen, 28
Bundesministerium für Vertriebene, Flüchtlinge und Kriegsgeschädigte, 62, 63, 82
Burchett, Wilfred G., 128
Burck, Gilbert, 372, 373
Burden of Guilt, 97
Burke, James W., 674
Business Week, 425, 530
Butler, Harold, 374
Butterworth, Emma M., 8
Byford-Jones, Wilfred, 129
By the Rivers of Babylon, 323

Cambridge University. Dept. of Experimental Medicine, 286
Camp of All Saints, 791
Canadian Forum, 345, 464, 559
Cannibal, 695
Captain Pax, 19

Care and Help for Expellees, Refugees, Victims of Material War Damage, 28
Carey, Jane P. C., 375
Cargas, Harry J., 928
Caritas, 324
Carleton, Verna B., 675
Carmichael, Joel, 376
Cassidy, Velma H., 130
Castle on the Border, 592
Catholic World, 423, 478, 484, 514
Cavert, Samuel M., 377
Ceram, C. W., 103
Challenge. See *Ruf*
Chemie und Liebe, 748
Chesney, Inga L., 9
Child of Hitler, 39
Child of the Revolution, 58
Children Are Civilians Too, 602
Children, Mothers, and a General. See *Kinder, Mütter, und ein General*
Children of Vienna, 641
Christen, Peter, 10
Christian Century, 341, 344, 348, 359, 360, 377, 378, 390, 394, 399, 412, 453, 456, 497, 516, 527, 564, 577, 578
City on Leave, 918
Civil Affairs and Military Government, 844
Civis Germanicus [pseud.], 379
Clark, Delbert, 131
Clark, Penny, 835
Clay, Lucius D., 132
Clockmaker of Heidelberg, 680
Clown, 603
Cohn, David L., 380
Cold War in Germany, 128
Cole, John A., 133
Colliers, 524

Collins, Sarah M., 134, 135
Collis, Robert, 136
Colossus Again, 858
Come as a Conqueror, 143
Comeback for Germany, 749
Comeback: Germany, 1945-1952, 212
Coming Home from the War, 633
Commentary, 403
Commercial and Financial Chronicle, 368, 526
Committee Against Mass Expulsions, 11
Commonweal, 346, 382, 438, 463, 518, 520
Condemned of Altona, 723
Conference on Health and Human Relations in Germany, 137
Confessions of the "Old Wizard", 80
Conlon, William H., 138
Connell, Brian, 139
Conner, Sydney, 140
Conover, Denise O., 836
Conover, Helen F., 929, 930
Conqueror's Peace, 184
Conte, Manfred, 608
Contemporary Review, 349, 379, 413, 420, 515, 540, 547, 566
Control Commission for Germany (British Element), 123, 144, 247
Control of Germany, 107
Cornhill Magazine, 470
Coser, Lewis A., 382
Cotterell, Geoffrey, 676
Cottrell, Donald P., 383
Cousins, Norman, 384
Crack in the Wall, 55
Craig, Gordon A., 837

Crane, 657
Crane, Edward M., 164
Crawley, Aidan, 838, 839
Crazy in Berlin, 667
Creating a New State, 13
Crime of Our Age, 162
Critical Bibliography of German Literature, 959
Cross, James. See Parry, H. J.
Crossman, R. H. S., 386, 387, 388, 389
Crowd Is Not Company, 191
Cruelest Night, 843
Crusade in Nuremberg, 840
Crutches, 623
Cultural Relations as an Instrument of United States Foreign Policy, 868
Cultural Relations with the Occupied Countries, 270
Cumulated Fiction Index, 931
Current History, 410, 452, 563
Curtain Falls, 113

Dachau: The Harrowing of Hell, 268
Dance of Death, 50
Dancing Bear, 155, 647
Dangerous Spring, 593
Danger Spot of Europe, 125
Daniel, Eugene L., 141
Daniell, Raymond, 392
Daniel, Vera, 349
Dark Arena, 722
Dark City, 105
Darkness over the Land, 726
Darkness over the Valley, 88
Darton, Laurence, 309
Dastrup, Boyd L., 840
Davenport, John, 393
Davidson, Basil, 142
Davidson, David A., 678
Davidson, Eugene, 841

Davis, Franklin M., 143
Davis, Jerome, 394
Day before Sunrise, 733
Day, Ingeborg, 12
Dear Fatherland, Rest Quietly, 119
Death and Life of Germany, 841
Death in Berlin, 699
Death in Rome, 634
Decision in Germany, 132
Decision to Divide Germany, 826
Defeat in the East. See *Flight in the Winter*
Degens, T., 609
Denazification, 850
Denazification, Occupation and Control of Germany, 279
Deneke, Helena, 144
Dependent Baggage, 295
Derrick, Michael, 396
Desperate Moment, 586
Deutsche Bibliothek (Frankfurt am Main), 932
Deutscher Nachkriegsfilm 1946-48, 963
Devil on My Shoulder, 4
De Zayas, Alfred M., 842
Diary of a Nightmare, 49
Dibner, Martin, 679
Dickens, Arthur G., 145
Dickson, Alec, 397
Dietrich, Hermann R., 13
Dilemma of Postwar Germany, 866
Dimont, Charles, 398
Diplomat among Warriors, 228
Discourse with Shadows, 712
Dismantling the Ruhr Valley, 37
Displaced Person, 669
Displaced Persons Analytical Bibliography, 929

Displaced Persons: A Selected Bibliography, 939
Displaced Persons Operations, 327
Divided Germany, 750
Dobie, J. Frank, 402
Döblin, Alfred, 403
Dobran, Edward A., 146
Dobson, Christopher, 843
Documents of Humanity during the Mass Expulsions, 56
Documents on Germany under Occupation, 896
Documents on the Expulsion of the Germans, 82
Documents on the Expulsion of the Sudeten Germans, 94
Doernberg, Stefan, 14
Dog Years, 619
Donner, Jörn, 147
Donnison, Frank S., 844
Dos Passos, John, 148
Doutiné, Heike, 610
Doyle, Frederick J., 845
Drath, Viola H., 846
Dreher, Carl, 404
Dresden 1945, 881
Duns Review, 503
Dushnyck, Walter, 149

Earth and Fire, 598
Eastern Zone and Soviet Policy in Germany, 888
East Prussian Journal. See *Token of a Covenant*
Ebsworth, Raymond, 150
Eckardt, Wolfgang, 407
Ecke, Wolfgang, 611
Economic Policies, Programs and Requirements in Occupied Germany, 151

Economic Recovery in the Countries Assisted by UNRRA, 328
Economist, 406, 426
Edding, Friedrich, 847
Edge of Darkness. See *Edge of Night*
Edge of Night, 721
Edmonds, Henry M., 680
Edmondson, Paul, 681
Education, 481
Edwards, Julia, 682
Egan, Eileen M., 310
Ehe der Maria Braun, 751
Ehe im Schatten, 752
Eich, Hermann, 15
Einsiedel, Heinrich, Graf von, 16
1-2-3 [Eins-Zwei-Drei] Corona, 753
Embattled Witness, 36
Embers Still Burn, 177
Emigration, 31
Emmrich, Kurt, 17
Enactments and Approved Papers of the Control Council, 152
End of a Berlin Diary, 263, 543
Enemies Are Human, 75
Enough, No More, 100
Enser, A. G. S., 933, 934
Epitaph on Nuremberg. See *Victor's Justice*
Erika. See *Fräulein*
Escape from Germany, 838
Es Liegt an Dir, 754
Ethnic German in Austria, 894
Europe and the German Refugees, 42
European Historical Fiction and Biography for Children, 943

European Refugees, 1939-52, 245
European Witness, 274
Europe 1945/46, 153
Europe's Homeless Millions, 315
Europe's Suicide in Germany, 217
Evangelische Kirche in Deutschland, 311, 312, 313
Evil of Time, 666
Expellees Are Working, 74
Expellees in the German Federal Republic, 62
Experiment in Education, 862
Experiment in Germany, 236
Experiment in International Cultural Relations, 271
Exploding Star, 69

Facts about Occupied Germany, 154
Faecke, Peter, 612
Fährmann, Willi, 613
Fall, Cyril, 409
Fanger, Horst, 614
Farewell to Europe, 704
Farewell to Germany, 22
Farm Work and Friendship, 835
Farquharson, John E., 848
Father Land, 898
Faulk, Henry, 849
Faustball Tunnel, 885
Faviell, Frances. See Parker, Olivia
Fay, Sidney B., 410
Federal Republic of Germany, 964
Fehling, Helmut M., 16
Ferguson, Clarence, 156
Fernau, Joachim, 19
Fetter, Joseph, 157

Fey, Harold E., 412
Fielding, Gabriel. See Barnsley, Alan G.
50 Facts about UNRRA, 331
Film ohne Titel, 755
Films on UNRRA and Related Subjects, 935
Film without Name. See *Film ohne Titel*
Final Ball, 616
Finale, 756
Firebugs, 612
Fire in the Ashes, 298
First Steps into a New Germany, 14
Fischer, Alfred J., 413
Fischer, Bertha, 615
Fittkau, Gerhard A., 20
Fitzgibbon, Constantine, 850
Flee the Wolf, 83
Flight and Resettlement, 887
Flight in the Winter, 93
Flight of Cranes, 607
Flight towards Home, 611
Floore, Frances B., 314
Fly Away Home, 642
Food Situation in Continental Europe, 330
Forced March to Freedom, 127
Forced to be Free, 884
Foreign Affair, 757
Forell, Clemens. See Bauer, Josef M.
Forests of the Night, 660
Forman, James, 685
Fortnightly, 435, 454, 496, 517, 531, 551
Fortress, 626
Fortune, 372, 373, 393
Forum, 358, 407
For You the War Is Over, 851
Four-Power Control in Germany and Austria, 830

Index

Four Year Report, 158
Foy, David A., 851
Fraenkel, Heinrich, 22, 23, 415, 416, 417
Fragebogen. See *Answers of Ernst von Salomon*
Francke, Gunhild, 24
Frat Wagon, 731
Fräulein, 708
Frederiksen, Oliver J., 852
Freedom and Union, 354
Free Land. See *Freies Land*
Freeman, Dexter L., 159
Freies Land, 758
French in Germany, 917
Friedmann, Wolfgang, 160
Friedrich, Carl J., 140, 161
Friedrich, Otto, 686
Friends Committee for Refugees and Aliens, 309
Friends in High Places, 729
Frisch, Max, 25
Fritsch, Ludwig A., 162
From Military Government to State Department, 10
From Scratch, a Report in Pictures, 43
From the Ashes of Disgrace, 273
From the Ruins of the Reich, 832
Funk, Arthur L., 936, 937, 938
Furmanski, H. R. R., 26
Fuss, Felicia, 939
Future of Germany, 865

Gainham, Sarah, 687
Gaiser, Gerd, 616
Gansberg, Judith M., 853
Gant, Roland, 163
Gardiner, Gerald, 419
Gardner, Brian, 854
Garten, Hugo F., 420
Garthaus, Ils M., 27

Gaskill, Gordon, 421
Gathering Evidence: A Memoir, 5
Geissler, Christian, 617
General, 643
Generation without Farewell, 671
Genet, 422
German Attempts at Picturing Germany, 301
German Book Publishing and Allied Subjects, a Report, 164
German Catastrophe, 67
German Children, 759
German Community under American Occupation, 856
German Diary, 124
German Exodus, 890
German Expellee Problem, 28
German Expellees, 63, 864
German Faces, 285
German Federal Republic. Bundesministerium für. See Bundesministerium für ...
Germania, Anno Zero, 760
German Journey, 213
German Lesson, 636
German Mentality, 292
German Notebook, 208
German Officer, 690
"German Prisoners of War in the Southwest United States," 845
"German Reaction to the American Occupation," 833
German Realities, 283
German Requiem, 610
Germans, 257, 838

175

Germans: An Indictment of My People, 91
Germans from the East, 901
Germans on Trial, 207
Germans: Public Opinion Polls, 72
German Talks Back, 38
German Universities after the Surrender, 892
Germany, 761, 762, 763
Germany after the Fall, 764
Germany and Austria in May-June 1947, 265
Germany and the Future of Europe, 225
Germany, a Series of Photos of the U.S. Zone, 165
Germany, Bridge or Battleground, 296
Germany Divided, 244, 765
Germany--Handle with Care!, 766
Germany in Defeat, 196
Germany in Our Time, 859
Germany in World Politics, 846
Germany, Key to Europe, 767
Germany, Key to Peace, 916
Germany: Key to Peace in Europe, 120
Germany, My Host, 133
Germany, Nation or No-Man's Land, 297
Germany, 1947-1949, 130
Germany Revisited, 166
Germany's Eastern Frontiers, 908
Germany's Eastern Neighbours, 919
Germany Surrenders, 768
Germany Today, 769
Germany under Direct Controls, 829
Germany under Occupation, 241

Germany, What Now, 142, 189
Germany, Year Zero. See *Germania, Anno Zero*
Germany: Yesterday and Tomorrow, 68
Ghost Waltz: A Memoir, 12
Gibbons, W. J., 149
Gibbs, Philip H., 688
Gift Horse, 51
Gillyflower Kid, 697
Gimbel, John, 855, 856, 857
Girl Survives, 289
Gittler, Lewis F., 429
Glaeser, Ernst, 618
Glaser, Daniel, 430
Glaser, Hermann, 29
God and Caesar in East Germany, 904
God for Tomorrow, 679
Goldsmith, M. K., 562
Gollancz, Victor, 166, 167, 168, 169, 170, 431, 432
Gollwitzer, Helmut, 30
Goodykoontz, Bess, 433
Gordon, Selwyn, 434
Gordon Walker, Patrick C., 171
Gorer, Geoffrey, 435
Göttinger Arbeitskreis, 31, 56
Governing Postwar Germany, 205
Grass, Günter, 619, 620
Grau, Karl F., 32
Greene, Harris, 689
Green Frontier, 632
Gregor, Manfred, 621
Griffiths, Eldon W., 436
Grimm, Hans, 33
Grosser, Alfred, 858, 859
Group Captives, 849
Group Portrait with Lady, 604
Groussard, Serge, 690
Grube Morgenrot, 770
Gruesome Harvest, 193

Index

Grund, Josef C., 622
Grün, Max von der, 34
Guide to Studies of the Historical Division, 950
Gulgowski, Paul W., 860
Gunnison, Royal A., 437
Gurian, Waldemar, 438

Habe, Hans. See Bekessy, Jean
Hagen, Paul, 439
Hagen, Renate, 96
Hahn, Lili, 35
Hale, William H., 440
Hall, Adam [pseud.], 694
Hallo Fraülein, 771
Hanser, Richard, 441
Häring, Bernhard, 36
Harkort, G., 442
Harold, John E., 940
Harper's, 353, 361, 440, 498
Harrington, Gordon, 443
Härtling, Peter, 623
Hasenack, Wilhelm, 37
Hauser, Ernest O., 444, 445, 446
Hauser, Heinrich, 38
Hausfrau at War, 101
Havighurst, Robert J., 173
Hawkes, John, 695
Hawkins, Thomas, 447
Health Conditions among the Civilian Population, 319
Health Recovery in Europe, 210
Hearnden, Arthur, 861
Heaven Pays No Dividends, 627
Heck, Alfons, 39
Heinrich, Willi, 624, 625
Hell Above and Hell Below, 204
Hell in Siberia, 73
Helt, Marie E., 941
Helt, Richard C., 941
Here Is Germany, 772
Heritage, 637

Hermans, Ferdinand A., 449
Herman, Stewart W., 174
Herr vom andern Stern, 773
Hersch, Gisela, 942
Herzkönig, 774
Hesse, a New German State, 159
Heymont, Irving, 175
Hibbs, Ben, 450
Hidden Damage, 281
High Cost of Vengeance, 288
Hilldring, John A., 451
Hill, Russell, 176
Hirsch, Felix E., 452
Hirschmann, Ira A., 177
Hitler's War and the Germans, 906
Hocking, William E., 862
Hoehler, Fred K., 315
Hoemberg, Elisabeth S., 178
Hogan, Michael J., 863
Hogerziel, Hans, 136
Holborn, Hajo, 179
Holborn, Louise W., 316
Holler, Joanne E., 864
Holm, Anne, 696
Holocaust: An Annotated Bibliography, 928
Holocaust in Books and Films, 961
Hommen, Willi, 454
Hoover, Herbert C., 180
Hopman, A. N., 455
Hornstein, Erika von, 40
Horses of Anger, 685
Horstmann, Lali von Schwabach, 41
Hotchkiss, Jeanette, 943
House on the Rhine, 683
Howard, Elizabeth F., 317
Howell, Forrest W., 181
Howley, Frank L., 182
How Like a Wilderness, 163
Howl Like the Wolves, 34

How Wars End, 262
Hughes, William R., 183
Hulme, Kathryn, 318
Hunger, 775
Hunger's Rogues, 255
Hutchinson, Paul, 456
Hutchinson, Ray C., 697
Hutchison, Keith, 457
Hutton, Oram C., 184

Ich War 19, 776
I Did Not Interview the Dead, 308
If Thine Eye Offend Thee, 648
I Joined the Russians, 16
I Lived under Hitler, 110
Illustrated London News, 409, 458
In Another Country, 665
In Darkest Germany, 167
Index to Documents Series of UNRRA, 944
Information Bulletin, 185
In Germany Now, 238
In jenen Tagen, 777
Inside Story of UNRRA, 322
Inside the Vicious Heart, 824
Instead of Arms, 114
Institut zur Förderung Öffentlicher Angelegenheiten, 42
Integration of Refugees into German Life, 186
International Affairs, 342
International Committee of the Red Cross, 319, 320
International Journal, 471
International Labour Review, 468
International Refugee Organization, 316, 321
Inter Nationes, 956

In the Presence of Mine Enemies, 141
In the Wake of Battle, 201
In the Wake of the Armies, 329
In Those Days. See *In jenen Tagen*
Investigating Officer, 700
Invisible Flag, 17
Irgendwo in Berlin, 778
Is There Still a Chance for Germany?, 121
It's Up to You. See *Es Liegt an Dir I Was 19*. See *Ich War 19*

Jaeger, Henry, 626
Jaenicke, Wolfgang, 43
"James F. Byrnes, Germany, and the Cold War," 836
Jameson, Storm, 698
Janowitz, Morris, 460
Jaspers, Karl, 187, 865
Jeopardy, 608
Jerome, V. J., 188
Joesten, Joachim, 189, 461
Johnsen, Julia E., 866
Jordan, Philip, 462
Jordy, William H., 463
Journal of a Retread, 106
Journal of Central European Affairs, 535, 574, 584
Journal of Modern History, 947, 948, 949
Journey into Desolation, 240
Justice Comes to Germany, 779

Kahn, Arthur D., 190
Kalow, Gert, 44
Kanaar, A. C., 465
Kanter, Trudi, 45
Kaps, Johannes, 46, 47, 48
Kardorff, Ursula von, 49
Kaufmann, Richard, 627

Index

Kaye, Mary M., 699
Keefe, Frederick L., 700
Keefe, William F., 192
Keeling, Ralph F., 193
Kee, Robert, 191, 867
Kehr, Helen, 945, 946
Kein Platz für Liebe, 780
Kelber, Magda, 466, 467
Kellermann, Henry J., 868
Kellogg, Virginia, 701
Kelly, Matthew A., 468
Kern, Erich, 50
Kern, Harry, 469
Kessell, Mary, 470
Keyserlingk, Robert W., 471
Kimball, Warren F., 869
Kinder, Mütter, und ein General, 781
Kirkpatrick, Clifford, 472
Kirstein, Lincoln, 473
Kirst, Hans H., 628
Klaas, Joe, 702
Klaussner, Wolf, 629
Klemme, Marvin, 322
Klimov, Gregory, 194
Knappen, Marshall M., 195
Knauth, Percy, 196, 474, 475, 476
Knef, Hildegard, 51
Knickerbocker Weekly, 571
Knop, Werner G., 197, 477
Know Your Germans, 6
Koehn, Ilse, 52, 630
Koeppen, Wolfgang, 631
Köhler, Albert, 53
Konstantin, Prinz von Bayern, 54
Koop, Allen V., 870
Kopelev, Lev, 198
Kormann, John G., 871
Körner, Wolfgang, 632
Kospoth, B. J., 199
Krammer, Arnold, 872

Krantz, Paul, 200
Kraus, Charles H., 201
Krause, Walter C., 202
Krebs, Richard J. H. [pseud., Valtin, Jan], 728
Kriegie, 264
Kriegsgefangenen, 219
Kriegsgefangener 3074, Prisoner-of-War, 156
Krüger, Horst, 55
Kruger, Rayne, 703
Kruk, Zofia, 203
Krüss, James, 633
Kuby, Erich, 873
Kuehnelt-Leddihn, Erick von, 478
Kuklick, Bruce, 874
Kunzig, Robert L., 479
Kupferne Hochzeit, 782
Küpper, Heinz, 634
Kurth, K. O., 56
Kurtz, Michael J., 875

Lach, Donald F., 947
Ladies Home Journal, 583
Landauer, Carl, 948, 949
Land of the Dead, 11
Landscape in Concrete, 638
Lang, Daniel, 876
Langgässer, Elisabeth, 635
Lang Ist der Weg, 783
Langmaid, Janet, 946
Lania, Leo, 480
Laqueur, Walter, 704
Larson, Ruth, 481
Last Days and the First, 84
Last of the Conquerors, 725
Last Train West, 24
Lattimore, Betram G., 877
Lawson, Robert F., 878
Leaving Them to Their Fate, 168
Lee, Guy A., 950
Lehndorff, Hans von, 57

179

Index

Lenz, Siegfried, 636, 637
Leonhard, Wolfgang, 58
Lest I Fall, 732
Let Not Your Flight Be in Winter, 659
Letters from Germany, 59
Let Us Live, 784
Lewis, Richard H., 204
Library Journal, 513
Library of Congress Author Catalog: Films, 951
Lid Lifts, 171
Liebe '47, 785
Life, 343, 400, 474, 476, 522, 529, 585
Life Can Be Cruel, 26
Life for a Life, 614
Lindeman, Eduard C., 485
Lind, Jakov, 638
List of World War II Historical Studies, 952
Litchfield, Edward H., 205
Litvinoff, Emanuel, 705
Living Conditions in Germany in 1947, 311
Living with Crisis, 89
Loewengard, Heide H., 586
Logan, Andy, 486, 487
Lonely Conqueror, 624
Long Way Home, 594
Lost Europeans, 705
Loucheim, Katie, 488
Love '47. See *Liebe '47*
Löwenstein, Prinz Hubertus, 60
Löwenthal, Fritz, 61
Lowie, Robert H., 879
Lübeck Diary, 145
Ludwig, Emil, 206
Lukaschek, Hans, 62, 63
Lunau, Heinz, 207
Lundholm, Anja, 639

Mabley, Edward, 706
McCormick, Anne O., 489
McDougall, Ian, 208
McGovern, James W., 707, 708, 709
MacInnes, Colin, 710
McInnis, Edgar, 880
McKee, Alexander, 881
McKee, Ilse, 64
Mackenzie, Norman, 490
Mackinnon, Marianne, 65
McMahon, Finn, 711
McMillan, Lewis K., 209
MacNalty, Arthur S., 210
McNeill, Margaret, 323
McSweeney, Edward, 324
Magill, Frank N., 953, 954
Magill's Survey of Cinema: Foreign Language Films, 953
Magill's Survey of Contemporary Literature, 954
Maginnis, John J., 211
Mainsprings of German Revival, 915
Mair, J., 830
Malcolm, Jean, 712
Man Between, 786
Mann, Anthony, 212
Mannin, Ethel, 213, 713
Man Outside, 606
March the Ninth, 697
Marcus, Alan, 714
Marcuse, Ludwig, 491
Mark of Shame, 625
Marriage in the Shadow. See *Ehe im Schatten*
Marriage of Maria Braun. See *Die Ehe der Maria Braun*
Marrus, Michael R., 882
Marshall, Bruce, 715
Marshall Plan, 863
Marshall Plan Summer, 109
Martin, James S., 214

Martin, Kingsley, 492
Martyrdom and Heroism of the Women of East Germany, 46
Martyrdom of Silesian Priests, 47
Maschmann, Milita, 66
Maser, Clifford, 325
Master Race, 670
Max's Gang, 589
Maybe I'm Dead, 702
Mayer, Arthur L., 493, 494
Mayer, Milton S., 215
Meinecke, Friedrich, 67
Mellor, W. Franklin, 210
Melrose, Georgiana, 216
Memoirs, 1945-1953, 1
Memo to America, the DP Story, 883
Men, 650
Menace of the Miracle, 823
Menck, Clara, 495
Mende, Tibor, 217, 496
Menschen in Gottes Hand, 787
Men without the Rights of Men, 12
Merkl, Peter H., 68
Merritt, Anna J., 218, 955
Merritt, Richard L., 218
Metcalf, Clayton G., 219
Metternich, Tatiana, 220
Michelfelder, Sylvester C., 497
Middle of Midnight, 668
Middleton, Drew, 221
Military Government Gazette, 222
Military Government Journal, 211
Millar, George R., 716
Miller, Douglas, 499
Miller, John, 843
Millin, Sarah G., 223
Mins, Leonard, 706

Mischling, Second Degree, 52
Misse Sine Nomine. See *Tidings*
Mission on the Rhine, 910
Model Childhood, 655
Molden, Fritz, 69
Mönning, Richard, 956, 957
Monroe, James L., 958
Montgomery, John D., 884
Monthly Report of the Military Governor, 224
Moore, John H., 885
Moosdorf, Johanna, 640
Moral Conquest of Germany, 206
Mörder Sind unter Uns, 788
Morgan, Bayard Q., 959
Morgan, Roger, 886
Morgen Ist alles Besser, 789
Morgenthau, Hans J., 225
Morituri, 790
Mosley, Leonard O., 226
Motion Pictures 1940-1969, 960
Mozart Leaves at Nine, 689
Muffs, Judith H., 961
Muhlen, Norbert, 227, 500
Muir, Malcolm, 501
Müller, Traudie W., 70
Murderers Are among Us. See *Die Mörder Sind unter Uns*
Murphy, Henry B. M., 887
Murphy, Robert D., 228
My Disappearance in Providence, 587
My Host Michel. See *Germany, My Host*
My Name is Celia, 703
My Past Was an Evil River, 716
My Road to Freedom, 85
My Thirty-third Year, 20

Nabokov, Nicolas, 229
Naked before My Captors, 718

Naked Years, 65
Napoli, Joseph F., 502
Napp, Ralph R., 77
Nassauer, Rudolf, 717
Nation, 340, 364, 376, 457, 462, 473, 509, 552, 557
Nationale Front des Demokratischen Deutschland, 71
National Geographic Magazine, 402
National Review, 397, 553
National Union Catalog: Motion Pictures and Film Strips, 962
Nation Divided, 23
Nation's Business, 370, 499, 523, 581
Nation's Gethsemane, 276
Nazi Childhood, 99
Nazi Era, 1919-1945, 946
Nazi Prisoners of War in America, 872
Nelson, Saul, 503
Nemesis at Potsdam, 842
Nettle, Peter, 504
Nettl, J. P., 888
Neumann, Robert, 641
Neven-du-Mont, Jürgen, 889
Newell, Bergen F., 718
New German Republic Born, 791
New Republic, 424, 485, 493, 504, 546, 580
News from Soviet Germany, 61
New Statesman and Nation, 365, 366, 367, 386, 387, 388, 389, 391, 398, 415, 416, 431, 432, 459, 483, 490, 492, 508, 533, 572
Newsweek, 469, 501, 506, 519
New Yorker, 422, 486, 487, 539

New York Times Encyclopedia of Film, 927
New York Times Magazine, 392, 489, 538, 544, 562
Next Door, 640
Nina, 645
1945: The World We Fought For, 867
Nineteenth Century and After, 362, 465, 568, 582
Nizer, Louis, 230
Noelle-Neumann, Elisabeth, 72
No Jail for Thought. See *To Be Preserved Forever*
No Place for Love. See *Kein Platz für Liebe*
Nora's Ark. See *Arche Nora*
Nork, Karl, 73
Norman, Albert, 231
Norris, Betty, 144
North to Freedom, 696
No Ruined Castles, 709
Nöstlinger, Christine, 642
Noth, Ernst E., 232
Nothing but Tears. See *We Chose to Stay*
Nowakowski, Tadeusz, 719
Nuremberg, 792
Nuremberg Trials, 793
Nürnberg, 1948. See *Nuremberg*
Nürnberg und seine Lehren, 794

Oberländer, Theodor, 74
Oberländer Trust, 282
Occupation of Germany, 233
Occupiers, 682
O'Donnell, James P., 506
O'Donnell, Joseph P., 234
Office of Military Government for Berlin Sector, U.S., 158

Office of Military Government, U.S. Zone, 151, 222, 224, 242, 261
Official Gazette of the Control Council, 235
Off Limits, 692
Old Friends and New Music, 229
One Great Prison, 18
One-Two-Three Corona. See *Eins-Zwei-Drei Corona*
Only Way: How Can the Germans Be Cured?, 3
On the Other Side, 102
Operational Analysis Papers, 330
Operation Thunderbolt, 795
Opitz, Karlludwig, 643
Ordeal by Fire, 294
Ordinary German, 239
Origins of the Marshall Plan, 857
Other Price of Hitler's War, 905
Our German Policy, 231
Our Love Affair With Germany, 172
Our Threatened Values, 169

Pabel, Reinhold, 75
Padover, Saul K., 236, 509, 510, 511
Paikert, G. C., 890
Pakenham, Lord, 237
Palace Hotel. See *Zwischen Gestern und Morgan*
Paquin, Grete, 96
Pargiello, Jan S., 512
Parker, Olivia [pseud., Faviell, Frances], 155, 683
Parliament, 565
Parry, H. J. [pseud., Cross, James], 677

Past Is Myself. See *Ride out the Dark*
Payne, Ronald, 843
Peiss, Reuben, 513
Peterson, Edward N., 891
Peterson, Theodore C., 514
Peters, William, 238
Phillips, David, 892
Phoenix, 661
Pick, F. W., 515
Picton, Harold W., 239
Pie, Arthur B., 240
Pilgrims of the Night, 326
Piper, Otto A., 516
Pledge Betrayed, 834
Pleyer, Peter, 963
Plievier, Theodor, 644
Polish Review, 401, 512
Political Quarterly, 417
Political Refugees and Displaced Persons, 925
Politics, Economics, and Society in the Two Germanies, 955
Pollock, James K., 241
Poor in Spirit, 686
Popkin, Zelda, 720
Population of the U.S. Zone of Germany, 242
Post Bellum Blues, 711
Postwar Changes in German Education, 893
Postwar Germans, 252
Postwar Population Transfers in Europe, 899
Powell, Robert, 517
POW Odyssey, 275
P.O.W., the Story of an American Prisoner of War, 146
Prebble, John, 721

Prelude to the Long Happy Life of Maximilian Goodman, 651
Price, Arnold H., 964
Price, Hoyt, 243
Primal Vision, 596
Priming the German Economy, 827
Prisoners of War and Political Hostages, 958
Prittie, Terence C., 244
Private Worlds, 687
Problem of Germany, 243
Problem of 12 Million German Refugees in Today's Germany, 306
Proudfoot, Malcolm J., 245
Prowling Russia's Forbidden Zone, 197
Prussian Nights, 272
Public Opinion in Occupied Germany, 218
Public Opinion Quarterly, 576
Purgatory of Fools, 220
Puzo, Mario, 722

Quaker Relief, 338
Quarterly Review, 357, 548
Quest, 635
Quest for Christa T, 656
Question of German Guilt, 187
Questions and Answers Relative to the German Refugee Problem, 312
Quiller Memorandum, 694

Radspieler, Tony, 894
Rainbow in the Night, 639
Randle in Springtime, 676
Rape of Berlin, 87, 663
Ratchford, Benjamin, 246
Razzia, 796

Rebirth of the German Church, 174
Red Wins, 199
Re-educating Germany, 250
"Reform of the West German School System," 878
Refuge, 7
Refugee in the Post-War World, 914
Refugee Problem in Western Germany, 118
Refugees are People, 149
Refugees as a Burden, a Stimulus, and a Challenge, 847
Refugees Courageous, 76
Refugees in Germany Today, 902
Reinhold, H. A., 520
Reiss, Elizabeth C., 310
Remembrance Day, 658
Reparations, 717
Report from Berlin, 147
Report from Germany, 226
Report from Hamburg, 339
Report from Inside Germany in Late Summer and Early Autumn, 209
Report of the Control Commission for Germany (British Element), 247
Report of the Director General, 321
Report of the International Committee of the Red Cross, 320
Report of the United States Education Mission to Germany, 248
Report on Conditions in Central Europe, 305
Report on Germany, 126

Report on Germany for the Rockefeller Foundation, 173
Report on the Germans, 299
Report on the Refugee Situation, 797
Research in Germany on Pressing Social Problems, 282
Resettled Heifers for Resettled Refugees, 798
Responsibilities of Voluntary Agencies in Occupied Countries, 269
Restoring Democracy in Germany, 150
Resumé on the Development of the European Refugee Problem, 313
Return of Germany, 228
Return of Gunner Asch, 628
Review of Politics, 449, 495
Reynolds, J. Lacey, 523
Reynolds, Quentin, 524
Richards, Paul, 249
Richter, Werner, 250
Ride Out the Dark, 116
Ries, Henry, 285
Riess, Curt, 251
Right to Love, 615
Rings of Glass, 646
Rinser, Luise, 645, 646
Rise of Western Germany. See *Spoils of War*
Rise Up in Anger, 652
Road to Chaos, 277
Robinson, Donald R., 525
Rockefeller Foundation, 173
Rodenhauser, Reiner, 77
Rodnick, David, 252
Role of American Voluntary Agencies in Germany and Austria, 307

Rooney, Andy, 184
Roosenberg, Henriette, 253
Röpke, Wilhelm, 78, 526
Rose, Ben L., 527
Ross, Alan, 528
Ross, William D., 246
Roth, Günther, 895
Round-Up. See *Razzia*
Rowan Farm, 595
Rubble Years, 29
Ruf, 799
Ruhm von Oppen, Beate, 896
Rundell, Walter, 897
Rural Sociology, 541
Russell Sage Foundation, 939
Russians and Berlin, 1945, 873
Russians in My Home, 40
Russian Zone, 256
Rust, William, 254

Sag die Wahrheit, 800
Sailor in the Bottle, 597
Salomon, Ernst von, 79
Saltzman, Charles E., 532
Sandulescu, Jacques, 255
Sartre, Jean-Paul, 723
Saturday Evening Post, 197, 350, 351, 369, 444, 446, 450, 477, 549
Saturday Review, 384, 480, 706
Saturday Review of Literature, 561
Schacht, Hjalmar H. G., 80
Schaeffer, Karl-Heinz, 81
Schaffer, Gordon, 256, 534
Schaffner, Betram H., 898
Schalk, Adolph, 257
Schaper, Edzard H., 647
Schechtman, Joseph B., 535, 899
Schepses, Erwin, 536
Schieder, Theodor, 82
Schimansky, Stefan, 258

Index

Schirmbeck, Heinrich, 648
Schmeling, Marianne, 83
Schmid, Richard, 537
Schmidt, Dana A., 538
Schmitt, Hans A., 900
Schoenberg, Hans W., 901
Scholz, Hans, 649
Schönke, Adolf, 259
School and Society, 383, 455
School Life, 433
Schoonmaker, Frank, 539
Schorske, Carl E., 243
Schrobsdorff, Angelika, 650
Schulenburg, Tissa Hess, 84
Schütz, W. W., 540
Schwartz, Harry, 541
Schwarzenberger, Suse, 542
Schwarzer, H. Rudy, 85
Schwarz, Leo W., 902
Sealed Verdict, 724
Second World War, a Bibliography, 936
Second World War: A Select Bibliography, 937
Seeds of Destiny, 801
Seeds of Destruction, 111
Select Bibliography of Books on World War II, 938
Selected Reading List on United Nations Relief And Rehabilitation Administration, 965
Seltsamen Abenteuer des Herrn Fridolin B., 802
Settel, Arthur, 260, 261
Seven Thunders, 223
Sevruk, V., 262
Shadow of Hitler, 44
Shadow of Stalingrad. See *I Joined the Russians*
Shady Miracle, 618
Shaping of Postwar Germany, 880

Shapiro, Lionel, 724
Shelton, Regina M., 86
Shirer, William L., 263, 543
Shoe Leather Express, 234
Sibert, Edwin L., 544
Sigrid and the Sergeant, 673
Silesian Inferno, 32
Simmons, Kenneth W., 264
Simons, Dolph, 265
Simplicus 45, 634
Sington, Derrick, 266
Sins of the Fathers, 617
Sketchbook 1945-1949, 25
Skriabina, Elena, 267
Sky above Us. See *Und über uns der Himmel!*
Slater, Lisa, 87
Slatoff, Walter J., 546
Small Victory, 720
Smallwood, Russell, 547
Smith, Marcus J., 268
Smith, Myro, 966
Smith, Rennie, 548
Smith, William G., 725
Smoking Mountain, 672
Snell, John L., 903
Snyder, Harold E., 269, 270, 271
Social Research, 395
Social Service Review, 408, 536
Söhne des Herrn Gaspary, 803
So I Was a Sergeant, 202
Solberg, Richard W., 904
Solution of the German Problem, 78
Solzhenitsyn, Alexander, 272
Some Facts about Expellees in Germany, 28
Some Girls, Some Hats, and Hitler, 45
Somewhere in Berlin. See *Irgendwo in Berlin*
Sommers, Martin, 549
So Much to Forget, 278

186

Index

Sons of Herr Gaspary. See *Die Söhne des Herrn Gaspary*
Sorge, Martin K., 905
Sorio, Georges, 550
Soundings, 396
Soviet Russia Today, 534, 550
Sparrow's Song, 90
Späth, Gerold, 651
Spectator, 347, 374, 381, 419, 434, 443, 528, 560, 567, 570, 579
Speier, Hans, 273
Spender, Stephen, 274, 551
Spivey, Delmar T., 275
Spoils of the Victors, 681
Spoils of War, 839
Spotlight on Germany, 249
Spring, Henry P., 276, 277
Staden, Wendelgard von, 88
Stalag U.S.A., 853
Stalmann, Reinhart, 652
Stanké, Alain, 278
Stark Decency, 870
Starr, Joseph R., 279
Stars and Stripes, 280
Steeper Cliff, 678
Steinert, Marlis G., 906
Sternberg, Fritz, 89, 552
Sternberger, Adolf, 282
Stern, James A., 281
Stiles, Martha B., 726
Stoll, Irma, 90
Stolper, Gustav, 283
Stonborough, John, 553
Stone, Shepard, 554
Stone, Vernon W., 555
Story of U.N.R.R.A., 331
Stouffer, Samuel A., 284
Straight On, 136
Strange Occupation, 216
Strassenbekanntschaft, 804
Straw to Make Brick, 714
Strike, Clifford S., 556

Stringer, Ann, 285, 350
Struggle for Democracy in Germany, 825
Struggle for Germany, 176, 221
Studies of Undernutrition, Wuppertal, 286
Subject Bibliography of the Second World War, 933, 934
Sudeten German Picture Book, 95
Sudetens, a Moral Question, 157
Sullivan, Matthew B., 907
Summary of D.P. Population, 332
Survey, 356, 375, 555
Survey Graphic, 439
Survey Midmonthly, 418
Survive the Storm, 629
Swanstrom, Edward E., 326
Swords or Plowshares?, 869
Szaz, Zoltan M., 908

Taper, Bernard, 557
Taste of Fear, 203
Tauber, Kurt P., 909
Taylor, J. E., 558
Taylor, Philip H., 967
Technical Assistance Commission on the Integration of the Refugees in the German Republic, 186
Tell the Truth. See *Sag die Wahrheit*
Tempel, Gudrun, 91
Temper the Wind, 706
Ten Seconds to Hell, 662
Tent, James F., 910
Terror Machine, 194
Teschner, Richard, 559
Thayer, Charles W., 287
Theatre Arts, 494
They Came in Peace, 98

Index

They Thought They Were Free, 215
Thine Enemy, 688
This Is Germany, 260
Thompson, Dorothy, 561
Thomson, Stewart, 92
Thorwald, Jürgen, 93
Those Human Russians, 183
Thresholds of Peace, 907
Through the Night, 649
Thy People, My People, 178
Tidings, 654
Tilla, 630
Time, 414, 475, 505, 545
Time of Rape, 9
Time Out, 293
To Be Preserved Forever, 198
Todesmühlen, 805
Token of a Covenant, 57
To Lose a War, 86
Tomorrow and Yesterday, 605
Tomorrow the World, 64
Topical Autobiographies of Displaced People, 308
To the Victors the Spoils, 710
Tour of Duty, 148
Towards the Future Shore, 60
Toward Understanding Germany, 879
Tragedy of a People, 11
Tragedy of Silesia, 48
Transfer of the German Population from Poland, 912
Transfigured Night, 310
Translations from the German, 957
Transport 7-41-R, 609
Treatment of Defeated Germany, 188
Trevor-Roper, Hugh, 562
Trial, George T., 563
Tritschler, 165

Tully, Andrew, 912
Turner, Ewart E., 564
Turner, Philip, 565
Turnwald, Wilhelm K., 94, 95
Two Women and a War, 96
Two Years Before the Masthead, 192

Under the Bombs, 831
Und Finden Dereinst wir uns Wieder, 806
Und über uns der Himmel!, 807
Und wieder 48, 808
Union List of UNRRA Films, 968
United Nations Relief and Rehabilitation Administration, 327-35, 809, 935, 944, 965, 968
United States and Europe, 930
United States and Germany, 913
United States and West Germany, 886
United States Army in the Occupation of Germany, 921
United States in Germany, 1944-1955, 304
United States News, 405
United States Occupation of Germany, 812
United States Occupies Germany, 811
United States Policy toward Germany, 300
Unloved Germans, 15
Unquiet Germans, 287
UNRRA Goes into Action, 809
UNRRA in Europe, 330
UNRRA Monthly Review, 333
UNRRA: Organization, Aims, Progress, 331

Index

UNRRA Procurement of US Military Surpluses in Europe, 330
UNRRA Program of Relief and Rehabilitation Supplies, 334
UNRRA Review, 333
U.N.R.R.A., the History, 335
Unser Mittwochabend, 813
Unwanted, 882
Unwilling Journey, 30
Urgent Message from Germany, 115
Uris, Leon, 727
U.S. Denazification Policy in Germany, 871
U.S. Department of State, 130, 233, 248, 913
U.S. Displaced Persons Commission, 883
U.S. Forces in Europe, 810
U.S. High Commissioner for Germany, 185, 893, 950
U.S. Library of Congress, 922, 929, 930, 951, 960, 962, 964
U.S. National Archives, 926
U.S. Occupation in Europe after World War II, 900
Utley, Freda, 288

Vain Victory, 258
Valentin, Veit, 566
Vallance, Ute, 289
Valtin, Jan. See Krebs, Richard J. H.
Vansittart, Robert G., 290
Vassiltchikov, Marie, 291
Verboten, 701
Verlorene Gesicht, 814
Vernant, Jacques, 914
Verrina [pseud.], 292
Vespers in Vienna, 715

Viator, 567
Victor's Justice, 112
Vietor, John A., 293
Villard, Oswald G., 59
Virginia Quarterly Review, 404, 488
Visiting Committee of American Book Publishers, 164
Vogt, Hannah, 97
Voight, F. A., 568
Vor uns Liegt das Leben, 815

Wahle, Anne, 294
Walk in Darkness, 693
Wallich, Henry C., 915
Walls Came Tumbling Down, 253
Waln, Nora, 569
Walston, H. D., 570
Walt, H. P. van, 571
Wann, Marie D., 295
Warburg, James P., 296, 297, 572, 916
Wartime Origins of the East-West Dilemma over Germany, 903
Watcher on the Rhine, 139
Watson, Ann, 98
Way We Lived in Germany during World War II, 27
We Chose to Stay, 41
Wege im Zwielicht, 816
Weiskopf, F. C., 573
Weiss, Winfried, 99
Weitz, John, 729
Wells, Ingeborg, 100
Welt, Elly, 730
Wendel, Else, 101
Werlberger, Hans, 653
Werner, Alfred, 574
Western Allies and the Politics of Food, 848

West German Cinema since 1945, 941
We Thank You, 53
What Buchenwald Really Means, 170
What to Do with Germany, 230
What We Saw in Germany, 336
Where Is Germany Going, 254
Where No Birds Sing, 734
Whip My Homecoming, 70
Whispers of Death, 181
White Book on the American and British Policy of Intervention, 71
White Flags of Surrender, 35
White, Theodore H., 298
White, William L., 299
Whither Germany, 302
Whiting, Charles, 731, 732
Wiechert, Ernst E., 654
Wiener Library, 153, 945
Wild Place, 318
Williams, Frederick W., 576
Willis, Frank R., 917
Wilson, Francesca M., 337
Wilson, Iain, 577, 578
Wilson, Roger C., 338
Winds of History, 828
Windsor, Phillip, 918
Winterspelt, 588
Wintertime, 728
Wiseman, Thomas, 733
Wiskemann, Elizabeth, 919
Without Sanction, 653
Witness to History, 117
Wolf, Christa, 655, 656
Wolfe, Robert, 920
Wolfers, Arnold, 300
Wolff, Kurt H., 301, 895
Wolff-Mönckeberg, Mathilde, 102
Wolff, P., 165
Wolfson, Irving, 580

Woman in Berlin, 103
Woman in the House, 664
Women of Germany, 144
Woodbridge, George, 335
Wood, Junius B., 581
World Affairs (London), 352, 442, 466, 467, 542
World Council of Churches. Refugee Division, 339
World in Film, 817
World Report, 355, 385, 447, 575
World Today, 411, 427, 428, 448, 521
World War II, 966, 970
World War II from an American Perspective, 969
Worsley, R. H. M., 582
Wozzeck, 818
Wylie, I. A. R., 583
Wylie, Ida A., 734

Yale Review, 436
Year of Potsdam, 261
Year of the Wolves, 613
Year That Changed the World, 854
Your Job in Germany, 819

Zblinden, Hans, 302
Zeit mit Dir, 820
Ziegler, Janet, 970
Ziemke, Earl F., 921
Zimnik, Reiner, 657
Zink, Harold, 303, 304, 584
Zuckmayer, Carl, 585
Zugvögel, 821
Zwerenz, Gerhard, 658
Zwischen Gestern und Morgan, 822

Augsburg College
George Sverdrup Library
Minneapolis, MN 55454

Ref DD 257 .P3

Paul

The Germans after World War II